PSALM

Toby DOW and Caron TATE

"This first-time collaboration between Dow & Tate has produced a masterful piece of suspense and intrigue with plot twist after plot twist. Impossible to put down. Brilliant in its execution."
- Sandra Rasten, Book Reviewer

© Copyright, Toby Dow, 2020. All rights by all media reserved.

ALL RIGHTS RESERVED. This book contains material protected under International and Federal Copyright Laws and Treaties. Any unauthorized reprint or use of this material is prohibited. No part of this book may be reproduced or transmitted in any form or by any means, electronic or mechanical, including photocopying, recording, or by any information storage and retrieval system without express written permission from the author/publisher.

ISBN: 978-1-64184-424-6 (Paperback)
ISBN: 978-1-64184-425-3 (eBook)

About the authors

Toby Dow

Born and raised in Sydney's East, Toby always had a creative edge to him. With a passion for the thriller/horror genre, Toby went about piecing together a story he had conceived some years prior but never acted on. Toby's time was consumed first as a flight attendant and later starting his own successful business. Career and family life took priority while, over an eight-year period, Toby gradually developed the intricate, well-woven and well-researched plot of Psalm, his first foray into the world of literature.

Once he felt the work was ready for the next phase, Toby showed his fledgling manuscript to former best-selling author turned producer/literary agent, Lynn Santer. Immediately seeing the potential, Lynn introduced Toby to African American writer, Caron Tate, to finalize what is now his masterpiece.

Toby has already started work on the follow up book to Psalm.

Dedication

Toby would like to dedicate his work to his wife Marcela and his children Jayde and Braxton. "My family are my life."

Acknowledgements

Toby would like to thank Lynn Santer for her extensive input and guidance. "Without Lynn coming into my life this book would have never seen the light of day. Lynn is the best thing to happen to this project. I can't thank her enough for her input and professional assistance in getting Psalm over the line. She is a true friend for life."

Caron Tate

Caron Tate is a 2013 graduate of the University of Southern California's Master of Professional Writing program.

Her fiction, memoir, and poetry have appeared in various publications, and she's also written several award-winning plays. Her singing/song writing alter-ego, "Mumz da Wurd" has songs and video on her YouTube channel and includes the anti-gun violence "A Christmas Prayer." (https://www.youtube.com/watch?v=-IERyDMd3Ig)

Caron originally attended Howard University in 1968 as a voice major and worked as a performer—singing, acting, dancing, and modeling—in the DC/Maryland/Virginia area for many years. After moving to Los Angeles, and over 30 gap years, she resumed her undergrad education at Santa Monica College (SMC) and the University of Illinois. She's now an Instructional Assistant at SMC, helping students with their writing challenges.

Caron is currently at work on the second of a series of children's books called *Uncle Darrow and the Kreole Kids*.

Dedication

Caron would like to dedicate her work on this book to her mom Dorothy Cash, a woman who knows the value of hard work and perseverance.

Acknowledgements

Caron would like to thank Laura Eimiller and the Media Relations office of the Los Angeles Federal Bureau of Investigation for all the help and information.

She would also like to thank the members of the MPW Second Act Club/Writers Unblocked Sunday writing group for a year of feedback and support. Write on Kids!

Many thanks to Devo Cutler-Rubenstein for the introduction that started this train down the track.

Contents

Chapter 1	WEDNESDAY – Los Angeles	1
Chapter 2	FRIDAY – Los Angeles	10
Chapter 3	THURSDAY – 16 Hours Earlier: New York	20
Chapter 4	FRIDAY – FBI Office: Los Angeles	36
Chapter 5	DAY – New York	47
Chapter 6	FRIDAY – Later: Los Angeles	53
Chapter 7	FRIDAY – Afternoon: San Francisco	69
Chapter 8	FRIDAY – Night: New York	85
Chapter 9	SATURDAY – Early morning: Washington, DC	94
Chapter 10	MONDAY – Morning: Los Angeles	105
Chapter 11	MONDAY – Morning: Washington, DC	120
Chapter 12	MONDAY – Afternoon: Los Angeles	133
Chapter 13	TUESDAY – Morning: San Diego	152
Chapter 14	TUESDAY – Afternoon: Washington, DC	166
Chapter 15	TUESDAY – Afternoon: San Francisco	174
Chapter 16	TUESDAY – Afternoon: Los Angeles	180
Chapter 17	TUESDAY – Afternoon: San Francisco	187
Chapter 18	TUESDAY – Afternoon: Los Angeles	195
Chapter 19	TUESDAY – Evening: Los Angeles	206
Chapter 20	TUESDAY – Night: Pescadero	217

Chapter 21	TUESDAY – Night: Los Angeles	228
Chapter 22	TUESDAY – Night: Los Angeles	236
Chapter 23	TUESDAY – Late Night: Los Angeles	243
Chapter 24	TUESDAY – Late Night: Los Angeles	247
Chapter 25	FBI Office – Los Angeles	253
Chapter 26	Night – Dallas, Texas	259
Chapter 27	FBI Office – Los Angeles	263
Chapter 28	FBI Office – Los Angeles	269
Chapter 29	Nov. 22nd – Dallas, Texas	276
Chapter 30	Nov. 22nd – Los Angeles, CA	283
Chapter 31	Dallas – Texas	294
Chapter 32	Five days later – Los Angeles, CA	302

Chapter 1

WEDNESDAY – Los Angeles

A man stood motionless at the window of a hotel room in Hollywood, his arms open and welcoming, his face lifted toward heaven, as a storm raged outside. The ferocious crashes of thunder, the searing flashes of lightning tore their way through the darkened sky. He trembled at each one as if touched by a lover. "Fire," he whispered. "Fire in my bones."

His image in the wet glass shivered and distorted as the storm buffeted the old building, causing the window to rattle and vibrate in the casement, but he didn't notice. He couldn't. He could not see his own reflection. Mirrors, reflective glass of any kind, appeared to him like empty black holes leading to the Abyss. And that was all he saw and what he knew to be true about this decadent place he was looking down on.

Each flash revealed more of its dark ugliness; each rumbling vibration seemed to unearth and release more evil. "City of Angels," he sneered.

He knew the welcome rain, answer to millions of prayers in drought-stricken Southern California, would help to extinguish the raging wildfires that humans were powerless to control. But for him, it meant something else: This could be the sign he had been waiting for.

This storm, the kind of storm that 'never happens in Los Angeles' was an omen, a sign that the time had come to complete the next steps of the mission he had already embarked on.

There was no doubt, for he heard his 'Guiding Voices' again, speaking in him and through him, and this time they rode in on the storm—screeling, banshee voices telling him, *It's time. Now, tonight. It's time!*

He bowed his head in submission and slowly pulled the dingy, once-gold curtains shut. Even in the darkened room, his eyes gleamed with purpose. "Yes, it's time," he said resolutely.

He glanced at the ancient TV as he walked past. The sound was turned down as always, so the subversive messages could not enter his brain or attempt to deter him from his purpose. He paused for a moment when President Mitchell and his consort, the so-called first lady, appeared on the screen. The ridiculous caption read, "Mother of the World: America's Mom Talks about First Baby." They were hiding their true natures behind their smiles, as always, coiled around each other trying to project their supposed love and devotion. They reminded him of two writhing moray eels: their vicious, grinning teeth were bad enough, but the other hidden jaw; that was what did the real damage. They didn't know, but they were the king and queen of a doomed, rotting realm, supreme symbols of the evil that surrounded him. Proof that it was everywhere. But not for long. He turned them off.

The man turned on a table lamp, checked his watch, put on rubber gloves, and began to move purposefully around the small room, easily finishing the minimal cleaning still left undone. Every piece of clothing, every scrap of paper, every item that belonged to him, except for those on one small table, the closet, and one wall, were put into a trash bag. He wiped, dusted, straightened the furniture, folded and bagged the sheets he'd bought, cleaned the bathroom, went over and over the room using the small vacuum cleaner he had purchased just days before, and finished by removing the bag from the vacuum and adding it to the trash bag.

He moved quickly to the small closet, checking the pockets of the soft leather coat that hung there next to three other hangers with a baseball cap and belt clipped to one and a shirt and a pair of pants, both black, hanging from the other two.

"And now the end begins," he whispered.

He touched the space on the pole between each hanger and felt a moment of satisfaction, noting that they were all exactly two finger-widths apart. On the floor below them, centered between the four hangers, was a pair of black leather Doc Martens boots next to a black leather case. He dressed hurriedly, paused a moment, staring proudly at one wall, which was covered with photos and printed-out information.

He put the case next to the table, upon which were a glass of wine, a crust of bread, two white candles in glass cylinders, and an open Bible on top of a white piece of fabric. He caressed it gently, noting the two holes near one corner. He knelt before his makeshift altar, opened the case, and pulled out a piece of paper. He read over the handwritten message, product of weeks of work, held it to his heart, and placed it reverently on top of the Bible.

"Yes, I hear you," he whispered and pulled two other items from his coat pockets and placed them on the table: a gun and a knife. He lit the candles, bowed his head, and began reciting new versions of Bible verses that he had been given.

"Take, eat: these are the bodies which shall be broken for you: this do in remembrance of me," he intoned and ate the bread. Then, "This cup is the new testament in their blood," and he drank the wine.

The man picked up the gun and the knife and held them over the twin flames while chanting, "There is nothing hidden that will not be revealed. There is nothing kept secret that will not come to light." When he felt the burning heat reach his hands, he cried out, his tortured voice joining the thunder and lightning. "This is my new testament: I will rain down upon the wicked. Fire and brimstone and burning wind will be the portion of their cup."

And for the first time in years, he smiled.

* * *

By the time he took the fire escape out of the building, carrying his black case and trash bag, the storm had subsided somewhat. He walked through the neighborhood he had come to know in the past weeks . . . the peculiar Hollywood mix of gullible, ogling tourists, pimps who looked like businessmen, and entitled females exiting exclusive clubs who looked like prostitutes. He tried not to notice the tiny skirts that barely covered crotches and bare midriffs below voluptuous breasts, but he wasn't always successful. He turned away angrily, refocused on his mission, and as he listened to the staccato rhythm of stilettos on the sidewalk, he thought they were all whores, all streetwalkers. They deserved what was coming.

The ones dressed like him were everywhere too. All black was the other Hollywood theme. They were the ones who sneered at color and glitter and slavish adherence to fashion trends. They were intentional outsiders, but their tattoos and piercings were another trendy adherence. They probably thought he was one of them. But they were outsiders by choice. He had never had a choice. Any of these lost souls, any of them, would be the easiest prey, but he knew they couldn't be. What he had to do was specific, preordained. There could be no deviations. He checked his watch: fifteen minutes. Not much longer now.

He wandered into a souvenir store that had the usual wide-open front and cheap, cheesy items for sale. He grabbed a Red Bull from the cooler and walked toward the register but stopped to listen to a couple arguing in the middle of the aisle. He could not have described the skinny young man very well later, but the girl was a tall, striking blonde with porcelain, almost transparent skin and large gray eyes. Long ago, before he became what he now was, when mirrors still held his reflection, before what an ignorant therapist once labeled a delusion; he remembered his own eyes were gray. He thought she looked like one of the sweet, gently feminine statues of female saints that he'd grown up looking at. But the purity ended at her chin. Why did she bother with underwear when every inch of her could be seen through the lacy, hot pink jumpsuit she was wearing under her cheap, brown plastic jacket? She was beautiful, he thought, even with her slutty attire, but she was still repulsive. Despite the "dumb bitches" and "fuck you's" spewing from the couples' mouths, they would probably finish the disagreement, which seemed so important, by going home and having disgusting sex. That was the way these things usually ended; he'd heard.

It could be them, he thought. *I could change things up and make it these two,* like the couple from so long ago, Hartnell and Shepard. *They could be my sacrifices.* But he knew he wouldn't. He could not and would not change the plan. Each correct piece added to the puzzle which must be completed. The picture would then be done, whole, and ready to be observed and understood by the world. The truth. He must not waiver from his plan.

He walked to the counter, added a pack of Kools, and paid for both, lighting up the moment he stepped outside. He walked to the intersection of Hollywood Boulevard and Schrader and waited there, sipping his drink and smoking and feeling his adrenalin rise. The moment was approaching.

He glanced at his watch and frowned. He could not be late. But when he looked up, a dark blue Toyota turned the corner onto Schrader, and the smiling African American driver pulled over to the curb and turned off his Lyft sign.

The man took one last drag, dropped the fiery butt of his cigarette to the ground, stomped it out, and slipped into the backseat.

"Good to see you again, how . . ." the driver began, but he was cut off by an angry, "It's 9:32, Fred."

The harsh tone wiped the smile from the driver's face. "Sorry, yeah, two minutes. I am late, sorry, traffic. Uh, the usual?" After receiving a curt nod Fred hit the gas and immediately moved out into traffic. "Okay, 3898 E. Washington it is. And don't worry, we'll be there by 10:00. I'll make up the two minutes easy."

"This isn't on your record, right?" the man asked, curtly.

The smile returned to the driver's face. "My friend," Fred said, "as I've explained before, my twins and the other two don't care if their formula and clothes are on the record or off, and neither do the exes. We all love a man who pays triple."

He whipped around, making an illegal U-turn, took the right back onto Hollywood, and, in a couple of blocks, turned left on Cahuenga. Moments later, they were on the 101 Freeway and headed south, away from the Hollywood area. The 101 was loaded with traffic as usual but the driver threaded effortlessly through every opening.

"See," he said, indicating his phone GPS, "arrival at 9:58. We're good."

His passenger nodded, opened his black case and removed five $10 bills, which he tossed on the front seat. The driver looked down, gasped, and glanced curiously in the rearview mirror. "Uh, wow, thanks! I mean, I wasn't saying that about the twins for sympathy or dry begging or whatever, but for real, man, thanks. You're really helping a brother out, big time Mr. And I still don't even know your name."

After a moment's silence, he added: "I know I said this before, but every time I hear your voice, I think I ought to know you. From before, I mean, before I started picking you up."

His passenger just said, "This is the last time, Fred. Last time we'll take this ride."

"Sorry to hear that. Really sorry to hear that. So whatever you're working on, it's done? You're finished? I noticed you were carrying a little heavier load this time," Fred said jovially. But the smile dropped off his face like a clown mask when he saw the bone chilling gray stare that met his eyes in the mirror. "Look," he continued shakily, forcing his eyes back to the road, "Whatever it is, it's really none of my damn business. You're here doing your thing for what you need to do, and I'm doing the same. I'm just making conversation. Not questioning or judging."

"My task is begun but not done," the man said, his hand caressing the fabric in his still open case. "Like you, I have a greater purpose. We both understand what we have to do."

"Sure. Sure we do."

Both were silent for another few minutes, until the driver said, "Here we are, usual place on E. Washington, and as usual, nothing much here but sidewalk, industrial parks, and us."

He pulled to the curb, scooped up the bills, and leaned forward to put them in a small pouch he had hanging from the dash, and started to turn to his right, "So I guess this is it, I won't see—" but he froze as he realized his passenger had taken off the cap and donned a hood with eyeholes cut into it.

"What—what the hell kind of Klan shit is—" he began, and stopped once more, looking down at the gun in his passenger's right, now gloved, hand.

Of course the pathetic loser would think of something racist; something to feel like a victim instead of a piece of a holy plan. "Turn around," the man said softly, and the driver complied immediately.

"Look man, you don't have to do this." Fred held up the pouch without looking back. "Take your money and all the rest of it. I don't care, just take it."

"I don't want your money."

Now, Fred's eyes grew even larger. "Look, brother, I know I said I remember you, but I was just running my mouth. Even if I did know anything, I'm not a snitch. Go about your business, I don't care what you're doing. Far as I'm concerned, I never saw you."

The man shook his head, leaned forward, and placed the muzzle of the gun at the driver's right temple. "As you said, we both have to do what we need to do."

"Naw, please, please man please! Kids! I got—" but his last words were cut off by the "pop" of the silenced gun.

The brains and blood exploding onto the driver's side window felt louder to him than the shot. The killer watched the blood spray from the exit wound near the man's left eye, and as the body slumped forward onto the wheel, he closed his eyes and for just a moment enjoyed the intoxicating feeling of power that surged through his veins—he didn't want it to end.

But then he was back to business. He grabbed the coded message and a Ziploc bag out of his case, exited on the curb side, quickly checking to make sure there was no one around, and slipped into the front seat. In moments, he had pulled the knife out of his pocket, sliced off a section of the dead man's shirt, sealed it in the bag, and slipped it into his pocket. He placed the coded message on the dashboard in front of his victim.

Dousing the tip of his leather glove in the blood from the side of the driver's head he began to draw on the windshield. "Let this be a sign unto you," he said as he finished by drawing a circle with a large cross dividing it into quarters. "In this cipher is our identity. The way has been prepared. The Zodiac has led, and I must follow. You are all in the crosshairs, and my aim is true."

He removed his gloves, turning them inside out, and put them in his pockets. For just a second, he self-indulgently sat back in his seat, drew in a satisfied breath and dug his heels into the floor of the vehicle. Stiffening his body as though to extend himself in size, he made fists with his toes inside his footwear, silently dislodging whatever may have been collected in the tread. This step was done.

He walked a few blocks to his parked Ford Bronco, unlocked it and slipped in behind the wheel. Yes, this step was done, and the plans for the next were already underway.

Chapter 2

FRIDAY – Los Angeles

Harrison Carter was instantly awake when his buzzing cell phone broke the early morning silence. For just a moment before he looked at the display, his sense memory zapped him back to his days as a surgical resident, and the old, gut-tightening tension grabbed him as he wondered what catastrophe or crime would call him in to the ER before first sunlight. It was during his time as a resident that Harrison stood a test that would change his life forever, placing a wedge between himself and his father. Harrison Sr. was Chief of Surgery at Cedars Sinai in Los Angeles. Over the years he had performed surgery on some of the country's elite, including past presidents and so many celebrities he'd lost count. During his career, the older man had received some of the highest honors for his dedication to the medical profession. Naturally he had expected the same for his son. Harrison Jr. shook the memory away, checking the display as he sat up in bed, snapping back to the present. The moment of disorientation left him, and he was able to exhale. It was replaced by a different kind of tension; it was more positive anticipation because he knew this call from his boss, FBI

Los Angeles Assistant Director Phil Stanton, meant a new case or an important break in an existing one.

"It's Carter Boss," he said.

"Carter, good, you're up. It's about those two cases you keep bringing up," Stanton said in his usual clipped tones. "There's been another one right here in the LA area. I think you're right. I think we have a new kind of serial killer. I'm putting together a task force, and you're on it. Gather anything you've put together on those cases; we have to get ahead of this thing. How soon can you get here?"

"Half an hour sir, tops," Harrison responded, and Stanton clicked off with a quick, "Good," before he could say another word.

Harrison rose naked from his bed and hurried to the shower. The warm spray on his body woke him up the rest of the way, but it couldn't stop the small feeling of panic that was creeping up. This was what he had been waiting for. This was the opportunity that he knew, or at least hoped, would come from the moment he arrived at the Bureau a few years ago. But now, almost as bad as the dread he used to feel before assisting with a major surgical procedure, came the feeling that maybe he would fail. Maybe, as his father always said, he wouldn't be able to cut it.

He heard his dad's voice echoing in his head, as it had all his life. When Harrison told his parents about his decision to leave medicine for the FBI, his mother had sat silently, lovely head bowed, as his father excoriated him. "You'll fail, as you should," he'd sneered. "This is not what you're supposed to do. You're a Winston Carter. You're supposed to be a doctor, goddamit, or at least a politician like your grandfather. How have you lost your identity? I don't understand, son. Why would you want to move lower instead of higher? Anyone who truly wanted to save people, to help them, would choose medicine over the FBI without thinking twice!"

His father's voice had taken on a confused, contemplative tone that was even worse than the angry one. "Are you trying to rebel against me, or are you ill? I don't know what's going on with you. This is how bipolar disordered patients behave—one person one day and someone else the next. It's like you feel a need to atone for privilege."

And he finally sighed, like he was giving up. "I don't understand. But . . . you know I'm only telling you this because I care."

These 'discussions' usually ended that way. He'd heard things like that from his superstar father his entire life. He'd often wished his parents had had another child, so the weight of all of their hopes and dreams wouldn't rest on his shoulders alone. But they hadn't. He thought his Mom probably didn't want to be fat again or take the chance she might never get her figure back. Even as a young teen, he'd realized that Harrison Winston Carter, Sr., Chief of Surgery at celebrity hospital Cedars Sinai, frequent TV news and talk show expert guest, and bestselling author of *Cutting Edges: A Surgeon's Life* (later joined by six other books); was more than a regular doctor and that he, Jr., would probably never, ever measure up. His mother's adoration didn't help. After all, as his father felt obligated to point out, she had been a flight attendant, and they both wanted more than that for their son, as they should. She usually smiled her dazzling smile after one of these "events" and went shopping.

Harrison stood before his closet and allowed the order to calm him. His breathing slowed as he regarded numerous dark suits on identical hangers and shirts and ties coordinated by color. He didn't care if it looked like one of those Closet World TV commercials; for him, it was relaxing. He always understood when he heard about people on the autism spectrum who were comforted by color or repetition or sameness of some kind. This made sense to him.

He grabbed a dark blue Michael Kors plaid suit with one of his favorite Tasso Elba shirts: white with a subtle blue diamond checked pattern. He took a moment in the mirror to reassure himself that everything was all right and was startled as always to see the duplicate of his father's handsome, angular face and gray blue eyes staring back at him. *But never the disapproving sneer, never that,* he'd promised himself since he was a boy.

He snatched a protein drink from the fridge, grabbed the keys to his Mustang and was out the door of his condo in moments.

The midnight blue Mustang and his wardrobe were his only surrenders to the kind of entitled life he'd grown up in. He wasn't interested in hanging out at Polo clubs or being introduced to Judges or Mayors to enhance his job prospects. His passion had never been in the medical or political worlds, much to his father's chagrin. Not that the FBI couldn't offer him a generous career. Many a great politician had forged their career from there. But Harrison Sr. wasn't interested in such thoughts. He was only interested in how his highly influential friends and family members would react to his son's chosen career path.

Driving out of the garage and up the alley, Harrison turned left onto Inglewood Boulevard, noting the mix of small businesses and apartments, not one over four stories. He had to smile; even his clean, safe, but certainly not upscale, Mar Vista neighborhood was something that grated on his father's nerves. Bel Air it was not.

He loved driving at this time when almost no one was out, and the first rays of the sun were beginning to show. It was his favorite time of the day for thinking and allowing the pieces of any crime puzzles he was working on to fall into place. This same focus had worked for him with diagnoses and in surgery. He would concentrate on an issue or problem in the quiet, and he could see the questions swirling around almost as if they were three-dimensional. They would connect to each other, snap into place like a Rubik's cube, and the answer would be right there before him.

This was why he'd continued thinking about the two cases Stanton had mentioned. From the time he'd made the decision that the FBI was the place for him, he had obsessively kept up with FBI unsolved murders all over the country and those handled by the Violent Crimes Against Children task force. He had focused on one such case in Little Rock, Arkansas. The victim was seven-year-old, blonde Jocelyn Simmons, a local child beauty pageant queen, found strangled in the basement of a 5-bedroom home on upscale Valley Creek Crest. She had gone missing the day after the owners left for a vacation in the Bahamas. When they returned, they found the body, hands bound and mouth duct-taped, under a white blanket.

It took very little time for anyone who still remembered the case to make the connection: this was either a copycat or they were being haunted by the same monster who murdered JonBenét Ramsey more than twenty years earlier. The Little Rock FBI was called in immediately and began a sweeping investigation, but there was very little for them to go on. The only "clues" were planted, intentional links to the original murder, down to a tampered-with basement window and the white bowl with a spoon and some pineapple on the kitchen table. Even the five-bedroom, gabled house was clearly chosen for its similarity to the Ramsey home, but that was it. There was nothing linking anything left in the house to the killer.

As in the earlier case, the first suspects were the homeowners, but their travel itinerary quickly cleared them. The FBI ran down every possibility. They checked every person they thought might be connected in any way: pedophiles, the girl's own family, murderers, every name on the registered sex offender list, but nothing.

Harrison stayed in touch with the local office and received updates to the point where he could tell he was annoying the agents handling the case. They couldn't seem to convince him that they really were doing all they could. He had no more answers than they did, but something kept bringing him back to the case. What Harrison knew was this killer was meticulous and cunning with an unrivaled attention to detail. He had to know the house, the family's plans, the weekend location of the little girl, how to snatch her and keep her hidden long enough to do the crime, and of course, all the public details of the JBR case. Harrison could see the pieces swirling: If it was the original killer, how old might he be now? Why here? Why now? Why this girl? Was it the physical similarity between the two young beauty queens? Was there a deeper meaning? And if a copycat, some of the same questions presented themselves to him, but there were no answers. Not yet.

He stopped at a red light before crossing Olympic Boulevard, even though there was no one else in sight in any direction. He thought again of his father. His dad always told him to follow the rules. Of course, in his father's books that didn't just mean "the rules", although it meant that as well, it also meant following the family rules—tradition. In that respect at least, Harrison had to concede he was the rule breaker. He had always felt more in sync with the blokes at college who hung out in sweaters rather than the spoiled rich brats who behaved like entitled wankers. His mother may not have been born to wealth but her soul and heart were rich. It was these qualities that mattered more to Harrison. What's right and what's wrong. Okay, sure, being in medicine could help save lives but that was no less true in the FBI. His father's way was not the only way and he was "entitled" for his way to be his own. He decided now might not be the time to start being his dad.

He turned his thoughts back to the other bizarre case, this one in Tulsa, Oklahoma. The murders had happened across several months, but the bodies of seven young men were found at the same time in an abandoned house just weeks after the child in Little Rock. Someone made an anonymous phone call to the police, claiming that a horrible odor was coming from the premises.

The bodies were found under the floorboards, some stacked on top of others and sprinkled with quicklime to speed up decomposition and mask the smell. One of the upstairs rooms had been converted into a sex chamber with chains and bondage equipment. There were thick, soft leather straps used to tie around a victim's throat, and crotchless leather shorts. There was also an assortment of dildos, whips and paddles.

Because the victims were all prostitutes or runaways, some hadn't even been reported missing; no one was looking for them.

But this time he had made the connection before anyone else. The crimes in the two cities were nothing alike: a single little girl; multiple male prostitutes, probably lured by a potential customer; the girl strangled; one man stabbed, the rest strangled with a tourniquet or asphyxiated (sometimes with their own underwear); one crime was executed in a day or two, the other taking place across months. The agents working the case were looking for someone who had issues with homosexuality or prostitution or both, but certainly not the type of criminal who got-off on snatching innocent young girls.

Despite the differences, Harrison saw something that almost went unnoticed in the corner of one of the Tulsa pictures: there was a dirty red clown nose and a broken pogo stick lying in the junk strewn around the floor in the room above the buried bodies. The pieces clicked into place, and a name entered his head: John Wayne Gacy, the serial killer from Cook County, Illinois who did his crimes in the 1970s while running a business and also entertaining as a kid's party clown called Pogo. Gacy's known victim count was over thirty, but it was almost as if the current killer was doing a sampling to show anyone paying attention that he wanted to remind them of the clown killer's monstrous deeds.

And there was something else: three of the asphyxiated victims had paper stuffed down their throats, and some of that paper was pages torn from a Bible. In the case of the little girl there was a Bible, open to the Book of Psalms, left in the room by the monster who had committed this vile crime. Harrison thought he saw a mark next to one of the verses, but he couldn't be sure.

What if, Harrison had begun to wonder, someone was replicating infamous murders in different parts of the country? A new puzzle was laid before him with the biggest question being: why? . . . And the Bible thing . . . was there a message?

He made his right turn on Wilshire Boulevard and drove the short distance to the Federal Building at 11000. Minutes later, he was on the 17th floor.

When he entered the FBI offices in 1700, the first person he encountered was his partner, the beautiful Kate. That's how he always thought of Special Agent Katherine Fleming. Even clearly too rushed this morning to put on much makeup or pull together one of her classy outfits, she was, at almost six feet tall with straight black hair and piercing green eyes, still a stunner.

"Good morning," he said, determined to keep it professional when he really wanted to say *you're gorgeous*. "What do we have?"

He started printing out the notes he had on the two killings and added them to what he'd brought from home.

"Hi," she smiled, looking at him with what he hoped was appreciation. "Why do you look like you've been up for hours? Don't you sleep?"

"Well, yes I . . . ." he began confused, but she shook her head and waved it aside.

"That was a joke, literal boy," she said. "We don't have all the details yet, but there's a new case that has something to do with your research. Looks like you're on deck. We need to hurry; Stanton wants everyone down in the briefing room ASAP."

Kate pressed the elevator button, and they stood in silence for a moment as they waited. Finally, Harrison turned and looked at her, her eyes almost on a level with his because of her heels. "We haven't had much time to talk. I've been thinking about . . . well, it's been a year since—"

"Since Dale. I know," she responded, taking a deep breath.

"You don't have to talk about it if you don't want to, but if you do, I'm here," he said softly.

The elevator door opened, and she stepped on, holding the door for him. "I know," she said. "Thanks partner. I will. I know I can always talk to you. You know, the more I think about him and the way he did things, the more I realize that I just wasn't his priority. The whole Batman and Robin BS. He and—"

"Hold it!" a male voice called out, and Kate instantly hit the Door Open button.

Skip Jennings rushed onto the elevator. The muscular, spiky haired Agent looked, as usual, as if he were going to burst out of his shirt. Harrison knew he spent much of his free time working out and perfecting his martial arts. Skip was generous with that kind of information.

"Thanks, Katy," he grinned at her, ignoring Harrison. "You look . . ." he started, shaking his head, "Well, you know."

She frowned, pressing the button to take them down. "Harrison and I were talking about the case. This is going to be something different. He thinks that . . ."

"Yeah, I'm sure Dr. Detective has some amazing insights for us all," he said, his back still to Harrison. "Katey, you know, it's about a year since my partner, our partner—"

"Thanks, I know. I don't want to talk about it," she snapped at him.

He glanced at Harrison in time to catch a small smirk at the corner of his mouth. "Wow," he said to Kate, as he sadly shook his head. "You know, I miss him too."

He sounded phony to Harrison, but Kate's face softened. "I'm sorry," she said, "of course you do. Maybe we'll do a memorial of some kind. I'll get in touch with his sister and let you know. But let's . . . well I'd rather think about the case right now."

"Sure. I'm cool with that." He turned to Harrison as if just noticing him. "So, Doc, you're presenting for the first time. Guess that means you'll get the lead on this one," he said sarcastically. "Better get those nerves under control. You're looking a little shaky there, champ."

"He's fine," Kate said as the elevator doors slid open.

"Thanks for your concern, Jennings," Harrison said, keeping his voice cool and steady, "because if I'm right about what I think is going on, we all have plenty to be nervous about. It's good we'll be working on this together though. We'll need some brawn along with our brains."

Kate stifled a chuckle, and Harrison stoically enjoyed the way Skip's jaw tightened. The doors opened, and they all stepped off the elevator.

Chapter 3

THURSDAY – 16 Hours Earlier: New York

"Thanks everybody, that's a wrap," the photographer called out to the loft that was teaming with male models, stylists, makeup artists, and camera assistants.

"More beauty, more money," he added, handing off his camera to his assistant and doing a small victory dance. "I do great work, right, riiiight?" he called out, hand to ear with pretend neediness.

There was a chorus of, "Of course you do, Bodey/You're the best/Sure, definitely," and some halfhearted "Woohoos," before they all laughed with Bodey joining them.

"Seriously though," he continued, "It's been a long day, but this will be a foldout inside front covers, billboards, and of course online. Thanks for everybody's hard work, and may it mean more of the same for all of us."

"Amen, brother," the lighting tech said. "Anybody down for drinks at Pera?"

"On Thompson, right?" Bree, the makeup artist, called over.

"Yep, best cocktails in Soho and mega-cheap happy hour. You in, Bree?"

"Sure," she replied, turning to the stylist. "Mary, you coming with?"

Mary Kelly, who was sitting at her laptop looking from a photo on the screen to its subject, one of four sculpted male underwear models, didn't appear to have heard her.

Bree stepped up behind her and looked over her shoulder, leaning close to her ear. "Since you've been imagining the poor guy without his briefs all day long, why don't you put your tongue back in and go help him get dressed."

"Shush, he can hear you," Mary whispered, shutting her laptop and pretending not to notice the model grinning at her as her face turned first pink then red. "I told you, I don't mix business and pleasure. Nothing worse than getting involved with somebody and having to see them on a job after it all goes to the crapper. Besides, male models are jerks. They spend more time in the mirror than the women."

"Well you need to get laid somehow," Bree whispered back loudly. "You're wound too tight, and a little schtupp goes a long way. Come with us, I know he'll go if you go." They both glanced at the man who now had a tee-shirt on that did nothing to mask the chest and six pack Mary had been ogling.

"OMG he is mad fine. He looks even better *in* clothes, if that's possible." Mary paused a moment in packing up her belongings. "I'd really like to. Maybe . . ." But she stopped herself and shook her head resolutely. "No, no. I have a shoot tomorrow day, and I'm helping at Owen tonight at an art opening."

"Really? Really Kelly?" Bree said, slightly annoyed. "You seriously think working all the time like this is going to get you a social life? Bae, you're 31, perimenopause is just around the corner."

"There are more important things than partying all the time." Mary put her jacket on and jammed her red fedora on her head, making sure to adjust the brim so it was just above her eyes. "And I do have a social life."

"That cat doesn't count," Bree shot back.

"Oh, bye!" Mary said, escaping out the door.

She knew Bree was right: she did need to have more fun. And she certainly wasn't going to get a boyfriend by never going anywhere and working every waking moment. But on the other hand, she didn't leave Starkville, Mississippi with $117.52 and end up in a two bedroom in Soho . . . with a killer view . . . by partying and going from man to man like the other young women she knew. She could honestly say she did not drink her twenties away as some of her girlfriends had.

And what did they know, anyway? Most of them couldn't even define the word "poverty", let alone live it and survive it and come out on top, as she had.

The afternoon was coming to a close as sunshine gave way to clouds that were slowly gathering overhead. She did her usual no-nonsense, brisk, "New York strut", as she liked to think of it. People would have thought she was odd back home, charging down the street like this. And as always, she let the hum and energy of The City move through her like that TENS device her chiropractor used to run a little electric current through her muscles. Just moving through her neighborhood lifted her spirits. Loneliness? *Poo poo on that noise.* She laughed out loud as she inwardly used her mother's strongest condemnation. She didn't even care when a couple of people steered away from her as they would a homeless kook.

She was hungry, but she first made a detour to Bond 07 by Selima. After all, Mary thought, she'd worked like crazy for the last couple of months; it was time for a reward. And what better reward than good vintage? It took her only a few minutes to blow half the check she was expecting on a pair of boots and a 70s era jacket that she had been stalking for a few weeks. It was a lot, but she was worth every cent. Besides, she received her stylist discount, so it was a bargain. She walked out with a big grin on her face.

She was even further cheered when there were only two people in line at Tomoe Sushi—in her mind, a small miracle. Mary looked at the place that was on her "4 D's" list: dinky, dive, but food so dynamite, she could eat it and die happy. She looked forward to the day when she could share her inner clever world with someone who would get it. And her.

She observed the usual crowd of down-to-earth sushi lovers mixed with the trendy networking types. She wondered if they were trying to show the world how important they were, or actually hoping for a real connection of some kind. *Whatever! Too deep on an empty stomach* she thought. Right now, she had yummy grilled yellowtail, shrimp dumplings and a salad on her brain. "Hamachi Kama, Shumai, and a seaweed salad, to go please." After her usual smile and wave from the chefs she was soon on her way home.

Mary had only walked a few minutes when something changed her mood. For some reason, she started to feel uneasy. She knew that feeling. From before, in the days when her financial situation dictated a lot of ramen noodles and late notices from her landlords and calls from Mom saying in *that voice, "Honey, y'all can just come on back home. That's a try, not a failure. Maybe that place just isn't for you."*

But there was no reason now. Except, it was happening. She felt her heartbeat increase and her palms become moist. Something wasn't right. She felt like someone was watching her, like they were right behind her, creeping up. She swung around quickly, but no one was even close. And no one was paying attention to her. Nevertheless, she hooked her clothing bag over her left shoulder and put her hand into her pocket, clutching her mace spray. The knuckles of her other hand, clutching her carryout bag with a tense fist, had gone white.

The sun dropped, and the damp chill in the air didn't help. She picked up her pace. She didn't see anything, but it didn't matter. She felt . . . something. Something off, wrong. She was at Minetta Lane and 6th Ave minutes later and rushing up to the door of her building. She fumbled for her keys and, struggling for control, she opened the front security door, stepped quickly inside, and turned once again to see . . . nothing. She shut her eyes, leaned against the wall, and inhaled a few slow, shaky breaths, regaining her composure as she'd been taught by her hypnotherapist some years ago. *What the hell?* was all she could think. Maybe Bree was right: maybe she just needed a little sexual healing, so she could relax. She tried to laugh, but she couldn't get it out.

"You okay, Miss?" she heard Greg's concerned voice call out to her from behind the front desk.

"Fine, thanks, Greg," she said a little too brightly. "Too much shopping, I guess. It'll tire you out every time. You guys get that alarm fixed?" she added quickly, hoping he wouldn't ask anything more.

"Yeah, I think so. But I tell everybody, treat it like it's the real thing. You never know. *Some people* didn't come down last time," he said pointedly.

"Ok. I hear you, Greg. Hope it's fixed though."

She took the elevator to six and hurried to her apartment, still feeling the last of the uneasiness like a cold hand on the back of her neck. "Jones?" she called as she put her packages down and hurried through the apartment, switching on lights in every room.

She heard a slight noise behind her and turned to see her cat rushing toward her, tail in the air. He leapt into her arms, and she hugged him close, nuzzling his warm fur as he loudly shared the details of his day.

"Really? You did? Well, that's fine and dandy," she said, noting that her heart and breathing had slowed. She gave him a kiss and put him gently on the floor. "Let's dinner. I have to go back out tonight." She opened a can of Jones' favorite salmon and put her food on *good* plates as her mother used to say to describe the few plates they had had that matched and weren't chipped. Of course, one of her saucers now cost more than all their dishes combined.

She was feeling much better as she poured a glass of a gorgeous merlot given to her by gallery owner Charles Owen. It tasted extra good because she knew it had cost a couple hundred dollars at least. The wine and food finished the job of mellowing her out completely. She remembered to follow her personal rule of once a day looking around her showplace apartment and out at her million-dollar view and thanking God and all the angels and her poor childhood for bringing her to this lifestyle in this place and time.

"Mine was great, how about yours?" she asked Jones when she was done. "Yummy to your tummy is good too," she responded to his purred answer.

She put her dishes in the dishwasher, grabbed her phone and a second glass of wine, and went to the bedroom closet. "Okay, what to wear." She began pulling garments as she would for a client: dress, choices of matching shoes, a group of accessories, a jacket or two. She put more down, took some away, and dialed her best friend Miranda as she continued to sip and decide.

"Mar!" she heard her friend say as she had for over 25 years, and she responded as she always did with, "Mir!"

"What's the good word?" Miranda continued their pattern.

"Just you baby bird," Mary said. "And the actual good word for right now is wine. Very goooood wine." She giggled and took another sip. "You're still coming tonight, right?"

"Not only that, I'm probably buying," Miranda said. "We're redoing the beach house, and I've heard this guy is supposed to be a wizard with pastels.

Maybe I can build a room around something. What are you wearing?"

"Black on black," Mary replied. "But you know what that means."

"Yep, your makeup is going to look like you just stepped off a runway, and women everywhere will be handcuffing themselves to their husbands."

"Well, they don't have to worry," Mary said as she began hanging up all her rejected possibilities. "I want only one, and I want him to be mine, all mine."

"Speaking of, any prospects? Any swipes in the right direction?" Miranda asked.

"No, none of those. Well, there was kind of a hottie at the shoot today, but . . . Anyhow, speaking of swiping right, how's my Dave boy?"

"The usual: a wolf at work, I hear, and a teddy bear at home, I know."

"That's okay. We love a rich, generous, wolfen teddy."

Miranda giggled and said, "Now that's the wine talking. But if you're serious, Dave has a fellow wolf who would just love to be your teddy bear. I think he showed him a picture of you. His name is—"

"No please, not another one. Dave is cool, but those guys he works with make me feel like the fashion I shop for. I can tell they're always looking for a superior item that looks just as good or better."

"Well you can't wait forever, Mar. You know we aren't exactly—"

"Would you let it go, please? I wish everybody would leave me alone about it! I'll meet someone when I do," she snapped.

There was a moment's silence before Miranda said gently, "You okay? I didn't mean anything, I was just—"

"I'm sorry, Mir," Mary jumped in. "Too much wine, and not enough dating.

You're actually saying what I've been thinking, and it kind of bothers me that—"

Woooo!Woooo!Woooo! interrupted her, blaring throughout the apartment.

"Oh my God!" Mary screamed as she jumped, and Jones disappeared under the sofa.

"Is that that stupid fire alarm?" Miranda yelled, as if the noise were on her side of the call.

"Yes, and I can't ignore it again," Mary yelled back. "Look, I'll call you when I come back up. I can't hear a thing."

She clicked off, grabbed her jacket and keys, and hurried down the six flights of stairs, grumbling the whole way. She was joined by other tenants who seemed to feel exactly the same as she did about the inconvenience.

Greg was holding the door to the lobby open, doing his best "in charge, calm voice-of-authority" routine. "Keep moving folks, hurry please, but be careful, it'll be over soon, thanks for your cooperation."

But the looks and remarks, which he chose to ignore, were far from cooperative.

Mary frowned and shifted from foot to foot, worrying about her appointment at the gallery.

"What is this, like the third time this month?" an annoyed male voice said from behind her.

"I think it's the—" she began as she turned and stopped, mouth still open as she looked up at a pair of intense gray eyes that took her breath away, "—fourth or . . . fifth or . . . something." The dark haired, slim but muscular man was looking down at her like he couldn't quite believe what he was seeing.

"Pretty annoying," the man said in a soft, bemused voice, "unless, of course, something interesting happens while you're hanging around on the sidewalk."

There was a moment of silence as they both stared at each other.

"I'm sorry to stare at you like that," Mary said, looking around, embarrassed, at the other people milling on the sidewalk. "This is going to sound crazy, but your eyes are the same color as my cat's."

"Uh, thank you? I guess?" he said. He smiled. "Is he a real cool cat?"

"He's kind of a perfect cat, actually," she laughed.

"I've been thinking about getting a cat. But, I don't know. Is it a good idea to have one in an apartment when you have to leave them alone a lot?"

"Well Jones, he's fine with it."

"Jones, ha, I like that. What kind of cat is he?"

"He's a Balinese long hair."

"Oh that's like . . .?"

"Kind of a Siamese,"

"Oh, yeah, they're pretty. I like their—"

"—eyes," they said at the same time, as she looked up at his, and he looked away.

"My name is Matthew," he said awkwardly, extending his hand to shake.

"Mary. I haven't seen you around." She thought his hand felt strong and warm and just rough enough.

"I've only been here a few months. I haven't seen you either. If I had, I definitely would have remembered. Oh boy, that sounded creepy didn't it?"

"No, no it didn't, not at all," Mary said quickly.

"I live on 9, 913. I um . . . Do you like living here? It seems like a really good place.

How long have you been here?" He stopped, grimacing with annoyance. "Oh no, too many questions, Ugh, I'm sorry, I'm doing it again."

"No, It's okay, it's okay really," she couldn't stop giggling, "I'm in 601. I've met some creepy guys, and believe me, they never, ever worry about being creepy."

"Again, thanks, I guess? So uh . . ." He stammered as she admired his awkward cuteness. "Uh, do you like plants?"

"Plants?" she asked, confused.

"Sorry, I mean like flowering plants. For your apartment. They kind of brighten the place up."

"Well, it's like you and the cats; I'm not sure being in my apartment would be healthy for plants. I think much violent death would ensue. Plant death, that is."

"No, see," he leaned toward her earnestly, "that just means someone chose the wrong one. Some plants are really low maintenance and really pretty at the same time."

"Oh, like me," Mary said flippantly and immediately blushed. *The wine must have me flirting like this*, she thought.

"Well, I don't know about the low maintenance part, but—" Matthew began, but he was cut off by Greg calling out, "All clear! Thanks for your patience everyone, you can come back in now. False alarm."

"Patience!" one woman hissed at him. "My evening is ruined. Why can't you people get this thing fixed? It's ridiculous."

"Uh oh, poor Greg," Matthew said softly.

The two walked past as the woman, flanked by other fuming tenants, followed the retreating Greg to the front desk.

They waited silently with a small group of complainers for one of the elevators to come back down.

Their silence continued on the way up, as they shared looks and smiles, while others looked straight ahead or checked their phones.

At the sixth floor, Mary stepped out and turned around, her arm stopping the door from closing, aware that everyone was looking at her.

"Well, so . . ." she began, not quite knowing what to say.

"I'll see you soon, I hope," Matthew said, "Maybe—"

"Could we go now?" an exasperated man snapped. "Some of us have things to do."

"Sorry," Mary said, stepping back as Matthew waved and gave her a small shrug.

She went back to her apartment on a whole different kind of energy. She rushed through showering and excitedly dialed Miranda the minute she was done. She put her phone on speaker and dressed hurriedly.

"Mir! Guess what? I've met somebody!"

"What? Like, now? Where? In your living room?? Just because we talked about--"

"Mir, I'm not joking. One Mississippi."

"Two Mississippi," Miranda replied in their girlhood code for the absolute truth. "Wow. So, who is he? Where did he come from?"

"A new guy in the building, well, here for a few months," Mary replied. "We met waiting for the all clear. And Mir, he's cute and kind of sweet and shy and intense at the same time. He likes cats, and he collects plants."

"Well thank you, broken fire alarm." Miranda said, laughing. "So what happened, did he get your number or ask you to coffee or anything?"

"He didn't get a chance to, but I know he's on nine, and he knows where I am. And I have a really good feeling about this. I know. It's stupid."

"It's not stupid at all," Miranda said. "Just take your time and be careful. And I'll start picking a matron of honor dress."

"Now y'all are just silleh," Mary said in their childhood Mississippi accent and giggled.

"But now that you mention it, I was thinking peach or apricot."

Miranda let out a pained "Ugh", and they both dissolved in laughter which was interrupted by Mary's doorbell buzzer.

She groaned with annoyance. "Who the heck is this?"

"Maybe it's makeup borrowing Betty," Miranda offered.

"It better not be. I keep telling her to call first. I have to go."

She peeked out the eyehole before jumping back. "Oh my god, Mir, it's him!" she whispered, as if he could hear through the door.

"You mean—"

"Yes! Him. Matthew. What should I do?"

"Uh, open the door maybe?"

"Ohmygod, ohmygod. Ok, stay on the phone, ok?"

"No, I will not. I'll see you at Owen later, and you can tell me all about it. Bye Mar."

"Bye, Mir."

"Ok, ok," Mary said, composing herself as she put the phone down and slowly opened the door.

"Uh hi," Matthew said. He was in a fresh shirt and jacket and was holding a potted plant with white flowers and dark green leaves. Once again, he stood open-mouthed for a moment. "Wow, you changed. You look . . . Uh, it's for you," he said holding out the plant nervously, as if he thought she might not take it.

Mary took it, and he sighed in relief. "It's beautiful. I love it. I have the perfect place for it." She walked to the table next to her sofa.

"It's called Oxalis," he said from the doorway. "I have one with pink flowers too, but I thought the white would go with anything." His voice became louder as she got farther away.

She turned and looked back at him.

"Well," he said, "well, so I wanted to . . . I'll see you again soon, I hope. Really beautiful. That's what I was going to say. You look really beautiful." He grabbed the door handle and began to pull it shut.

"Matthew you're just going to plant me now and dig me later?"

"What?" he looked genuinely confused.

"My mother used to . . . Nevermind," she said. "Just come on in. I promise I won't bite."

He stepped slowly in and closed the door, took a few more steps, put his hands awkwardly in his pockets and stopped, taking the place in like a kid walking into Disneyland. "Wow, this place looks amazing. Are you an artist or something? Or just like really, really rich?"

"More the first one, I'm a stylist."

"Oh, like a hair stylist?"

"You are hilarious," she laughed as she moved a small sculpture and put the plant in the middle of the table. "So pretty. What do you think?"

"Beautiful," he said, looking at her as he approached.

"I meant the plant." She turned away from his intense gaze, noticing how fast her heart was beating. *What if he's the one? What if?* she kept thinking. Jones took that moment to rescue her by jumping into her arms and staring defiantly at Matthew.

"That must be Jones," he said. "Impressive looking guy."

"Yes he is," she said and put him on the sofa.

"So his eyes really look like mine?" he asked. She thought he just wanted her to look at him, so she did before turning her attention nervously back to the plant.

"Yes they do," she whispered. "Um, these leaves," she touched one gently, "they remind me of shamrocks."

"You noticed!" he said, triumphantly. "I knew you would."

"You did? Why?" She turned and looked at him again.

"Well, with a good Irish name like Mary Kelly, how could you not?"

"Oh. Yes, of c . . ." and the smile faded from her face. "I never told you my last name."

"Well, no, but it's on your mailbox along with the apartment number," he said.

"No, no it isn't," she said, taking a couple of steps back from him.

"All right, I admit it. I slipped Greg a few bucks to find out. But please don't get him in trouble," he said, moving toward her, his palms open. "I just wanted to know about you. And Mary Kelly is a wonderful name. Why in the 19th century, it was world famous. Didn't you know?"

"Nineteenth century? What are you . . . ??"

There was a moment where neither of them breathed or moved. Then she knew. She knew what was coming.

"You're talking about Jack the Ripper, aren't you?"

"You are beautiful," was all he said.

She looked toward her door, but he was standing between it and her. "Look," she pleaded, panicked, "just get out, I won't scream, I won't say anything. Just leave. Please! Please don't hurt me!"

She grabbed the gift plant, the heaviest thing close to her, to throw at him, but he grabbed her wrist and twisted it, forcing her to drop it. She took in a breath to scream, but his right hand, that strong, just rough enough hand, clamped on her throat like a vise, and all she could manage was a tiny, choked squeal.

Scratch him! I can scratch his face, his eyes! But before she could finish the thought, he had twisted her arm behind her and flipped her body around like a doll, pressing her back to him and now squeezing her throat with his forearm. From somewhere, he pulled a knife that looked to her like a sword.

She quivered and struggled, moaning and crying, trying to kick him, but it was like being held in an iron cage underwater: she could not breathe. She was beginning to lose consciousness when she heard him say words she used to hear every year at Christmas. But something was wrong with them, something off and different.

"Fear not, Mary, for thou has found favor with God. The power of the Highest overshadows thee now. Greater love has no one than this, that she give up her life for the greater good."

He brandished his sword in the air and cried out to somebody, "In the day of great slaughter, the Tower will fall."

Mom! Mommy! Come and help me! Nothing beats a failure! Mommy!! One Mississippi, Two Mississippi---

And he slashed her throat, cutting to the bone in one movement.

As her blood mixed with white petals and dirt on the floor, the man stepped briskly to the front door, opened it, and brought in the large leather bag he had waiting outside. He carried her body to the bedroom and put her on the bed. He took a Tyvek Hazmat suit out of his bag and replaced it with his jacket. "So beautiful," he said, looking at her face and body for the last time before he began to cut.

Jones hopped down from the sofa where he had been cowering, one of his paws landing in her blood. He stopped to carefully lick it off before trotting nonchalantly to his favorite hiding place behind the living room curtain.

Chapter 4

FRIDAY – FBI Office: Los Angeles

Harrison had never felt this kind of nervous tension entering the conference room. He'd never liked speaking before a crowd, but this was far worse. He actually wondered, briefly, if he was going to have to take a break to go and throw up. But he dismissed that feeling as ridiculous, and imagining what his father might have to say about that kind of weakness helped to steady him immediately.

Believing that they had someone special in their midst, Bureau chiefs had acted quickly to offer Harrison a position at their Los Angeles headquarters to work and study.

Only the elite were ever offered a position. After a compressed training regime at Quantico, the Bureau's academy in Virginia, Harrison was ushered off to Los Angeles to work with a specialist team. He knew that from day one he would have to be on his toes and prove himself to his peers if he was going to gain any of their respect. Still relatively young, he was a perfect fit for the Bureau. It would allow them to mould him into the Agent they believed he could be. To prove his worth to those who took a chance with this unknown commodity, Harrison would often stay back at work to pick the brains of those more experienced. This was no place for egos, this was where the best of the best worked side-by-side to try and read the minds of killers and to predict their next move.

Snapping back to the task at hand, Harrison told himself this wasn't actually a "crowd." In addition to the three of them, there were Kate's good friend Agent Jeanne Conrad and three other agents whose names he didn't know. He recognized an administrative assistant, Laurie something, who'd been with the Bureau for many years. She smiled and gave him a little wave and went back to her cell phone. His attention was really drawn by a freckled, African American guy with wild hair who hardly looked out of his teens, though he must have been at least 23 to be an agent. To Harrison, he appeared to be eager and excited, like a kid standing in line for the circus.

Kate took a seat at the long conference table beside Jeanne. As he'd seen them do before, they gave each other a deadpan stare then said, "S'up," and "S'up," like two hardened gang boys. Then both grinned at each other: clearly some inside joke between them. Jeanne definitely looked like she might legitimately know a gang greeting or two. He liked her but once again wondered about their friendship; in his opinion, they couldn't be more different. Jeanne: African American, with that Marine-looking, almost Mohawk haircut he knew was called a "high and tight" and who looked like she could break Kate in half on her way to win an arm wrestling match with Skip Jennings. She never wore short sleeves during working hours, but when she did, like for playing baseball or working out, her pecan brown skin was light enough so he could see she had some kind of tattoos on her arms. And then there was model beautiful (in his opinion, anyhow) Kate. But maybe neither one really belonged. Maybe, like him, they felt like outsiders, and that was the connection.

He walked toward the seat on Kate's other side only to be cut off, like a rude, asshole highway driver, by Skip Jennings planting his bulk in the seat next to hers. Kate barely acknowledged him, and Jeanne glanced at him and made a face like a little kid smelling something "vewy stinky." Harrison liked her even better at that moment.

Phil Stanton swept in, followed by his Chief of Staff, Malik Daniels. Daniels was usually the lighter, more easygoing foil to Stanton's unbending professionalism, but today, Harrison thought both looked absolutely grim. *They think I'm right* he said to himself. He had an odd feeling of being glad and proud while simultaneously being ashamed of feeling that way. A potential serial killer was nothing to high five himself about.

Stanton went directly to the head of the table and set down a mug of still steaming black coffee. Everyone else quickly took seats, waiting expectantly.

"Good morning everyone," Stanton said. "Let's get right to it. As you know, you're now part of a task force formed in response to a series of crimes. We'll be working with other local Bureaus and agencies across the country. I'll explain more about our purpose shortly. First: introductions. You all know Special Agent in Charge of the Criminal Division, Malik Daniels."

Daniels gave a small wave to everyone, looking around the table. To Harrison, he smiled and nodded. Harrison knew that smile from his mentor was one of encouragement. Malik and his wife Sharon were the anchors that had kept him steady in his time at the Bureau. Despite the glaring differences between them, like race and their Catholicism versus his agnosticism, he thought of them as his "other parents." Whenever he started feeling insecure or began wondering if he'd made the right choice, all he had to do was go to Daniels for advice, and a few words would set him back on the right track. And the irony, which he knew, and Malik would unfailingly point out, was that all of it was in his imagination. He had been on a steady trend upward since he entered the Bureau, and he knew that when it came to education, laser focus, and determination, he was in a class by himself. But in his head, where, he sometimes felt, Harrison Carter, Sr. reigned, things weren't as clear.

A dinner invitation from Sharon Daniels meant that Malik had gone home and told her something like, "Our boy needs some help." Harrison would never have said it out loud, but sometimes he couldn't help thinking how different things would be if his parents were more like the Daniels. *And wouldn't that be interesting,* he thought, watching Daniels' confident, strong demeanor. *What if I'd been adopted by a black Catholic couple as an infant?* Yes, his life would definitely be different.

He stopped his mind from its nervous, random wanderings and brought his focus back to Stanton. He had tuned out while his boss introduced the agents and Laurie, the admin.

He turned to Malik and said, "Agent Daniels is more familiar with our other member, so if you'll introduce him, Malik."

"Sure Boss," Malik said indicating the eager young guy. "Despite appearances, this young person is out of high school, and he is our brilliant IT person Othello Cook. Don't let his youthfulness fool you, he is a fully credentialed agent, was number one in his class, and anything we need with regard to computers or information, he's our guy."

Malik turned to Stanton. "Back to you, sir." He took a seat on Harrison's side of the table.

The Director began, "Thanks. Now I'm going to—" Othello spoke up loudly and eagerly. "Sir? Uh, Sorry sir I just want you to know, everybody to know, I'm really excited about being on the team, and any information, anything you want to find online, locate, anything IT related, I can make it happen. I know we're here for a serious purpose, but I just have to say I'm so stoked to be a part of this. My life is amazing right now. New job, new girl. You know that feeling people talk about when you've had just the right amount of ecstasy and you're kind of floating? Well it's kind of like that. Hashtag dream job. And I . . ." He paused and looked around him at the bemused and disbelieving looks mumbled, "Talking too much."

Kate chuckled and said, "It's okay. You're fine. And interesting."

"Definitely that," Jeanne threw in.

There was a moment of amused silence before Stanton said, "Well, congratulations on . . . all that. I appreciate your enthusiasm. With the kind of cases we'll be working on, I hope you can hold onto it."

"And congratulations on the new relationship," Malik said, stifling a laugh. "Let us know when the wedding date is set."

Othello blushed, making his freckles even more prominent, and Stanton went back to business.

"I'm sure all of you remember, about nine months ago in Little Rock, the murder of little beauty queen Jocelyn Simmons. There was speculation at the time that it may have been a copycat who was trying to emulate the JonBenét Ramsey case. And of course, you'll all be familiar with the multiple cases in Tulsa, Oklahoma where there were seven murdered men, most of whom appeared to be involved in prostitution. That one mirrored the John Wayne Gacy murders. Both cases were as identical as someone could make them to the originals, using publicly available pictures and information. What you may not know is Agent Harrison Carter has held a belief for some time that these murders were committed by the same individual."

"Yeah, we did hear about his little serial killer theory," Skip said, "but unfortunately, we never heard anything about proof. Some of these newer agents see a serial killer behind every rock."

Stanton gave Skip a look that silenced him immediately. "What's truly unfortunate is, you're all here right now because it looks like it's a lot more than a theory. Harrison, are you ready to show us what you've put together?"

Harrison swallowed. All eyes were on him. He was the center of attention. A difficult surgery, confronting his father, *anything* would be better than this.

He cleared his throat and stood up. The moment before he started talking, he looked across at Kate and decided he'd just try to focus on her. "Okay. Everybody. What I noticed in the two cases was not only that they were clearly copies of the earlier famous murders, but also there was something else: something about them made me wonder about a link between the crimes. Now, it wasn't method. Obviously, the single murder and the multiples were very different, but . . . uh, well. It's more of a mindset or mentality."

He felt his throat getting dry and bit his tongue to make more moisture. "What I mean is, if you think of it like . . . ok, in medicine, there may be multiple symptoms that present at different times. Maybe some point in one direction and some in another, but when you take them all together, the diagnosis may lead to a completely different place than first expected."

Skip rolled his eyes and muttered, "Thanks, Dr. Obvious," and pointedly looked away.

Kate shushed him then looked back at Harrison and nodded encouragingly. He hit a few keys on the laptop in front of him and continued, "I can show you here what I'm talking about. I guess . . ." he looked around at everyone, "we can kind-of pass it down so you can all—"

"Want me to put it on the big screen?" Othello asked, already up and reaching for Harrison's laptop.

"Thanks," Harrison said and used the small break to take a sip of water.

"Yeah thanks," Skip said, just loud enough for those closest to hear. "Grateful for *somebody* who knows what he's doing."

No one commented, and Harrison found himself imagining his fist knowing its way to Skip's face.

"Here you go," Othello said returning to his seat.

Harrison stepped up to the lectern where the laptop was placed and clicked on the first of the side-by-side pictures he'd been studying for months.

When the images of the two beautiful little blonde victims flashed on the screen, he could feel the reaction in the room. Some of them had never seen the two tragedies in direct, graphic comparison. "As you can see," he said, going from slide to slide and pointing out the eerie similarities, "someone very precise and meticulous studied this case and replicated it, down to the way the knots were tied and the break in the basement window."

He showed some of the bodies in the Tulsa killings beside Gacy photos. "Same thing here," he said, grateful for the focus being on the screen instead of on him. "Both scenes were recreated with clinical precision and also devoid of a hint of the killer's DNA. Other than the connecting clues that were left behind intentionally, the relevant areas of each scene were almost surgically scrubbed."

"So we're looking for a homicidal doctor?" Skip asked, feigning confusion.

Harrison ignored him and continued, gaining confidence from Skip's boorishness; he must be doing pretty well. "There are two other elements that helped me to come to a conclusion." He put up another slide with a picture of a Bible, open to the Book of Psalms, and clicked to the next one of a crumpled Psalm torn out of a different Bible.

"These were left behind at the two scenes. The Simmons one is third chapter, verse one: 'I have so many enemies, Lord, so many who turn against me.' And the one from the Tulsa case, stuffed in the mouth of the apparent final victim was Psalm 54:6 which says, 'I will gladly offer you a sacrifice, O Lord; I will give you thanks because you are good.'"

"Do you know what those mean?" one of the other agents asked.

"No, only speculation so far. I thought about perhaps the victims being the sacrifices referred to. It's possible that all of them, including the little girl, were symbols of something in the killer's life."

"You're pretty sure it's only one killer?" a different, female voice asked.

"Well no, I'm not sure. Especially with so many young male victims in Tulsa. That's just one of the possibilities right now."

"So this 'similarity' that you're talking about," it was Skip doing his best disbelieving, confused voice, "is based on . . . in the first case . . . a Psalm from a bible, being related to paper found in the throat of one of the victims of the other crime? I read about those cases too. There was underwear in a couple of the guys' throats, and little Jocelyn had on underwear. Does that tie them together too?"

In his mind at that moment, Harrison saw himself launching across the table and ending up with his hands around Skip's throat, but before he could come up with a response that would be more acceptable for a grown up meeting, Jeanne said, "Damn, jerk much, Jennings?"

"People!" Stanton rapped out, the steel in his voice unmistakable. He looked from one to the other. "If there's something going on here that has nothing to do with the cases we're working on but might somehow interfere, it's going away. Right now. When Harrison is done, we have more to tell you."

"Thanks, sir. I'm done." Harrison drew a relieved breath and walked back to his seat, noting a smiling Kate giving him two thumbs up. He couldn't resist winking at Skip and was pleased to see his jaw tighten again.

"Good. Thanks, Harrison. Now let's get to why you're all here. About two hours ago, I received a phone call from Det. Davi Silva, City of Vernon. You probably heard about finding the body of the murdered Lyft driver in East LA last night. Well, of the details that haven't been made public are two salient facts: there was a symbol left on the car window . . . a circle on a cross, and also—"

"Zodiac!" Harrison blurted out involuntarily.

"Yes. This scene is a duplicate of one of the Zodiac killings, a taxi driver named Paul Stine. Also, there was a coded letter that, when deciphered, spells out a Psalm. For those who don't know, the Zodiac was a serial killer operating in Northern California in the late 60s and early 70s. He would leave his symbol and also puzzles and codes to taunt law enforcement at every crime scene. It's clear our killer has studied him. The Psalm thing, though, that's new and is not characteristic of any of these past perpetrators. The current one is chapter 10, verse 12. It reads 'O Lord, punish those wicked men! Remember those who are suffering!'

"As with the two Psalms left in the other cases, this verse could have any of a dozen meanings. This killer is trying to tell us something, and we're going to find out what it is. Here's the game plan: we're bringing in a Bible expert to help us try and figure out some kind of meaning, how these verses are connected.

"Agents Carter and Fleming, Det. Davi Silva will be waiting for you to arrive at the East LA location in about 45 minutes. On our request, they haven't moved the car. Katherine, you know we can't actually take over their case, but make sure they know we're working nationally, not just locally, and they need to cooperate.

"Agents Conrad and Jennings will be coordinating with Little Rock and Tulsa, respectively. Update them and find out anything more current that they have on their cases. And share whatever we have. Everyone else, you've been assigned different tasks that Laurie has forwarded to you.

"Othello will be inputting all the information we have from the three cases we know of so far and cross checking for any kind of similarities beyond what we already know. Make sure to funnel anything you find to him, so everyone is updated at all times.

"Malik, I know you really know your Bible, so feel free to jump in with any insights you may have. And that goes for everyone." He stood up and looked at the team. "Any questions? Fine, then we'll—"

"Uh sir," Skip said, "I think I could be of much more use at an active crime scene. Since Carter already has a relationship with the people in Tulsa, wouldn't it make more sense—?"

"It would not," Stanton cut him off. He allowed the tension to grow for a few moments before saying quietly, "If everyone can please get to their tasks. Now." Everyone began quickly gathering their things as he turned and strode to his office.

Jennings was the first out of the door and Jeanne hurried behind him calling sweetly, "Hold that please, Skipper."

Kate walked up beside Harrison shaking her head and laughing. "She shouldn't mess with him like that. He hates being called Skipper."

"Well I'll try to remember not to do that," Harrison said. "Are you ready?"

"Yep. You drive. And bring your laptop. I want to look at your notes on the way."

"Harrison, let me holler at you before you go," he heard Malik say from behind him.

"Won't take long, Kate."

Harrison threw a look at Kate, shrugged, and followed him to his office.

Moments later, Daniels was sitting at his desk looking up at Harrison. He drummed his fingers a few times and finally said, "I'm not going to ask you what's going on with you and Jennings, but I don't have to tell you how important this case, these cases, are. You're on this task force because the Director and I are looking at your future. You haven't been here that long, but we think you can handle it. Can you? This is a team, and you're more of a solo kind of player. You have to be able to work with everybody, everybody on the team, no matter what kind of asshole they may be."

"No worries, sir. I can handle whatever asshole exposes itself to me."

Malik tried and failed to hold back his laughter. "Ok son," he said waving Harrison toward the door. Almost as an afterthought, he threw in, "And while you're avoiding the assholes, don't let any angels distract you either."

Harrison turned back toward him, mouth open. "I don't know what—"

"Too smart to play dumb Harrison! Keep your head in the game. Stay focused. This is a great opportunity for you. Don't let anything or anyone mess it up. Run on now. *Kate's* waiting." He winked at Harrison who kept opening and closing his mouth trying to come up with some snappy comeback that would show Malik he was wrong, but he had nothing. He realized he must look like a drowning fish, flopping on a beach, so he gave up and left the office.

Chapter 5

DAY – New York

Miranda had waited long enough. She'd called Mary repeatedly from the moment she arrived at Owen and realized her friend hadn't shown. This was not Mary: she never, ever missed a job or flaked on a promise to be somewhere. Even when she was sick, she was the one who would be sent home by a boss before just not showing up. And tonight: no show and no call. And gallery owner Charles Owen was not smiling.

She knew Mar had met someone, but they'd never even been out, and she absolutely would not, *ever*, do a sleepover or even have sex the first night. It wasn't only about her focus on work; that kind of thing was completely out of character.

Miranda bought two paintings from Owen and made sure to emphasize that she wouldn't have come if it hadn't been for Mary.

"Well," he said, his tone a little less chilly than before she put more mileage on her AMEX Platinum card, "when you talk to her, you tell her I need to hear from her *post haste*. I've never known her to be so irresponsible. We had people needing advice on displays, not to mention models waiting for her."

"Believe me, Charles, it was something important. She'll call you with an explanation tomorrow, I'm sure," Miranda said.

People were still coming in when she left the gallery at midnight. She'd stayed as long as she could, hoping her friend would show up late, but she knew Mary would have called or at least texted to let her know that. While riding in her limo, she left yet another message for Mary. She had gone from, "Hey where are you?" through, "Call right now, this isn't funny!" and her next to last was, "You're really worrying me." Finally she couldn't take it any longer. She leaned over and gave her driver Mary's address and called one last time. "Mary, I'm coming to your apartment, and if you're scaring me like this because of some guy, I will kill you. One Mississippi." *That guy. What if?* She tossed her phone on the seat and tried to fight back the panic that was rising in her belly. She leaned forward and snapped, "Hurry!!" She closed her eyes and began to pray.

* * *

When she arrived at the building, Greg buzzed her right in, obviously trying to hide his surprise at the late hour. "Good evening, Miss, is everything—"

"Greg, have you seen Mary, Miss Kelly, this evening?" she interrupted.

"Oh, your friend, sixth floor, right? I'm pretty sure I saw her when we had a fire alarm. It was another false alarm, you know. But better to be safe, don't you think? People get pretty upset with me, but I can't fix it. I don't get it. We had it fixed twice, and the same thing keeps happening. Weird, you know? But—"

"Greg!" she snapped, "Did you see her leave later, like dressed up to go out?"

"No, Miss. She didn't go out. It's been real quiet since the alarm. And your friend, when she dresses up, people take notice, you know?"

Now Miranda was actually shaking. "She was supposed to meet me, and she's not answering my calls. Something's wrong, Greg. We have to go up there."

"Uh, now wait a minute, Miss. I can't go barging into someone's apartment at this time of the night. Plenty of people are grousing and complaining already today, like I had some kind of control over a technical problem. But it ain't my fault. You know, she's probably just asleep. But here, tellya what, since you're so worried, I can call her."

He picked up the internal phone and hit four numbers. Both were silent as it rang and rang again six more times. Miranda was rocking from foot to foot like she had to use the toilet. She looked frantically from him to the phone, waiting for him to hang up and finally burst out, "She's not answering! I'm telling you something's wrong! She met some guy who showed up at her door, she missed a job, and now she's not answering the phone. We have to go up there right now!"

"A guy? She met a guy?" Greg raised his chin indignantly before giving her a knowing look. "I see. Well, maybe the issue is she doesn't exactly want to be disturbed right now, if you know what I mean."

"No, you don't—"

He leaned toward her and said kindly. "But anyhow, she hasn't had any visitors this evening, so you're probably wrong about that. So nothing to be jealous about, you know? She'll probably take your calls tomorrow when she's had time to think about . . . whatever."

"What? What?!" Miranda yelled, "You fucking idiot, we aren't girlfriends. The guy wouldn't have come past you; he lives in the building. The new single guy, Matthew something . . . moved on the ninth floor a couple of months ago."

Greg froze, his eyes growing larger and larger. "We haven't had a new tenant on nine for five years."

"Oh no," was all she could choke out.

Greg was galvanized into action. He grabbed a key from a somewhere on the desk, ran to the elevators, and repeatedly slapped the three buttons.

All Miranda could do was hug herself, pray, and try to breathe as the swiftly moving car took years to get to the sixth floor.

When it stopped, Greg erupted out of the elevator flanked by Miranda, and both raced to Mary's door. Greg knocked, listened, knocked again and was about to knock a third time when Miranda screamed, "Dammit, Greg, open the door!"

He threw her a worried look, put the key in the lock and opened the door.

"Miss? Miss Kelly? It's me, Greg from the front desk. I'm with your friend, and she—"

"Jesus Keriste! Get out of the way!" Miranda yelled, shoving her way past him. She ran three quick steps into the room before she stopped like she'd slammed into a wall. She heard her own breath mimicking the sound of a defective vacuum cleaner. Then, she held it for a very long time.

Blood.

Blood on the carpet.

Blood with dirt and white flowers strewn in it like a sweet little decorative dark red pond.

She stood; her head twisting in every direction, hoping not to see what she knew must be there. "Mar! Mar are you here? Mary Kelly where the hell are you?"

"Miss!" she heard an intense whisper behind her. "We have to get out of here. We need to go and call the police now."

Miranda waved him away and continued looking.

"Miss," he said more urgently, "Someone may still be in here. We have to go." She felt his hand on her arm, and she clawed at it like he was attacking her.

"Ow! Dammit!" he said. "Fine, I'm going downstairs to let the police in. Come or not. Up to you."

Miranda didn't hear him.

She saw the trail of blood leading down the hall to Mary's bedroom and began to follow it, whispering, "Nonono, please no, please," over and over as she crept toward the bedroom.

But she knew. The acrid smell of blood grew stronger and stronger as she moved closer. Finally, she was there, at Mary's bedroom door, and she had no choice but to push it open the rest of the way and step inside.

But once the door was open, there was no more movement: no breathing, no blinking, not even a whimper.

Still years later—when she tried to tell herself that she should be past it by now—her best friend haunted her dreams and called out to her from some monstrous torture chamber in the darkest corners of hell. Her mind took a snapshot at that moment, and the image implanted itself between her eyes and the living world. For the rest of her life.

Mary, what used to be Mary, was on the bed looking at her. That is, the head was turned toward her. But the rest of the body wasn't right. Something about it wasn't right. *Things are gone. Things are gone away. She doesn't have on any clothes. Her breasts: where are Mary's breasts? And everything has gone from her abdomen. Mary's pretty, flat little tummy that wanted to have babies. How many was it? Three? Or was it four? Four kids? But you can't have kids when your liver is over there and your stomach is—and don't you need a vagina? But Mary doesn't have one anymore. And the blood is all over: over everything. And somebody wrote on Mary's wall. Was that red paint? It says Psalm 46:9 and over there, FROM HELL. Yes, it does look like hell in here, doesn't it? That big flap of something on the dresser and another one on the floor: that was Mary's skin, wasn't it? How is she supposed to hold her girl parts in with no skin on the outside, and where is her heart? Where is her heart?*

"Mary where's your heart? Mar, where's your heart? Mar? Mar? Where's your heart?"

Miranda heard a voice screaming that same refrain over and over, but she had screamed herself to silence before she realized it was hers.

Chapter 6

FRIDAY – Later: Los Angeles

As they approached the crime scene, Harrison and Kate drove for a long, unbroken block—the equivalent of three or more normal city blocks. They saw nothing in the area but sidewalk and telephone poles next to a cinderblock and metal fence topped by barbed wire. On the right side of the street, behind the fence, were acres of empty semitrailers lined up side by side. Across the street, also fenced in, railroad tracks ran parallel to the sidewalk next to row after row of what looked like industrial-sized red dollies, probably for loading large items on freight trains. The overcast sky made the area look even more dismal and deserted.

"Pretty lonely out here," Kate said. "I'll bet no one walks these few blocks from one week to the next."

"True. And late at night, there would be almost no traffic," Harrison said. "Unlike right now," he groused, as he braked for a traffic jam ahead. As usual, police cars and yellow crime scene tape were like magnets for people foolishly hoping to discover what was going on, by driving slowly and ogling.

"Our friends the 'LA Lookie-Loos,'" Kate said with exasperation after they'd sat motionless for several minutes. "Times like this, I wish we still had a good, old-fashioned gumball to slap on top of the car. We'd be out of this in no time."

"Yeah, and a siren package right along with it," Harrison said. "But I wouldn't give up my baby and drive a company car just for a flashy light. She'd never forgive me."

Moments later, the two pulled over behind several police cars and parked. They were immediately approached by a serious looking detective who flashed his badge on the way. "Detective Davi Silva," he said, extending his hand to shake Kate's. "Agent Fleming?"

"Right, and this is Special Agent Harrison Carter." She took his hand briefly, and Harrison saw her recoil just enough for him to notice.

When he in turn greeted the man and shook his hand, he realized why: Silva, although neatly dressed in a dark suit and crisp white shirt, his face clean shaven, and his black, wavy hair cut close; smelled like he'd chain-smoked a whole carton of cigarettes in a locked closet.

Silva threw an admiring look at the Mustang and said, "Nice," before he turned and briskly walked back toward the murdered man's car, occasionally talking over his shoulder. They grimaced empathetically at each other before following.

"Not sure what details you have already," Silva said. "Call came late last night, but looks like it happened late Wednesday, maybe between ten and midnight. African American male. Shot right temple at close range. Weapon maybe even touching his head at the time. We know the driver had been working in the Hollywood area earlier in the evening."

"Were you able to find out anything from his records?" Kate asked. "I can't believe this person would really have arranged for a Lyft, when they get all your info, including a picture."

"Oh, that. Sorry, no such luck, Agent. The driver wasn't actually working at that time. His Lyft sign was switched off. What we did find out was he was on duty until around nine. At a time when he was usually working the Hollywood neighborhood, he went dark and ended up here."

"I wonder why he picked here." Kate said, looking around at the few buildings in the distance. "There's pretty much nothing in the area: maybe because it's so isolated?"

"Well," Silva said, "isolated in a way, but still, day or night, a car could pass by at any time."

"Right. Do you know if the driver had taken this same ride or switched off while he was in Hollywood late before? Harrison has some theories . . ." She stopped and looked back at Harrison, who was turning slowly around in a circle surveying the area.

"Uh," the detective said, watching Harrison, "my partner's working on getting his records for the last couple of months, but if this is random, they won't help us."

"No, no, not random," Harrison said and nodded. "Washington Boulevard, Washington. Detective Silva, you know this area. What would you say the address of this location is?"

Silva, looking a little nonplussed, pointed to the nearest industrial building and said, "Well that's—"

"No," Harrison stopped him, "I mean if there was a building, an address, right here where the car is, approximately what would that address be?"

"Oh . . . uh," Silva glanced at Kate and looked back at Harrison as though wondering if this might be a joke of some kind, "Well, maybe 38-3900 or so, I guess. What?"

"Or 3898," Harrison said. "Thirty-eight ninety-eight Washington. That's where the Zodiac murdered Paul Stine. This is our guy."

"The Zodiac?" Silva's frown deepened. "What, you're thinking that symbol is real? That the Zodiac's back?"

"No, more likely a copycat. A different kind of copycat," Harrison responded.

"Jesus, all we need," the detective said.

They stopped at the blue Toyota and put on gloves, while Silva continued talking. "You'll be getting the forensics later, but so far, they didn't find anything useful. Couple of very small pieces of trash. They're looking at them, just in case. The victim, name's Fred Witherspoon, kept it pretty clean. You know these Lyft guys get complaints if their cars are dirty. But this one was too clean: not even fingerprints on the door handles. Think maybe our perp could be a pro?"

"Right now, anything's possible," Kate said. She began checking the backseat of the car while Harrison first examined, before sitting in, the front passenger seat.

Harrison minutely examined the Zodiac circle and cross on the front windshield. "So close to the original. He must have practiced."

"Nothing back here," Kate said. "Hope those few items they did find give us something." She leaned forward and looked at the blood spatter on the driver's side window. "Looks like he was sitting right here."

Both of them exited the car. Kate looked at the uniformed officers, some of whom were still walking the area, in case anything useful was left behind. "Detective, have you done any canvassing in the neighborhood?"

"Yep, Agent. Already thought of that, of course," he said with a bit of emphasis. "I've sent officers around to every business in both directions. Nobody knows anything. No break-ins, nobody working at the time this probably happened. We think he just told the driver to pull over, probably at gunpoint, and did the deed at a convenient time."

"No, even that was planned," Harrison said. "This murder happened at the time of Paul Stine's. And he planned his getaway. Whatever the end game is, this killer has mapped it out every step of the way."

Kate's phone rang, and she stepped away, "It's the Director, excuse me a moment."

"You say he was African American?" Harrison asked.

"Yep, divorced, three kids, three different baby mamas. Apparently, he and the current ex were close, but you never know. We'll be checking everything."

"Why African American? Why would he choose a black guy?" Harrison mused. He could tell by the look Silva gave him that the detective was beginning to think he was a little strange.

"Uh . . . why not?" he asked, his dark eyes fixed on Harrison.

"This killer, he plans everything. He studied the murders he's replicating down to the tiniest detail. He even made sure this one happened at the right time at the right address on the right street. The original guy, Paul Stine, was white. There are thousands of cabbies and Lyft drivers working who would have been closer to the original. Why would he veer so far away in this case?"

Silva shrugged, "Guess we'll have to ask him when we catch him."

Kate hurried back to them. "Harrison, looks like the Hollywood PD has found a motel room that might belong to our guy. Someone who's staying there left without checking out and left behind some evidence that could be tied to the Zodiac. He wants us to get there right now. We're meeting Det. Ken Hastings."

"Fine," Harrison said, "I think we're done here anyway." They took off their gloves, and the three walked toward Harrison's car.

"Detective, you'll make sure we have all the reports from the scene?" Kate said.

"Of course. Always happy to help the FBI."

Harrison thought he might have heard a hint of sarcasm, but Kate spoke up as if he was sincere. "Thanks, and we'll do the same. We think he's killed in at least three states, maybe as many as ten people. The only way we're going to get this guy is if we work together."

Silva, looking surprised, said, "Oh. I really appreciate that. I have to tell you, sometimes I feel that the Bureau could have a little more respect for us poor, ignorant local guys."

Ah hah, knew it, Harrison thought.

Kate said, "I'm sorry if you've had some bad experiences, but our Director's policy is that we work together and share information. Harrison has actually been studying this killer since before we realized the crimes were related; he can give you a good overview."

Harrison couldn't help thinking *Sure thing, ignorant local guy.* But he said, "Of course. Not to talk stereotypes, but I believe our killer is a white male, mid to late 30s. We already know that he can clean up a crime scene like a whole team of experts, and he may be a professional in some way. We know that he's not doing random killings, and he's not the typical serial killer who's targeting a specific type or population. There's something much, much bigger going on, at least in his mind. He may see himself as a man on a mission . . . a professional doing this for a living almost . . . or perhaps an artist or even a hero. But it's clear that whatever is driving him is something that he may not have control over. He's compelled. It's up to us to find out why."

"I'd like to go with you, if you wouldn't mind," Silva said, sounding much friendlier. "I want to see this motel room. Why don't we give you an escort?" He beckoned to one of the uniformed cops, who moved toward them. "Nothing like a siren to get across town fast."

"Sure," Kate said. "That'll be great."

Silva gave the address and instructions to the officer who got into one of the police cars. Harrison's hand was on his door when Silva, instead of getting in the black and white, came toward them eyeing Harrison's car. "I'll ride with you, if you don't mind. Can't pass up a chance to cruise in this baby."

Without waiting, he jumped in the backseat on the passenger side, and Harrison saw Kate's amused look across the top of the car. He knew the horror that must be on his face at the thought of the smoke smell that was now surely permeating his upholstery. She made a wry face at him and shrugged.

"Sorry, you're not catching her at her best, Detective," Harrison said. He half turned, so he was facing Kate and raised an eyebrow for her benefit. "I'm having it detailed tomorrow, so it'll be all shiny and new again."

Kate quickly turned her head as if she saw something out the window, but he could see her body shaking slightly with laughter. He held his breath most of the way to Hollywood.

* * *

When they arrived at the motel, a young, uniformed officer took them right up to the 5th floor on the ancient, creaky elevator. They were met at the door by a smiling, middle-aged black woman with gray hair pulled back into a long ponytail that whipped around when she moved, which she did constantly. "You're Agents Katherine Fleming and Harrison Carter, right? And . . . ?" she said, quickly shaking their hands while looking inquiringly at Davi.

"Detective Davi Silva," he said. "City of Vernon, where the victim was found. I'm just observing, but maybe your scene is connected with my murder."

She narrowed her eyes, tilted her head, and looked up at him. "Let me guess; smoker?"

He said, "Uh . . . yeah," clearly taken aback by her bluntness.

"None of my business, of course, but you should think about letting those things go. They'll kill you. Take you right out of here. It did my husband, so I'm kind of on a mission. But like I said, not my business."

"Uh . . ." he said again. "Okay. I'm actually thinking about quitting."

Harrison and Kate glanced at each other, and he mouthed "good" to her amusement.

Rather than let the awkward, if funny, moment go on longer, Harrison said, "I think we're supposed to talk to Detective Ken Hastings?"

"I am Ken Hastings," she responded, frowning up at him. She laughed and said, "I know. Long story: creative mother or Dad wanted a boy. Depends on which of them you believe."

She turned, ponytail whipping, and led them down the hall as she continued. On the way, they passed what appeared to be a forensics person carrying his lab kit.

"Anything?" Ken asked him. He shrugged, shook his head, and continued toward the elevator.

"Sounds like you two are having a really interesting day of it. Actually, if it hadn't been for the alert you guys put out, we wouldn't be here because no crime was committed. The guy didn't officially check out, but the bill was paid. Cash, of course."

She opened the door to room 59 and turned back to them. "I've never seen anything quite like this. You can check the room if you like, but it's clean like a movie set or a model home: as if no one ever stayed here. We've had forensics go over it anyway, but as far as we can tell, it's clinically clean except for . . . well, look at this."

She stepped all the way into the room and threw out her right hand, like Vanna White showing people what they've won on WHEEL OF FORTUNE.

The three followed her in and stood looking at the clipping and picture-covered wall to the right of the door. Every photo and article was on letter-sized paper and taped in precise grids; it resembled a colorful, many-paned picture window. The three stood for a moment like visitors at an art gallery. Finally, Kate said, "I'm guessing this is all familiar to you, Harrison."

"Oh yes," Harrison said. He walked a few more steps, minutely examining the photos and printed copies. "There's something here about every single known Zodiac crime."

"Hey, this cab driver one: this is the one you were talking about, right?" Davi asked, leaning close to one of the articles. "Jesus, it sounds exactly like my case."

"Yes. Paul Kline. He left all of this on purpose," Harrison said, standing in front of the Zodiac's sign, painted in red over several of the pictures. "This guy wants us to know without a doubt what his inspiration was."

"Harrison, your notes said the Zodiac would sometimes leave clues about what he's planning next. Do you think he may have left one for us?" Kate asked.

"That might be one," Det. Hastings said, pointing to the Zodiac symbol, "But who knows what it means. The pictures are certainly untraceable. They're printouts from the internet."

"You sure were right about clinically clean," Davi said. "The car at my crime scene was clean like this too. Don't think you'll find much here."

"He didn't leave DNA, or he tried not to," Harrison said, "but look at what he did leave."

Davi looked around, confused. "What do you mean?"

"The way this bed is made. Not a wrinkle anywhere. That old saying, 'you could bounce a quarter on it,' could apply here."

Ken said, "I noticed that."

Sure you did, Harrison thought.

"Are you thinking military?" Ken continued.

"No, it's . . . something else. The exact placement of the pillow, the tucking and folding. And this." He walked to the closet and pointed to the hangers and their precision spacing. "Is this how he left it?"

"According to the desk clerk, they didn't touch a thing because it was so clean, they didn't have to," Ken said. "Just spooked them when they saw all the murder info on the wall."

"Exactly the same amount of space between each hanger," Harrison noted. "Like he measured it."

"Yeah," Davi said, "So he's neat. But what does that mean?"

It means I wish you'd go outside for a smoke, and let me think, Harrison wanted to say.

"Don't worry," Kate jumped in, clearly sensing his annoyance. "If it does mean something, we'll find out what soon enough."

Harrison went to the tiny bathroom and noted that the traps had been taken out of both the basin and the shower. Ken, who was right behind him said, "You've probably guessed that he took them out and cleaned them like brand new. Probably got rid of years of gunk. I need this guy at my house."

"And what's this?" Harrison asked, indicating a neatly stacked pile of obviously unused sheets, towels, and washcloths.

"Not sure, but looks like he took them in and never used them. Probably supplied his own, if he even slept here."

"Did you get any details from the staff? What do we know about him?" Harrison asked.

She turned and called out, "Officer Brown, bring in Mr. Stallings, please." The young cop who had brought them up called out a "Yes, Ma'am, he's right here," from the hall.

"There isn't much of a 'staff' per se," Ken said, "three desk people only, who trade off eight-hour shifts, and a part time cleaner who comes through as needed. We've questioned the daytime clerk, Stallings, but he doesn't seem to know anything."

Moments later, a person walked in who might have been auditioning for the role of "prim and proper male librarian" in a low budget movie. He was maybe 5'5" in his good shoes, had on a mauve cable knit cardigan sweater over a beige shirt, both of which were buttoned all the way up, and was sporting a neat mustache so thin it could have been drawn on with an eyebrow pencil. He held his chin up at an angle as if there were a key light that he needed to make sure touched his face in the correct way, and his lips were pressed and pursed together in a tight little circle. Harrison thought he looked like he was continuously smelling something that he couldn't identify but didn't quite approve of.

"Hello, Mr. Stallings," Kate said, offering her hand. "I'm Special Agent Katherine Fleming, FBI, and this is Special Agent Carter and Detective Silva."

Stallings looked down at the proffered handshake without moving his head, only sweeping the general area with his eyes. He looked back up and said, "With apologies, Agent, I don't shake hands," and quickly closed his mouth again like he thought something might fly in.

Harrison, having heard the real thing, was reasonably sure his British-ish accent was phony.

"No worries," Kate said, "What can you tell us about the man who was staying here? Can you give us a description?"

"I have neither alternate nor concomitant information to what I have already shared with the detective here," he said, moving a finger just enough to indicate Ken. "P'haps you law enforcement mavens might consider sharing your . . . Intel, I think you call it, with one another. One does have duties to perform."

Harrison wasn't sure what his face looked like, but Kate's eyebrows had gone up about two inches. Ken, who had already experienced the guy, looked amused, and Silva clearly wanted to take him out back and discipline him: with extreme prejudice.

"Mr. Stallings," Harrison said, keeping his tone neutral, "I'm sure you don't know this, or you would most certainly be more cooperative, but this room, this hotel, may be part of an ongoing murder investigation. The sooner we get the information we need, the sooner we can leave. But if you want to slow things down, that's not a problem at all. We'll get what we need some other way: p'haps bringing some additional officers in to check the place out, slowly and thoroughly. After we evacuate everyone, I'm sure you'll be able to reopen in, say a week or so?"

The man's nostrils flared, and he raised his chin even higher. Harrison assumed this was his haughty look.

"I am most certainly not being uncooperative. I have a great respect for the local constabulary which keeps us all safe. Though I talked with the gentleman through his door, once or twice, I never actually saw him for myself. He checked in with one of the night people, who no longer works here, by the way, paid cash up front, and was no trouble of any kind."

"He never went out during the day? You never noticed someone new coming and going?"

Stallings gave an annoyed frown. "There are internal stairs as well as a fire escape. Any tenant can take either to the street, although almost none do. And besides, Agent, there many are new faces here on a daily basis, you understand. Our patrons are allowed to have guests in their rooms, as with any other hotel. Unlike this particular guest, most only stay a short time."

"Like a couple of hours short time?" Kate asked, pointedly.

"I know what you're implying, Agent. There are many non-nefarious reasons for our guests choosing to be with us for a limited period. They may just desire a respite from the challenges and travails of their day, not a long vacation. Providing they pay up front, they have the use of the accommodations."

"But you must have records, right? Credit cards for additional charges, that kind of thing?"

"Some of our clientele pay with credit cards, but most pay cash, which dispenses with the necessity for credit cards."

Did he really pronounce that word clee-on-tell?? Harrison thought for a moment and said, "That means no paper or virtual trail for wives or bosses, or in this case, law enforcement."

Stallings gave him a look, *Obviously, Styoopid.* "We do indeed have records, since we have a day rate, and it's quite easy to tell how many guests we've had from day to day. That is as much as we are required to ascertain."

"So you count the day rate, and all the extra from all the hourlies, guess that goes in someone's pocket?"

"With utmost respect, Agent," he said in a tone that contradicted his statement, "I am not the owner of this establishment. I am, speaking of hourly, paid by the hour. I do my job, which I'm blessed to have as I work on my Masters Degree in my dotage. I am obviously a mature student, but I plan, nevertheless, to achieve my goal. Annoying my employer, or his guests, with too many questions is not the way to preserve my current income stream."

"Detective Hastings tells us you have a cleaning person who comes through. How long was this guy here?" Harrison asked.

"Just over three weeks," Stallings replied.

"So his room must have been cleaned in that time."

"Well, not exactly."

"What does that mean?" Ken asked.

"Clean linens were left outside the room, per his instructions, and as you must have seen," he said pointing toward the bathroom, "they were never used."

"Do you think he slept on the floor?" Davi asked, looking at the aged carpet.

"Or maybe he brought his own linens and took them when he left. We can't even be sure if he actually slept here or if he was here every day," Kate said.

"When can we talk to the cleaning person and the desk person who actually saw him, the one he gave the money to?" Harrison asked.

"To be frank Agent," Stallings said, "neither of them works here anymore."

"Why is that?" Kate asked.

He shrugged slightly and said, "As I'm sure you are aware, everyone doesn't want to work, Agent. The cleaning position requires actual manual labor, and the desk position mandates interaction with the public on an ongoing basis. Not everyone is cut out for either one of those."

"Did they both quit at the same time?" Kate asked.

"They both stopped coming to work, around the same time. I had to do a double for the last few nights. Ragingly inconvenient," he sniffed.

The agents looked at each other. "We'll need phone numbers and addresses for them." Harrison told him.

"I will relay that to my employer. However, I wouldn't hold out much hope, were I you. Our staff are often transient. I'm not sure that our cleaning person has a steady address. We sometimes make our contribution by employing the domestically challenged to do cleaning."

"Do you mean homeless?" Davi said, not trying to mask his exasperated tone.

The man raised his eyebrows imperiously, "As I said," he replied.

"Does the property have security cameras?" Kate asked.

"I am sorry to say, no," Stallings replied. "There have been (which of course the man pronounced exactly as it was spelled) some maintenance issyoos in the last few months. We have had them looked at, but the problem seems to perzist."

"Right," Harrison, said. "And when we check, I think we're going to find that any security cameras in the area that may have caught someone coming and going from this building have had some maintenance issyoos."

The man's eyes narrowed, and Harrison managed to keep his face neutral.

"Yeah," Kate said, clearly frustrated. "Harrison you want to call the chief and update him?"

When Harrison reached Daniels, the Chief said, "I was about to call you. Do you have some good news for me?"

"Well, actually there's good and bad news."

"What's the good news?" Malik asked.

"I guess you could call it good news," Harrison said. "We've discovered that the Hollywood location is connected to the East LA murder. There was definitely a guy staying here, he was alone, and he thinks he's smarter than we are. He's leaving us hints."

"Well, that's definitely good news because eventually the ones who think they're smarter than we are always outsmart themselves. And the bad news?"

"Just like at the murder scene," Harrison told him, "The only evidence he left was the copycat, created evidence. Nothing else, at least not so far. They found one or two small items that they're checking, just in case. But you were going to call us?"

"Yes. More good news/bad news. The good news is, you're about to take a trip."

"A trip?" Harrison said.

"Yes, the bad news is, he's struck again. There's another victim, in New York this time. And Harrison, I hope you're both up-to-date on Jack the Ripper. You and Kate need to be wheels up ASAP. Pack quickly. We're flying you out on the next available transport."

Chapter 7

FRIDAY – Afternoon: San Francisco

When May Helmsly, better known online as MayHem, entered the broad double doors of Farley's, she paused as always to let the clientele take her in. And as always, there were a couple of people who stopped mid-conversation or halted their coffee halfway to their mouths to stare. *Of course they did*, she thought and smiled. She knew, as they did, that a 5'10" black (*very* black) woman, wearing all black, 4-inch heeled boots, a ginormous old school Afro, and bare cleavage down to here, was not exactly a common sight--anywhere.

She stalked to the counter and placed her usual order in her low, velvety contralto. "Black coffe with a double shot of mocha." She turned and regarded the room, and of course, many of the patrons were still staring. Like a queen, she proceeded slowly and spoke to every person who was looking in her direction before taking a seat at her usual table beside the front window. She sat with her back to the window and sensuously crossed her long legs. She watched, amused, as a young white guy with a scruffy beard whispered something, obviously about her, to his plump buddy who seemed to be disagreeing with him. Moments later, the bearded guy stood, looking from one direction to the other as if he couldn't decide whether to go to the corner with the magazines or check out the original art hanging on the wall closer to MayHem. When he walked slowly in her direction, it was obvious the art had won the day.

He turned away from a painting of a table with four different animal legs, shaking his head like a disapproving, haughty critic, and froze, mouth partly open, when he realized that MayHem was looking directly in his eyes, an amused, questioning look on her face.

He was not going to be able to pretend that he was noticing her for the first time.

"Oh . . . you," he started and cleared his throat. "You're MayHem, aren't you?"

"I am," she said, offering her hand as if she expected a ring to be kissed.

He looked back at his dumbstruck buddy and again at the hand; his widening eyes the only thing moving.

Finally, he took a deep breath and gave her hand a small shake, his eyes squeezed shut. "I knew it was you. My friend, Larry, that's Larry," he indicated his companion, "he said it wasn't you, but I knew it was. We're both, well we're—"

"Baby Blackbirds. You're part of my Murder of Crows. What is your name, my darling? How did you come to be following me?"

"Ray, my . . . well Raynard actually, but people call me . . . Well I, uh, we that is . . ." He cleared his throat again and said in a breathless rush, "My mom. That's why. I mean, she was killed. I didn't know what to do. I was looking around for help, for somebody to talk to, and all I could find was churchy people talking about God's will, and idiots telling me time would heal me. All of it bullshit. People started telling me how I needed help because I wasn't healing fast enough for them. Then I found you, that is, I found the BKA MAYHEM site, and that thing you said about 'death and life are one. To try to separate them is to—" MayHem joined him here, and they finished together: "dishonor God who brought us both."

"Well," MayHem said, "you really are a fan."

"Yeah I . . . I couldn't stop hating the person who did it. It kind of consumed my whole life, every waking minute. But when you talked about how all victims are perpetrators, all perpetrators victims . . . I can't explain it. All I know is, I felt better. All the hatred and rage was gone. Somehow, it helped. I think you . . . I think you saved my life."

"You saved your life, my darling. If I brought you benefit, remember followers like you are the reason I get up in the morning." She touched his arm gently.

"MayHem!" the barista called out.

"Exactly!" she responded as always and was about to stand when Ray said, "Please, let me. I'll get it." He ran over to the counter, and a young woman who'd been watching hopped up, phone in hand, and came to the table.

"Would you mind? A selfie?" she said, pushing her long hair off her shoulder.

"Of course," Mayhem said, raising her chin and tilting her head slightly.

The girl snapped several, rapidly changing her pose from smiles to duck lips to her version of MayHem's cool intensity. "You're like a star in San Francisco. I saw you on the news when you married that guy in prison to his girlfriend. That was crazy. She was so young, and he was like ancient. Weren't you scared? He'd killed like twenty people," she gushed.

"And he was paying for his crimes," MayHem responded. "There was no reason for fear. I embrace death as my friend and final comfort.

It will come when it comes. That person had the right to be married. I was glad to do it."

Ray stepped up, holding the coffee, and cleared his throat, but the girl didn't move.

"Wow, you're amazing," she said, giving Ray a dismissive glance. "Just like I thought you'd be in person. I want to be one of your Blackbirds."

"Uh, here's your . . ." Ray said, giving the girl an annoyed look as he shifted the hot cup to his other hand. She went back to her table, rolling her eyes at him as she passed.

"Thank you, Ray," Mayhem said and took a small sip. "Perfect!" She smiled at him and watched him fidget, deciding she might allow him to sit for a while, when she looked out the window and saw *Him*. It was that lovely man she'd talked to in Farley's a few times before. He too was a fan, but there was something special about him. He was the kind of guy she liked: older, well, late 30s, and so, older to her. And besides, he looked late 20s. He was sweetly handsome, shy, white but suntanned with gray eyes. He was also brilliant, intense, and in need of a firm hand to guide him. And she had just the hand.

"Thank you, my darling," she said dismissing Ray as the man came up the steps. "It really was nice speaking with you."

"Oh, okay," he said retreating sadly to his table.

"I hope to see you in here again," she called after him, immediately raising his spirits.

She leaned back and closed her eyes, knowing that when she opened them, the man would be standing there. And he was.

"Well, well," she purred, looking at him, "Good Christian men are hard to find." The momentarily shocked look on his face was not what she was expecting.

"Oh, you mean me," he said, laughing a little embarrassed as a blush warmed his cheeks.

"Well, your name is still Christian, isn't it?"

"I hope so." He glanced around the cafe, noticing a couple of guys glaring at him, and turned back to MayHem. "Okay if I sit down?"

"Of course." As she'd noticed the other times she'd seen him, he looked like his conservative mom had dressed him, or like he was a high school boy, unsure of how to dress for his first job interview. "I'm glad you came back."

"Well, I was hoping you would be here. I've been keeping up with what you've been doing on the site. I'll bet you have a lot more followers after that article on you."

"Oh, you're talking about 'Murder, She Tweeted.' It was cute. Not all accurate, though. Yes, I've communicated with some incarcerated people, but they weren't all serial killers. They weren't even all murderers."

"But the thing about that book? The one you're holding in your new homepage picture?"

"Oh that," she said waving her hand. "Yes, one of my fans made me a gift of a book that happened to have an anthropodermic cover."

"It's really, actually, bound in skin?"

"Aren't all really beautiful old books bound in skin?" she shot back, teasingly.

"But not human skin," he said, seriously.

She leaned back and regarded him for a long moment. "Why Christian, are you judging me, my Baby Blackbird?"

"No, I . . ." he looked out the window and then leaned toward her. "I think it's kind of amazing. It's like you don't care what people say about you or think about you. You're just you."

She laughed and watched him staring at her dazzling smile.

"Thank you, and yes I am. Who else can I be? But now, you have to tell me some more about you. I think your story is what's amazing."

He shrugged. "There's not much more to tell. You know about the orphanage, foster care. That's kind of my life. I started to work and travel, and I landed here in San Francisco. Kind of boring. But compared to you. Up to a million hits now, aren't you?"

"Oh no you don't Mr. Hayes. Growing up in an orphanage may be boring to you, since you lived it, but I can't even imagine. I know it can't be like watching a production of *Annie,* or *Oliver,* but those are the only references I have."

"Huh," he laughed a little, but there was no humor in it. "Not quite like that. I mean, we were never hungry. The food wasn't that good, but it wasn't bad either. And we got great educations. I knew how to research and write a pretty decent college level paper before I was 16. My math and French and Spanish aren't too bad, and I learned how to do handyman work and to rehab cars. Ever see that show PIMP MY RIDE? Well I could do any of that stuff."

"Oh really," she said, innocently, "So if I had a little car trouble, you could . . . get my engine started?" She couldn't help smiling at how embarrassed he looked.

"Yeah I could, I, well uh, I can build or fix just about anything. We had a good Catholic education."

"Oh yes, that. So what about those priests?"

He stopped moving for a moment. She thought he had actually stopped breathing. "What about them?" he asked.

"Well, I always heard priests and nuns could be crazy strict, kind of free with the rod so as not to spoil the child, so to speak."

"Well, yeah. They were strict," he said, his eyes darting to the side for a moment. "But so what? Parents are strict, right? Not that I'd really know."

"Do you know anything about them? Your parents, I mean."

"Oh, them," he said, suddenly appearing more comfortable. "Druggies who dumped me when I was a baby. Both dead of overdoses now."

"I'm sorry," she said, placing her hand gently on his arm.

He flinched a little, but didn't move away. His blush and slight smile showed that he may not have been touched much, but he liked the way it felt. As she had when they first met, she wondered if he might be a virgin.

"No, it's okay. Like you said, 'We are the power. We decide our own fates before we incarnate on this planet.' They made their decisions, and they had to live with them. Or die with them. And me too. If that orphanage was my fate, I guess I have to live with that choice and everything that's come after."

Ray and Larry left, calling out an attention-getting, "Bye MayHem," as they passed. She waved and smiled back. The two glared at Christian through the window as they walked away.

"Those are some of your followers, I guess. They weren't too happy to see me here. I guess all of us kind of . . . love you and want you to ourselves."

"Do you really?" she asked, putting chin in hand and leaning toward him with her elbow on the table.

"I mean . . . I just mean. All the things you talk about: nobody talks that way. Nobody will admit what's going on or how they really feel. That's why I, why so many people, follow you. And all the detail and inside information. Like your 10 Most Watched Murders list. How do you find out all that stuff? I know you write people in jail, but you have to be hearing from maybe law enforcement insiders too, right?"

MayHem only smiled and raised an eyebrow. "Well, the corniest joke ever right now would be to say, 'If I told you, I'd have to kill you.'"

They both laughed, and she drank another sip of her cappuccino followed by a sensuous, "Mmmm."

"I, uh, wondered . . ." he almost lost his train of thought for a moment watching her, but recovered with, "Oh yeah. This month's Most Watched - that theory you had about the murders in Little Rock and Tulsa being connected somehow. That seems like maybe you're hearing something from inside. But okay, I know you won't tell me."

She laughed again. "And you are exactly right. But I'll tell you this; BKA MAYHEM has many fans and supporters in all walks of life. Yes, I do believe there may be some connection between little Jocelyn, and those seven men in Oklahoma. And I'm not the only one. Almost any of my Babies who've studied famous killers of the past are already wondering. We're on the alert. It's an exciting time."

"Exciting," he repeated as if tasting the word. "I guess I wouldn't have thought of it that way. But you are kind of a fan. Of murderers, I mean."

After a long, thoughtful pause, MayHem said, "Despite what people think about me, I don't condone murder. I believe that even murderers still have some humanity. And since all of them won't be inside for the rest of their lives, who knows the difference a little human kindness might make in the way they behave once they're free again?"

"You're right. I respect that."

"But having said that, there is one case in which I do condone murder. People who hurt children deserve no mercy, none whatsoever. If I were to find out something about someone like that, I would do everything in my power to bring him or her to justice. Swift and final justice."

She watched as the color and all expression drained from his face. It looked like a hood had dropped over his head, leaving nothing visible but two holes for the eyes.

"Look I, I have to go," he said in a different, cold voice as he rapidly stood up. "Maybe I'll see you again sometime."

"Chris—" she began, but before she could complete his name, he was out the door, down the steps, and down the street.

Feeling the closest to embarrassed she could remember, MayHem left her coffee on the table and exited behind him.

* * *

After a quick stop at the grocery and hardware stores, Christian covered the nearly fifty miles south to Pescadero in just over an hour. Some would have been taking in the beauty of the Pacific Ocean that was on the right for most of the way, but his mind was swinging like a pendulum from what he wanted to do to what he had to do.

He couldn't get the image of MayHem out of his head, but he had work to do. He had promises to keep. He didn't have time for a relationship. *Relationship*: even the word sounded odd to him.

He tried to stop thinking about her eyes and her voice and how fascinating she was. What if he just spent a little more time with her? He could tell she'd like that. As he drove along North Street past the elementary school and St. Anthony's Church, he couldn't help imagining himself dropping off their kids, maybe taking them to one of the goat dairies or even, craziest thought of all, going to mass on Sundays. He laughed out loud at the ridiculousness. He was never going to set foot in a church again, and would MayHem ever be a church-going wife with little kids? He shook the thought out of his head like he was trying to wake from a nightmare and regained his focus. He hit the button on the CD player and his favorite Tears for Fears song began to play. As always, it calmed and centered him. He whispered the lyrics like a prayer, knowing they were surely sent to him by his Guiding Voices.

Welcome to your life
There's no turning back
Even while we sleep
We will find you.

Yes. He had work to do.

* * *

He drove through the weather-beaten fence and around behind the main house to the garage where he rented space. This was not one of the converted, upscale ex-farm houses in the area that were now worth multi-millions, but it was still a good-sized home, set in a woodsy area, very near the ocean. For him, it was all about privacy and quiet.

He went into the open back door of the main house, carrying the groceries he'd purchased and called out, "Doris, I'm back! The car keys are on the hook, and I've put the food on the table. Should I put it away for you?"

"Thanks," a woman's voice called back. "I'm cleaning in the bedroom. Are you joining me and Harry for dinner?"

"Yes, that'll be great, thank you," he replied as he put items in the refrigerator and cabinets.

"Ok. Be back over at seven," Doris responded.

Christian walked across the gravel-covered yard to the garage, noting that it was close to 3:30.

He unlocked the padlock and slid open the barn door he'd installed. He turned on the light and nodded with satisfaction as he looked around the room he had crafted. The curtains on the small, framed windows were each exactly the same distance apart. The books, including multiple versions of the Bible, were lined up in order of their height and thickness. The two chairs were exactly halfway under the table, the bed centered between the two windows, and everything was showroom clean.

Doris and Harry, the Sebrings, had allowed him to fix the place up however he wanted once he moved in. After the death of their only daughter in the eighties they had decided to sell their business and move to someplace quiet and nearer to the ocean. They were content to live out their days there, but after so many years with just the two of them, Christian had seemed like a gift from God, according to what they told him. He kept them company, ran errands, and did chores, and he knew they depended on him. They filled the parent space for him, and at the same time, they had the experience of having a son for the first time in their lives.

They had come out to his place occasionally at first, but once they realized it was immaculate all the time, and thanks to the intercom that Christian had installed, they usually just called him, so he could run across to them. They also wanted to respect his privacy. The occasional hint let him know they hoped the "boy" would maybe have a girlfriend one day. There were jokes every now and again about grandchildren.

He placed his supplies on the small dining table before moving a small chest that sat on an area rug at the back of the room. He lifted out the trap door he'd created from the floorboards and climbed down the stair ladder to the tiny room underneath. It had probably once been a storeroom of some kind, but that would have predated the Sebrings' move in by some decades.

It was something else now.

All along the walls, sectioned off by studs and lit with small spotlights, were pictures and documents relating to the most cunning and brilliant killers of the 19th and 20th century, some caught, some perhaps still alive and at large.

On the floor in front of each shrine area was a file box containing items related to the killings or the killer: the Ted Bundy area had not only pictures, a victim list, and some of his famous quotes pinned up, there was also a copy of the Ann Rule book about him, THE STRANGER BESIDE ME. On top of the Jeffrey Dahmer box was a Polaroid camera surrounded by old Polaroid's of men's heads and body parts.

And in front of the wall at the end of the room were neatly stacked and sealed boxes containing the information on his completed "projects." He called them projects just like Dennis Rader, the "Bind, Torture, Kill" murderer. Each had a label with the killer's or the case name: JonBenét Ramsey, Zodiac, Jack the Ripper; and each had taped neatly beside the label a verse from the Biblical BOOK OF PSALMS.

He turned on the computer that he spent hours on each evening and went immediately to a file that was full of photos he'd taken and uploaded. The COMPLETED section had all the pictures he'd taken of Jocelyn Simmons, Mary Kelly, and the others when he was preparing. It also included houses, apartments, neighborhoods—all the research he'd had to do to complete his projects seamlessly and perfectly.

He turned to his IN PROGRESS files. The next step. The next step had to be bigger, bolder, and guaranteed to garner even more attention than the earlier ones. There were a few possibilities, but he clicked on one, soaking in the details and information about his target.

He stood and walked to his project wall, strolling past each of the undone ones like a museum tourist. and stopped in front of one. When he felt the rush of energy and the whispers of approval, he knew it meant this was the one: maximum panic, maximum chaos. Yes.

He was swaying, with his arms crossed over his heart, enraptured, when his concentration was pierced with Doris' voice calling, "Dinner is served!" over the intercom.

He shut down the computer and made his way across the yard, stopping a moment to watch the russets, oranges, and gold left in the sky by the setting sun. "That's right, sundown," he whispered. "The end is coming whether you know it or not."

The Sebrings were already seated at the table when he came in through the back door.

"Mmm," was all he could say as the mixed fragrances of roasted turkey and rosemary potatoes met his nostrils.

"Come on, I know you're hungry after all that driving," Mary said.

He sat across from Doris with Harry at the head of the table, and as always, Doris took her husband's hand and reached for his.

"I know this isn't your favorite part, Christian, but come on, a little prayer won't hurt you."

"Well, anything to get at that turkey. You always cook like it's a celebration."

"Every day the Lord has given us is a reason to celebrate," Harry said, "But the truth is, she knows it's my favorite, and she's trying to entice me to stay." He winked at Christian as Doris shook her head and rolled her eyes.

They bowed their heads, and Christian felt himself tense up as Doris prayed. He heard her words bouncing around in his head with a rebuttal, almost like an insane tennis match.

"Dear Lord, thank you for this food we are about to receive."

Where were you when I needed you?

"Thank you for your wisdom,"

If you're so wise, how could you let that happen to us?

"your spiritual guidance,"

That's right, you led me here to this day. It was you!

"and the precious gift of life. Amen"

And more lives will be taken, thanks to you. Amen.

He opened his eyes to find both of them looking at him curiously.

"I think he got a little of the spirit there, D." Harry said. "That was one powerful hand squeeze Chris."

"I noticed," Doris said, looking at Christian and rubbing her hand.

"Oh, sorry," Christian said, "I didn't mean—"

"Joking, son. It's okay," Harry laughed, putting several dark meat turkey slices on Christian's plate before serving his wife and himself. "So what's on your radar for this week?"

"Well . . . there's this girl, well lady, so maybe, I don't know—"

"A girl? Tell me more," Doris leaned forward, expectantly.

"D, leave the boy alone. You'll chase her away before we ever lay eyes on her." He took a couple of bites then added offhandedly, "Hmmm. Granddad, grandpa, gramps . . . hmmm." They all laughed and continued eating as they chatted.

"Harry and I were thinking of going down to San Diego for a few days or so," Doris said. "There's some kind of antique and vintage show going on that sounds like fun. Feel free to bring your friend over and maybe make her some dinner. Women like a man who can cook." She glanced at her husband and whispered loudly to Christian, "Some of us even like men who can't cook."

"Some of us can cook where it counts," Harry said, provoking a whack on his arm from Doris and a fond laugh from Christian.

And once again, as he had so many times, he wondered *What if?*: what if he had been born to parents like these two instead of druggies who would dump him in an orphanage and then die, leaving him all alone?

"Don't worry, I'll watch the house. I have a job in LA, but it should only take a day or two, before I'm home."

"Well, I know you do quite well, with your special clients all over the place, but I'll be glad when you can do most of your building and rehabbing in the area, so you can be around more," Doris said.

"Me too," Christian said, wishing it were true. "I have to run a quick errand later, but I'll be back early."

They finished up, and Harry took his customary two bottles of Bud Light and settled himself on the front porch. Doris and Christian did the cleaning up as they had one of their usual chats. Afterward, he thanked her and kissed her on the cheek before heading back across the yard to get his jacket and keys.

He drove his Bronco this time, and shortly, he was back on the highway headed south.

It took only a few minutes to get to the Pigeon Point Lighthouse. It was one of his favorite places. It had been there for almost 150 years, waiting for the time when it was needed, lighting the way, and doing what it had to do to save people. It reminded him of himself: standing tall and alone, beat up, but not beat down. Still going.

He took out his current burner phone and dialed the FBI. After an electronic voice assured him the call would be recorded and took him through a list of choices, he pressed zero for the operator and was answered by a male voice.

"I was wondering if I could speak with Malik Daniels please." Christian said, in a plaintive, much younger-sounding, voice.

"Sir, we're actually closed for the day. May I take a message for you?"

"No, but . . . Will he be there on Monday?"

"I'm sorry, sir. I'm not really allowed to give out that information."

"Oh no!" Christian said, sounding near tears. "Please, you don't understand. I have to talk with Mr. Daniels. He gave me this card and he told me, if I found out anything about—well . . . please I just need to . . . I'll call back on Monday, but he'll be there. To help me. He'll be there, right?"

After a moment's pause, the voice said, "He will, but why don't you give me your name and tell me what—" Christian clicked off before the man could finish his sentence.

He stood watching the waves go in and out as the sense of purpose filled his heart. And he felt the pride of his accomplishments and his future mission so intensely, he thought he must be glowing as bright as the lighthouse. He whispered to himself, "They will slander me as an evildoer, but I will let my light so shine that they shall soon be cut down like the grass, and wither as the green herb."

Christian drove home and began to pack.

Chapter 8

FRIDAY – Night: New York

Harrison took another sip of his Jack Daniels, leaned back against the leather booth, and sighed. It had been one hell of a day. This morning, well yesterday morning, they had rushed into FBI headquarters in LA to join the serial killer task force. That was quickly followed by a trip to the murder scene in East LA, the hotel room in Hollywood, back home to grab a bag and be transported to LAX for the next available plane to New York, the horrific crime scene here, and finally a hotel where they could sit for a while and just breathe before hurrying back to LA in the morning. He told Kate he'd be here, hoping she might want to sit and talk for a while, but she preferred to go to her room and catch a few hours' sleep before their turnaround. He couldn't blame her. After what they'd seen in that Soho apartment, he wanted the day to end too.

The flight here was okay. He shook his head, sighed once more, and finished his drink in a long swallow. Part of him had hoped that maybe all those hours alone on the plane would be his chance to finally say to Kate what he had wanted to say for almost a year. But most of their time was spent on the case, and of course, since they were exhausted, sleeping. Besides, even though they had the good fortune to be in first class, never a guaranteed situation for agents who had to fly, it was essentially, a public place. They had to speak carefully and quietly about the case. Not that anyone would have understood. They'd gone over and over the Psalm left at the Lyft driver's murder.

"Hmm . . . 'punish those wicked men'," Harrison said. "Do you think Fred Witherspoon was somehow a surrogate for some group who've wronged him?"

"African American men, you mean?" Kate said. "Like maybe he was robbed or bullied in some way? Or a job that he wanted went to a black man?"

"Not likely, because look at his other victims—not even close to this one. That little girl couldn't possibly fit into that scenario. But there's some association, some connection between these crimes."

"The rest of the verse talks about remembering the suffering. So who's suffering here? Is he?" Kate wondered.

"Or maybe he feels he's actually helping them. Maybe he's putting people out of their misery. I can't tell yet. The pieces haven't fallen into place."

"'The pieces,'" Kate smiled. "You and your puzzle pieces."

"When it's right, when it's the right answer, I'll know," he'd said, staring at the crime scene photos they'd both received on their phones. He widened each photo, searching inch by inch.

"Do you always know when it's right?" Kate asked him.

Now, looking back, he wondered if maybe she wasn't *asking* him something, maybe she was trying to *tell* him something. *Loser!* If he'd looked into her eyes, maybe taken her hand at that moment! But no-o-o-o-o. Because that was when he saw it: the square of fabric missing from the Lyft driver's shirt.

"Look at this!" he said. "The Zodiac did this with Paul Stine's shirt: he cut a piece out and mailed it to the cops later with a coded note."

"So we may get one too."

"Let's hope so and hope it's just chockablock with fingerprints and DNA."

"Oh yeah, that'll happen," Kate chuckled ironically.

"I'll let them know about this the minute we land. If he does decide to send it to taunt us, we have to be on alert."

After that, they'd made small talk until they both fell asleep.

The drive to the murder scene was a blur, but once there—once they saw the horror that lay beyond the front door of one of the most amazing, beautifully decorated apartments he'd ever seen—everything came into crystal clarity. Despite training with cadavers and surgery on live people and seeing blood by the gallon going into and out of human bodies and despite studying the original Mary Kelly case, and being warned by the detectives on the way there, he wasn't expecting anything like what they encountered in that room. He knew people shot each other, stabbed each other, sometimes did worse, but he'd never before believed in monsters. The little boy inside him screamed and ran away and hid, but the doctor stepped forward and shut down his human feelings. If he hadn't, grown up Harrison would have run from the room and all the way back to LA.

"Oh. My. God." Kate whispered. They stared at each other a moment, he raised his eyebrows, and she whispered, "I'm okay, you?" He nodded, and they both began to work.

At most crime scenes, he was accustomed to chatter and discussions that ranged from crime related statistics gathering to weekend plans, but this one . . . it was almost as if they were afraid to make noise, as if the silence could stop it from being real. Even through his shoes and double booties, he thought he could feel the blood squishing under his feet, each step sounding like "pyick, pyick", as his feet stuck to the floor.

He stepped closer to the body, and a crazy voice in his head asked, *What butcher did this autopsy?* But this was no autopsy.

He prayed that she was dead before the beast started his work.

He leaned in, examining the slice across her throat that went all the way to her cervical spine. This was most likely the cause of death, and the rest came after. Good. He felt himself sighing with relief. He noted the vicious slash marks across what used to be her face, pieces of which were on the bed or hanging off by threads of cartilage. It was almost as if the perpetrator wanted to obliterate her—to go beyond just ending her life but to ending her existence.

One of her breasts was under her face, which was turned toward the door, and he thought he saw kidneys under there too, but knew he shouldn't move anything as yet. He located her other breast near her liver, which was between her feet. Everything which should have been inside her abdomen had been scooped or dug or hacked out and placed near her body or around the room.

He had to look away for a moment, but when he did, he was facing her dresser: the strip of thigh on top had knocked over some of her girlie, expensive-looking cosmetics. In the other direction was a little table and chair in front of a window. She had probably sat there reading or having coffee some mornings, but the thing on top of the table . . . that was a flap of skin from her abdomen. She wouldn't be sitting there anymore.

Unbidden, a part of that "Dry Bones" kids' song came to his mind:
The Hip bone connected from the thigh bone,
Thigh bone connected from the knee bone . . .

He waved his hand like a swarm of flies was in his face and forced himself back to the job at hand. Kate had said something, but he hadn't heard her. "What?" he asked.

"Medical training. I was asking if you thought he might have some kind of medical training."

He shook his head, partly to shake out the demons. "No. Like in the original case, these cuts are so crude, it doesn't even look like someone who knew anatomy; not even a butcher, let alone a medical practitioner."

"Well, guess we're not looking for a homicidal doctor," she said and tried, but failed, to smile. "Part of me thinks we should cover her body, but that would mean covering the whole room."

He squeezed her arm and said, "I know. Let's look at—"

"—something else," she finished for him.

They both walked to the wall to examine the message the killer had left.

"'From Hell'" Kate read. "This was how Jack the Ripper started one of the letters that he sent to the police with part of a kidney. He said he ate the other half."

Is our guy doing that right now? Harrison wondered as he looked around the bar at the few late hanging customers. What would they say, how they would react, if they knew what was walking among them right now. How many would make a stampede out of New York? But to escape this one, they might have to run a lot farther—like out of the country.

Even though he hadn't wanted to be a doctor, he was glad for his medical training. He wondered how he would have reacted to this particular scene without it. There wasn't much more to do at the scene. They couldn't interview the woman who found the body, a good friend of the deceased, because she apparently had gone into shock and was heavily sedated. The local agent had been told that they'd barely been able to stop her from screaming, and she probably wouldn't be able to talk lucidly for quite a long time, if ever again.

The front desk guy, Greg something, was no help. All he could tell them was that the victim thought the killer lived in the building and Greg was going to adopt her cat.

It was all information, bits and pieces, but no pattern. Why *these* murders? Why *these* people? Why go from state to state? There were hundreds of young Mary Kelly's right in California and alternately countless Lyft and Uber drivers all over the place in cities with Washington Streets and boulevards. Was he making sure the bureau had to be involved by crossing state lines? And those Psalms . . . was it some kind of game or pattern? He let the pieces swirl around and waited. Not yet, but it would come. It would come.

Harrison signaled for the check and was about to call it a night when Kate walked in. She had changed to a black shirt and form-fitting black pants which made her look even taller. Her face was scrubbed of all makeup, and he reflected again how she really didn't need any.

She had her phone in her hand and was clearly looking for him. She came over, plunked herself on the other side of the booth, and said, "For the first time, a little good news: one of those two pieces of trash in the back of Witherspoon's car might be something." She hit a button and showed him a text message forwarded from Laurie. It said:

> DNA found on cigarette butt in taxi.
> Running analysis through NCIC database.
> East LA will call with result.

"That is good news," Harrison said. He smiled, but she looked away and sighed.

Finally she said, "I couldn't sleep. I tried, but well, we know we have to get this guy. Period. Bottom line. But for right now, let's talk about something else. Anything other than the case."

"Okay. Ummm," was all he could manage. He said, "You were going to tell me about you and Dale. You called him Batman. I didn't get to know him all that well, but what about Batman?"

"Ha," Kate said. "I thought everybody knew. They called him and Skip Batman and Robin because they approached every case like they were the crusaders who were our last best hope before oblivion. Don't know how Skip felt about that. He probably either thought *he* was Batman or he wanted to be."

"Oh yeah, he would want to be the Batman, no doubt about it," Harrison said with a little more vigor than he'd intended.

She shot a probing look at him, and they both laughed.

"But did other people buy into that?" Harrison asked. "I mean, did they kind of look at him like a superhero?"

"You know," she said thoughtfully, "some may have, but I think he was more like the Dark Knight than hero Batman. We loved each other, but he had his issues."

She paused and looked at the table. "You know what's sad? Even as I say 'we loved each other,' I'm not a hundred percent sure about that. I know that I loved him, but I guess, truth be told, if you put a gun to his head and told him to choose between me and this job, I don't think there'd be any contest."

"Of course there wouldn't," Harrison said. "It would be you. Like you said, no contest." He stared at her for a moment, wondering if she could hear what he wasn't saying.

She raised her eyes and looked at him incredulously. He thought he may have seen tears, but he wasn't sure; she looked away too quickly. "No my friend," she said sadly. "No. The choice wouldn't have been me at all. As a matter of fact, you wouldn't even have needed the firearm, a few drinks, or get him somewhere private with just him and a couple of agents that he really trusted, like Skip, and he would have told the truth: it would be the FBI, no contest."

"Well, I don't mean to speak ill of the dead, but if that's true, he was an idiot."

The server came over, and Kate ordered a Sauvignon Blanc. They sat for a moment in silence.

"Dale and Skip," Harrison said, "They were best friends, no?"

"I . . . think so?" she responded. "Sometimes I thought they were closer than Dale and me, other times, I felt like they were more 'frenemies' than friends, and sometimes, it felt like the competition between them was more important than the friendship. I don't know, I'll never know. If you ask Skip these days, of course it was all love and loyalty between them: brothers forever."

"Well, I could understand the competition part, especially where you're concerned."

"What?" The tone of her voice and the look in her eyes were clear warnings, but he pressed forward anyway.

"Well . . . uh, I mean, you know. The way Skip feels about you, obviously—"

"The way he what? What are you talking about?" she said coldly.

"You . . . must have noticed," he said, unsure how to backtrack out of this dangerous territory. "I noticed."

"Ugh, Harrison," she scoffed, "How can you even say that when I've sat here and bared my soul about--Skip was my man's friend and partner.

We have that in common, nothing else. Sometimes Dale would cancel our hardly ever date night to be with his Robin. It was their bromance uber allies. He was my rival. As for anything else, Skip does not think of me that way, and I certainly don't think about him that way."

She sighed. "You know what, I think I'm tired now. I'm going to bed. I'll see you at the pickup in the morning."

"Kate, I'm sorry I didn't mean—"

"No, I know you didn't. I'm just . . . It's been a long day. Good night."

She walked out as the server arrived with her drink and set it on the table.

He wasn't totally sure what had happened, but he knew he was going to be thinking about it for the rest of the night. Maybe what he was missing was Kate's attraction to Skip. Maybe what he said made her feel guilty, and that was what upset her. And maybe he needed to call it a night and let this horrible day fade into history. He threw some money on the table and headed for the elevator.

Chapter 9

SATURDAY – Early morning: Washington, DC

The bedside clock read 5:30am, but President Jameson Harold Mitchell was already wide awake. As always, he took a few moments in bed to savor the fact that he had stopped living his dream long ago and was now living a fantasy even he couldn't have imagined. He moved his hand a few inches to feel the warmth of his wife's skin and sighed contentedly. *I may have the hardest, most challenging job on Earth, but it's put me in a position to help millions, hundreds of millions, of people. And besides, I have the best woman in the world to help me deal with it*, he thought. Not to mention a baby son and plans for number two. There might be a happier man on the planet, but he couldn't imagine that either.

Politics had never been his priority even while he was an undergrad studying law at Harvard. He had always seen himself as a crusader. Once he accepted that he would never be able to don a cape and mask and fight for the underdog, he was determined to find another way. From what he could see, most people needed someone to fight for them before the law at some time in their lives. It seemed that the poorest, those who needed knowledgeable help the most, usually could least afford it.

He thought becoming a public defender or community activist would suit him just fine. But things didn't turn out that way.

He hadn't accounted for the attention that leading Harvard's debate team, not to mention being a soloist with the Krokodiloes a capella group, would garner for him as an undergrad. He was doing what he loved and excelled at. But before he knew it, his name was popping up here and there, not only in the HARVARD CRIMSON paper, but also in the CAMBRIDGE CHRONICLE, and occasionally even in the BOSTON GLOBE. Once he entered the law school, he applied himself like other people's lives depended on it because as far as he was concerned, they did. Thanks to all the volunteer work he did, he was rewarded with, among other honors, a law award for Pro Bono Service.

Even now, he looked back at his work after law school as the most satisfying of his life. He had helped the incarcerated, homeless and other indigent people, and the undocumented. This last led him on a trek overseas visiting countries in the Middle East, South America, and Africa, where many refugees to the US originated. He spent his time volunteering and being a tourist to learn and understand why people left their countries and why they thought the United States was the place they should be. It was while he was in tiny Muizenberg, near Cape Town, South Africa, that he had first met the woman who would become his wife. From the moment he saw Pat Lee, he felt he knew her. Looking back, he knew it was love at first sight. She had smiled her sweet smile and shook her head when he hit her with what must have sounded like the corniest, oldest line ever dropped: "Don't I know you from somewhere?"

Of course, he didn't let that deter him for one second. She was the one. He knew it in his heart like he felt he knew her from before. They worked together sometimes, teaching children English or doing whatever they were asked. She was as driven and dedicated as he to help challenged and deserving young kids. She wouldn't go into her past too much, but he was able to glean that she'd been an orphan: had a rough, almost tragic, upbringing, and was determined, no matter what, to help kids just like herself. Even now, he sometimes wondered about the missing parts of her past that she didn't want to share, but he didn't care. He knew his girl. Nothing he could possibly find out would make her any less amazing or loveable.

He slipped carefully from bed to let her have her other hour of sleep before the baby would wake to demand breakfast. He softly hummed his personal theme song from *Oliver!* "Where is love, does it fall from skies above . . . Where is she, who I close my eyes to see." It made him laugh and smile because at the end he would always think, "Score! Answered!!"

The President knocked twice on their side of the family suite door and opened it to greet his favorite Secret Service Agent and head of his personal detail, Nathan Chen. With a quiet, "Good morning, Mr. President," Nathan delivered the iPad containing Jameson's daily briefing. This was also his time to acknowledge the military aide tasked with the burden of carrying the "nuclear football." Of course, the emergency satchel didn't look anything like a football, and it had nothing to do with games of any kind. This was the moment that sobered him each day and reminded him that he could use the contents to start a nuclear war. Like it or not, the fate of his country, and the planet, was in his hands at all times.

He went into the dining room where his usual light breakfast of oatmeal with dried cranberries and pecans was being served. The ever-dignified, white haired Charles served him like the professional he was, and Jameson mused, as he often did, about what would happen if he called Charles "Chuck" and tried to high-five him.

Instead, he said, "Good morning, Charles, how are you?" like a grownup, and Charles responded with his signature, "Outstanding, sir."

Jameson wondered if he would ever have that kind of dignified bearing. *Maybe in twenty years or so,* he hoped. "How's Ms. Louise doing?"

"Fine, Mr. President, thank you. She sends her regards."

"And Jelani. Did he make his A on that math test like he was hoping for?"

"Yes he did, Mr. President. He had no choice, once I told him the President of the United States was interested in the outcome of his math class. I tell you sir, he studied harder for that class than he has for any other subject since he's been in school. Of course, he'll always do the things he enjoys, writing and art and so on, but I never could get him to see the value of science and math. It seemed like his poor performance in those types of classes was discouraging him about school in general. You absolutely inspired him, and my wife and I will be eternally grateful because he really was kind of slacking off and losing hope. Sometimes it's just about who shows an interest, gives some positive input to a kid. Yours was the right input at just the right time."

"Well, my little input had some of that magic star quality that people attribute to this office, but you and your wife—you're the ones who've been there all the time. It's about years, a lifetime of input, not a few words from some random celebrity. The things that happen to our kids who don't have parents like you, well . . ." He shook his head.

"You should take that compliment, Mr. President, because you and your wife, young as you are, you're like the parents to the whole country. We all know how much you care. It shows in everything you two do and say and represent."

"Now you'd better to stop flattering me right now, Charles," Jameson said sternly. "You're not getting a bonus or a raise."

"I am wounded, sir," Charles said. "That was my best material." The two laughed and Charles began clearing dishes on his way out of the dining room. "Enjoy your breakfast, Mr. President."

"Thank you," Jameson said and continued to munch as he briefly checked his day's schedule on the iPad before turning to THE NEW YORK TIMES and THE WASHINGTON POST, which Charles had placed on the table in front of him. They were the only two hard copy newspapers he still received every day. He knew the same information was more easily and extensively available online, but somehow he felt it as an obligation—a link to the past.

He was comparing editorials on how the economy was doing when he heard the welcome sound of cooing and giggling before Pat entered the room carrying baby Aidan.

"Well if it isn't Mr. Perfect himself. Come right over here, my friend." He held his arms wide, and Pat transferred a soft towel from her shoulder to his and gave him the baby and a warm kiss. She kissed him again. "Mmm," he said, "You're beautiful. And if you're wearing that blue dress to entice me, it's working very, very well."

"You're the only man in the universe who finds baby fat beautiful."

"Baby fat? You mean that half an inch extra on your waist? You crack me up. But the truth is, you would look just as beautiful at any size or weight, and don't you forget it."

She raised an eyebrow. "Really? You think so? I'll bet you wouldn't even look at me twice if I weighed, say 80 or 90 pounds more."

"Truth to tell, I can't imagine you 80 or 90 pounds heavier, but then again, I can't imagine not loving you, so that you don't even have to worry about."

"I'm glad to hear that because I know that means you love me so much, you're going to listen to me."

"Uh oh," he said. "What am I going to listen to you about?"

"You know exactly what I'm talking about: the Dallas Ride."

"Oh, sweetheart, we already had this talk." He pulled Aidan closer and cradled him on his left side. He rocked him but kept his wary attention on his wife.

"I know we had this talk; we're about to have it again."

Jameson sighed and gave her a resigned, "Ok."

"I just don't think it's a good idea, Jamie. I believe if you drive through Dallas, like John Kennedy did, top down and all, you are begging for an assassination attempt. It's going to bring every crazy, every conspiracy theorist on the planet out of the woodwork to try and make history repeat itself. It'll be one of those insane links like people do between the Lincoln and Kennedy assassinations, and there's you . . . oh honey," she said, picking up the now sleeping Aidan from his lap, "we have a baby. You can't do this!"

"Pat, the country couldn't be more different now than it was. The American people need to know that their commander-in-chief trusts them with his life. I think if you give people the opportunity to be the best they can possibly be, they'll lean in. We've seen what happens when a leader brings out the worst in his fellow citizens. It starts from the top down. Besides, people love you: they absolutely adore you. And they like me because I was smart enough to marry you. We're finally coming back together as a country. All the vicious racism and divisiveness that has come out of past leadership is gone, hopefully forever. No one would ever want to hurt us."

"Stop that right now," Pat said, clearly trying to keep the frustration out of her voice.

"Stop making light of it. Neither one of us is that naïve. And you know Nathan Chen will back me up. Have you talked to Gordon about it?"

"Now why would I do that? I know what the inimitable VP Williams will say."

"And he would be right," Pat said.

"You know I always honor advice from wise, older gentlemen, but this is something I'm going to do."

She gave an exasperated sigh. "Yes, he's older, and yes, he's very wise. That's why you chose to run with him. You don't want to talk with him because he'll be on our side, telling you how crazy this is."

"Well he's not going, so it's kind of none of his business. Besides," he grinned, "his wife would stop him."

"And your wife is trying to stop you," she snapped.

Aidan whimpered a little, seeming to sense the discord, and Pat softened her tone immediately. "Jamie, many people love us, yes, but everybody doesn't. It's almost like greater love creates an equal and opposite hate. Remember that even though we've started to make some changes that are helping the country, the economy hasn't fully recovered from all the horrors that went on before. People are still angry and out of work, still having to declare bankruptcy and losing homes. And more relevant than that, still blaming whoever's in office for their woes. That hasn't changed."

"But they know it's changing. They know it's going to get better," he said.

She shifted the soft towel and baby to her other shoulder, turned and looked out the window, shaking her head.

"This ride is a part of it," he continued. "I have to show our people we love and trust them and believe in them, and we don't have to hide in the White House or in some megabillion dollar hotel or on a private golf course. We are people like them; we really are with them. My love, I know how I sound. But you're right: I'm not that naïve. I know it's dangerous, but this is a risk I want to take. I have to believe we've all turned the corner, and this is going to be the best time in the history of this country. Now you're their Mom, and they trust you, so you need to be on board with this. You see the vision, you agree with me, don't you?"

"Okay, dear," Pat said sweetly. "I'll let it go. For now."

He shook his head, deciding not to further engage and went back to the POST. She came over, placed their son in a bassinet next to the table and began to help herself to eggs, wheat toast, and strawberries. She reached across the table and borrowed his TIMES, as she often did, ignored the front page, and went straight to the New York section.

"Look at you, gossip girl. Don't you want to know the latest national news?" He asked teasingly.

"I have close connections with a very knowledgeable insider," she responded, raising her chin high. "If I need to know the latest on the national scene, I'll just roll over in bed and nibble his ear."

They were both absorbed for a few minutes when he heard her gasp, "Oh my!"

"What? What is it?"

"Go to the New York section. This woman was brutally murdered. Apparently, her body was mutilated. They're hinting she may have been dismembered. One of the officers was actually physically sick on the scene. It sounds horrible."

"Keep reading, I'll see what's online."

"This is beastly," he said after reading a few moments, "And nothing about suspects or capturing anyone. Wait, they've put together a couple of related links for me." He scanned the screen for a moment and clicked on a link. "It's by some blogger who calls herself 'MayHem,' now there's a name. Her title is 'Has the Ripper Risen?' Now this is odd: she's tying this murder to the ones in Tulsa and the Jocelyn Simmons murder."

Pat put the paper down and went around to peer over his shoulder. "Tying them together how?"

He ran a hand through his hair and leaned back. "This is . . . She's saying they all might have been done by some deranged person who's trying to replicate famous murders from different times."

"What? What the hell? Is she trying to start a panic?"

"Sure," Jameson said, "as she gets hundreds, maybe thousands more followers. And look at her picture. I'm sure plenty of curious people, especially men, will see that and decide to read what she has to say."

"Or offer her a turtle neck," Pat said disgustedly. "Scroll down some." She pointed to the left side of the screen. "Look, you're absolutely right about the followers. See, she's selling all kinds of merchandise."

"And all of it is murder related," Jameson responded. "Keychains, tee shirts, and . . . I don't believe this . . . letters and souvenirs from incarcerated murderers? Doesn't she have any morals? Or a conscience? How do you help people like that? People you know have done horrific things to other people? I mean, some of these people have hurt children."

"I don't know, honey," she said massaging his shoulders. "Maybe she thinks they deserve a second chance or, you know what, maybe, for her, it's just business."

"Business? Just business?" he spat out, his voice rising and his face reddening. "This book she's holding, it's made of human skin! And turning rapists and murderers into cool cult figures for fun and profit is not 'just business,' it's—"

"Jameson Harold, calm down," she said, hugging him and speaking softly into his ear. "We can't solve this right now. She has freedom of speech, so she can do this. We think it's wrong and disgusting; her followers," she leaned in to look closer at the screen again, "thousands of them apparently, think it's entertaining or grotesque or train wreck beautiful. But you are helping to make a country where people are too kind and caring to even dream of glorifying murderers and rapists. MayHem won't be around forever."

He sighed, patted her arm, and kissed it a couple of times. "You're right. She's only a blogger doing what she does. But I wonder if she has a point. What if one person is doing all this?"

"That would be monstrous. Well, why not give the FBI a call and get some more information?"

"I don't want to appear as if I'm interfering, but I can have Lila discretely find out who's working on it and have them give me a call."

"Ok, now finish your breakfast, Mr. President," his wife said. "You have work to do."

* * *

A short time later, Jameson received a call from Phil Stanton. "Phil, thanks for getting back to me so quickly. I know it was very early there when the call came through. Hope you weren't still asleep."

"No worries, Mr. President. I was already up. Nice speaking with you again."

"You too Phil, but I'm a bit confused," Jameson said. "Why am I hearing from you? Is Los Angeles working on this New York case? Or maybe the rumors I'm hearing are true?"

"Um, what rumors are we talking about, sir?" Stanton asked warily.

"That there's a serial killer. That there may be some copycat actually reenacting famous murders, like Jack the Ripper and John Wayne Gacy."

Jameson didn't like the obvious pause that happened at that moment, but he knew what it had to mean. "Well, Mr. President," Stanton said hesitantly, "We don't really know that for sure, but there is a strong possibility. And you're hearing from me because we have a task force working on some murders in different states that are apparently tied together."

"And no suspects yet?"

"Well, with respect, Mr. President, we don't want to get ahead of ourselves. We are not 100% sure we're looking for one person for all these crimes or even if they're all connected. If it's okay with you, may I update you when we have something more concrete? We don't want to alarm anyone."

"Of course. You're right. And I have full confidence in you and the Bureau. I wondered, especially after we saw this blog by a woman who calls herself MayHem. Blame my wife; you know how she always wants to take care of everyone. I guess both of us were kind of worried."

"Yes sir, I think the whole country knows how much she cares. And no worries, sir. It's wonderful to have a Commander-in-Chief who believes in us. We appreciate you checking, and I'll make sure you're in the loop on these cases. We're hoping it's not one person, but it doesn't matter. We are going to get this bad guy or guys and put them where they can't hurt anyone else."

"I like that. Talk to you later, Phil."

Chapter 10

MONDAY – Morning: Los Angeles

Early Monday morning, driving across the city and all the way to the office, Harrison's thoughts ricocheted between Kate and the case. He thought about the case because he didn't want to keep beating himself up about Kate. *You had your chance, you had your chance,* was the chorus his annoying, harpy thoughts screeched at him, but his answer to himself was *She's not ready. That's what she was trying to tell me. She's not over Dale. Or maybe it's really about that ass Skip. That was some overreaction.* Of course, the inner rebuttal was he was being weak and thinking up reasons to prevent his little feelings from being hurt. He almost felt like yelling out loud at himself to *Shut Up!* But that would just be weird.

They were back home that Saturday, and since there was no new information except Harrison's discovery about the missing shirt fabric and what they had gleaned so far from New York, Malik told them to "Take a break, and we'll bring fresh eyes to it on Monday." Harrison told himself if he'd known while they were still there, he might have suggested they stay another night. But he knew he didn't mean that. What if he asked something like that, and she flat out rejected him?

Standing in the parking lot at LAX, he gathered his courage to ask her to lunch or something, anything, but Kate had just said, "See you Monday," and stepped toward her car without looking back.

* * *

Exiting the elevator two days later, he almost bumped into Kate coming off the next one over. He felt her, "Morning," was a little strained, but maybe that was his imagination. They entered the conference room where the task force was working, and one of the first people to notice them was Skip, whose jaw tightened at seeing the two of them walk in together. Harrison knew what that look meant and couldn't resist raising an eyebrow and throwing him a sly "Yeah-we-came-here-together-she's-with-me" smile. Stupid, but he felt a little better.

The room was abuzz with activity. Team members were on computers and phones and sharing information with each other. Othello, wild hair floating like he was getting some kind of electrical charge from his keyboard, was alternating furious typing with running to the printer, grabbing copies, and adding them to the case update wall.

Jeanne's face lit up when her friend walked in. She gave them a wave and a thumbs-up and went back to her call.

Laurie walked over with two mugs of coffee and a sympathetic smile. "Thanks, Laurie." Harrison said taking the mug. "Looks like we're late to the party. Did we get the time wrong?"

"No. The Chief was only trying to give you a bit of a break after these last few days. Sounds like New York was a dumpster fire. But get ready to get back on your horse, because it's on and poppin'."

"Anything new since Saturday?" Kate asked.

"Nothing really helpful, but the Chief will catch you up. We've added a member."

She pointed toward Malik, who was standing in front of the case update wall in deep conversation with a serious-looking man in glasses. That wall, which had been nearly empty when they left, was now filled with pictures, labels, and information. It was divided into sections for the Jocelyn Simmons murder and one each for Tulsa, New York, and the Fred Witherspoon case. Othello added some information to the Witherspoon section.

Jeanne finished her call and walked over to them.

"Look at that," Kate said and sighed. "We're going to run out of wall."

"Not before we catch the son of a bitch," Jeanne said, followed by their usual "S'up."

There was a sign above the pictures on the evidence wall that Harrison pointed to. "Psalm Killer?" he asked. "He has a title now?"

"All Othello," Jeanne said. "That kid is a hoot. I think in his mind, we're hunting a super villain. He's the bomb though. Really knows his stuff."

"You guys have been busy," Kate said.

"Yeah. We're all caught up on the earlier two cases. And my man, Harrison, I must say you're a known commodity in both bureaus. And not in a good way," she grinned.

"I did Jocelyn, and our own little Skipper took care of Tulsa. He finally stopped sulking when he realized there were seven vic's, so that means he's got the biggest number!"

She did a little pelvic thrust with her hand near her crotch, a la Michael Jackson, and squealed, "Hee hee."

Kate shook her head and laughed, "Always trying to make trouble. Leave the poor guy alone; he's just trying to do his job. He's not as bad as you think."

Skip, appearing to sense he was the topic of conversation, strode over.

"Hey Katey, welcome back. Travel okay?"

"That part was fine. The crime scene . . ." she shook her head and glanced at Harrison. "Well, you'll see pictures later."

Skip took a step away, paused, turned back and faced Harrison. "Know what, Carter, you were right. I've been going over everything from the Tulsa cases and looking at the other evidence, and it's the same perp. You were right."

He turned abruptly and walked away, leaving both Harrison and Jeanne open-mouthed.

Kate looked at both of them, smiled and nodded.

"Oh good, you're back," Malik called over. "Come here, someone to meet."

When they joined him at the evidence wall, he said, "This is my friend and sometimes running buddy known in the grownup world as Professor Reginald Fletcher of Santa Monica College. Fletch has helped us out with a couple of cases in the past. This is the go-to guy when you have questions about the Bible, religion, or religious symbols."

After he introduced them and everyone shook hands, Daniels raised his voice and said, "Before we get back to more serious work, let me have everyone's attention for a moment."

When there was quiet, he continued, "Since we're all here, this is a perfect time to let you know that I'm under orders from Sharon Daniels to remind everyone about our anniversary party on Saturday. Be there or be very sorry next Monday."

There was a chorus of "We'll be there" and "Of course, sir".

"Is Saturday the actual anniversary, sir?" Othello asked.

"No, it's tomorrow," Malik answered.

"Thirty-eight years," Harrison said quietly, looking proudly at his mentor.

Daniels gave him a nod and smile, "Everyone should be so blessed. And Othello, feel free to bring that young lady you were talking about."

Othello's freckles, highlighted by his rosy blush, looked poised to jump off his embarrassed face. "Wow, sir. That's gangsta. Uh, I mean thank you, sir," he said. "She lives out of town, but I'll definitely ask her. Thanks."

"Yeah, OC. Anybody who makes you cheese like that all the time is definitely worth meeting," Jeanne said. "She might be my type."

"You wish," Othello replied with a grin.

"Okay, people," Daniels said. "Let's get back on it. Director Stanton and I would love a captured killer for my anniversary gift."

Everyone went back to work, and Malik said, "Fletch, why don't you share what you're thinking about these Psalms with Agents Carter and Fleming."

"Sure" Fletcher said, clearing his throat.

Harrison could tell that he was a definitely a college professor. He was short to Harrison, but his erect posture made him seem taller. He straightened his glasses, took out a slim stylus that he used as a pointer, and said, "When we encounter the kind of individual who links his crimes to religion or the Bible, he is generally either aligning himself with the two—that is, he feels that he is guiltless or acting in a way that would be accepted by his God, no matter what that means: murder, arson, theft, kidnapping—or he is rebelling in some way against them. His perception is that either religion or God has done something to him that leaves him no choice but to act in the way he is acting. This person knows what he's doing is wrong, at least in society's eyes, but he is compelled, forced to do what he does by that nasty bugaboo, religion."

"From what you've seen, can you tell which category our guy fits in to?" Kate asked.

"I haven't yet had time to look at all the evidence, but some thoughts: let's look at this first Psalm: 'I have so many enemies, Lord, so many who turn against me.' If we assume that he's using this scripture to speak on his behalf, it would appear that he does have some belief in God and that he feels victimized and isolated. Malik tells me that there doesn't appear to be any discernible connection between the child victim and the killer."

"Correct," Harrison said, "The agents in Little Rock checked it every way to Sunday. She was chosen, but not because she had anything to do with whatever his purpose is."

"Right," Fletcher said. "So it's not likely that this verse pertains to her. Someone is against him, and he needs help to fend him, or them, off. This little girl is a symbol or perhaps a sacrifice to facilitate that. There are examples all through scripture of people sacrificing living creatures to elicit a blessing from the Almighty. Which leads us to the second Psalm 54 verse 6. 'I will gladly offer you a sacrifice, O Lord.'"

"You think this refers to the actual bodies?" Kate shuddered. "I'd hate to meet the God he thinks would look kindly on that sacrifice."

"If each Psalm refers individually to each crime scene, that is the most likely assumption, but you should keep your mind open for possible connections between them or even other, less obvious, scenarios. When people, who may have some mental instability, begin to use the Bible to support their positions or to prove their hypotheses, they often find unexpected and creative ways to do so. You may perhaps have heard of the Bible Code?" he asked.

Harrison and Kate both shook their heads. "No," Harrison said. "I did grow up going to church, but I never heard of that."

"It mostly focuses on the Old Testament, the Torah to be more precise, and posits the idea that if one knows how to interpret certain sequences of the Hebrew in the correct way, they contain secret and predictive messages, kind of a Biblical Nostradamus. It's controversial, but there are many who see or create other codes and messages using the Bible. This person that you're hunting may, for example, be using the numbers of the verses or the letters in some way. That is not to discount the clear and obvious meaning of each verse."

Kate and Harrison looked at each other and then at Daniels.

"I know," Malik said. "Sounds like the more we know, the less we know, but let's just keep everything in mind and go from here."

"Yes, more pieces," Harrison said.

"Exactly," Malik said as he walked toward his office. "It will all come together. We're going to find this guy. When the Intel from New York comes in, Phil and I want everyone to go over it as a group."

* * *

Two hours later, Othello called out, "The file's come through from NYPD. Pictures attached. I'll forward to the Boss's office." He clicked on the attachment and leaned in eagerly, waiting for them to download. "You want me to post—" He began, but his body immobilized in that moment. Only his eyes moved, slowly opening wider and wider, until Harrison could see white all the way around his irises. Finally, he blinked a few times, cleared his throat, looked up at Kate and said hoarsely, "You want these posted?"

"Not all of them," Kate said, walking to the desk where he was working. "Scroll down." She touched some of the images. "Just these three for now. Pull up the picture of the original Jack the Ripper Mary Kelly murder, and put the one of the body side by side with this one from New York. A printout only, not on the screen. The rest . . . we'll make those available as needed."

He nodded, and a few minutes later walked to the evidence wall and posted the two pictures side by side along with two good shots of the bedroom wall.

Reginald joined several team members who approached the wall. He stepped back immediately, squeezing his eyes shut as if that would erase what he had already seen. "Dear God in heaven help us," he said. "This is . . . beastly."

"Yes." Harrison said. "As we've noticed before, this killer's attention to detail is unrivaled. Note the similarities in the head placement, what has been removed from her body, what's still there."

One of the men closest to the wall shook his head and said in a choked voice, "Sorry. Just had lunch. Right back," and hurried out of the room. Harrison knew he was going to part with that lunch momentarily.

"Understandable reaction to this madness," Harrison said. "That's exactly what the killer's hoping for. He wants us to recognize his power. He's sending a message about how easily he can replicate these scenarios. That takes time and dedication. And the things he can't exactly duplicate, he finds a way to suggest or indicate in such a way that we can't possibly mistake what he's trying to say to us. I think we hear him. The only question is the Psalms and how they fit in."

"Right," Kate continued. "As Harrison has discussed and Professor Fletcher has expanded on, there's most likely some deeper meaning. There has to be more than just the obvious interpretation of each Psalm."

Stanton and Daniels walked in and their faces made it clear they had opened the email. Everyone turned toward them and waited, but Stanton just said quietly, "Carry on."

"Thanks, sir. Professor Fletcher, did you have any other thoughts about the Psalms, now that you've seen most of what we have so far?" Kate asked.

Fletcher deliberately turned his back on the depictions of the recent carnage and faced the group.

"While there is still no certainty about what he may be trying to impart, I can give you a few more ideas of what to stay aware of. First, remember that each Psalm is only a part of the whole: one verse from a chapter that is one chapter in the collection of Psalms that are in the collection of books known as the Holy Bible. They exist in different forms in Christianity and Judaism, and there are even some very like those in the Quran. It means that when this person is making his murderous declarations and uses Psalms to help him, he is simultaneously using *and* striking out at all the major religions of the western world.

"You should also remember that there are many translations of the Christian Bible. His verses are from the *Good News Bible,* so probably his reference or background is Christian.

"If we look at the chapters he chose in their entirety, we find some themes are repeated: two of the chosen Psalms so far are called Prayers for Justice, the others are prayers for help and protection. Both three and fifty-four talk of others and their negative intent toward the psalmist and how God comes to save him. But seven and ten are hopes for an intervention from God and include graphic descriptions of what happens when he doesn't show up to help. Perhaps your guy doesn't believe God was there for him. Sorry, I don't suppose this is much help as yet, but I guess the bottom line is to be aware of and continue looking for patterns."

"Thanks, Fletch. If there's a pattern or code, our pattern whisperer Harrison will crack it," Malik said.

Stanton turned to Kate. "I know you've studied the Ripper cases, Katherine. Did you notice anything helpful comparing this scene to the original?"

"Unfortunately no, Boss. For those who don't know, this 'From Hell,'" she pointed to the wall pictures, "was the greeting in a letter the Ripper sent to the police. I guess our Psalm killer wanted to make sure we knew where to look for his reference. He used her blood to write it, and the Ripper claimed to have used the original Mary's blood as ink. Part of our Mary's liver was missing; the Ripper wrote that he made a meal of a piece of his victim's liver. Did our guy do the same? We don't know. What we can say so far is that he seems to almost embody, or morph into, these killers. For instance, if he continues to stay true to his idols' examples, we can expect that shirt swatch from the Lyft driver to turn up.

"Something else we know: he appears to be a clever actor, a chameleon. We know from New York that he's an attractive, seemingly normal, guy who convinced his victim that he'd moved into the building. According to what she told a friend, there was a romantic interest, and she was very quickly comfortable enough with him to let him into her apartment."

The door to the conference room opened, and Laurie came in, scanning the group around the wall. When Harrison turned, she pointed to him and beckoned. He walked over to her knowing it had to be important. "That City of Vernon detective who's working on the Lyft driver case, Davi Silva—he's calling. He wanted to speak with the Director, but I told him about the meeting. He says he has to speak with you urgently."

"Thanks, Laurie. Maybe it's good news," Harrison said and hurried to the phone.

"Hi, Davi. It's Harrison. The team is in a meeting, but Laurie said it was urgent."

"You're gonna love this, Carter," Davi said. "We have the results from the DNA on that cigarette butt."

"Okay."

"It belongs to a guy named Michael John Hitchings. He's in the database because he joined the Weekend Warriors."

"The what?"

"Army Reserve. They routinely take DNA of all recruits. He wasn't in very long but long enough. This is our guy."

"Uh, you're moving a little fast, aren't you? He could have been one of a hundred passengers Witherspoon had over the last week."

"But wait there's more," Davi said annoyingly, like one of those late-night infomercials. "We found out he was raised in a Catholic orphanage, and he brought a lawsuit against three of the priests for sexual assault. After a six-week trial, the jury acquitted all three, and Hitchings dropped off the map. We've been trying to find out where he is, but the only thing we came up with was a friend from the orphanage that he stayed in contact with. There's the religion connection, the right age range, losing that case—a perfect motive—and we have no idea where he is. Obviously he could be here or traveling the country. Well? What do you think?"

Harrison felt it: a significant piece of the puzzle stopped swirling and fell into place. That bed in the Hollywood hotel room, the precisely spaced hangers. Someone who had rigidly controlled training in his youth yet felt completely helpless. Chaos within the appearance of calm. "Yes, I think you're right. You're right. Thank you. This friend, did you find him?"

"Yep, his name's George Franks. He was in the San Diego area, but that may be old news. I'll send over all the info we have on him along with my Hitchings update."

"Tremendous work, detective," Harrison said. "We'll pay him a visit and definitely keep you in the loop."

"Always happy to help out the FBI," Silva said. Harrison thought he sounded sincere.

Harrison startled everyone, bursting breathlessly into the room. "I think we may have a name! I think we've ID'd the guy." His excitement was instantly transmitted to the group, who began to pepper him with questions.

"Okay, everyone," Malik said, "let him speak."

Once Harrison shared what he'd learned from Davi, the group was galvanized into action once again.

Othello hurried back to the computer. "I'll see what else I can find on him. If there are any young images, I can do some age progression. We'll see what he might look like now. Let you know as soon as the new information gets here from East LA."

"Finally something concrete to look for," Kate said.

"Yeah, but a couple of things you have to wonder about," Jeanne said.

"Like what?" Kate asked.

"Like why not the priests? Or any priests," she answered.

"Yeah. Why go after these random people that don't seem to have anything to do with what happened to this guy as a kid?" Skip added.

"Good points," Malik said. "Maybe this Franks can give us some answers. Try to get a current address, Othello."

"I think I know your other question," Harrison said. "It bothers me too: why the slip up with the cigarette butt? How do we go from vacuuming and sterilizing and gloves to a nice, convenient, DNA-laden butt?"

"You think he did it on purpose?" Jeanne asked.

"It's possible. But, since he's a smoker, maybe it was something simple and unconscious: he's smoking, Witherspoon arrives, and he has to put it out. What would a normal smoker do when there's no ashtray around?"

"Stamp it out with a shoe or boot. Probably grind it into the sidewalk." Kate suggested.

"And if the shoes had some decent tread—" Jeanne added.

"Like those ugly boots you love," Kate glanced at Harrison as she threw in her two cent's worth.

"Exactly. I think we've had a huge stroke of luck," Harrison almost whispered, with a slight sideways nod of satisfaction directed at Kate.

"Or maybe the God whom he seems to have lost faith in is helping us out when we need it most," Malik mused, glancing heavenward.

"Amen," Fletcher almost prayed. "And if it helps, Psalm 54:5 talks about God using their own evil to punish his enemies. Ten says the wicked believe they will never fail, never be in trouble. There's a lot of language about helpless victims, and in verse 18, the Psalmist refers to the cries of the oppressed and the orphans. It does sound like you may be on the right track."

"I concur," Malik agreed. "Let's find out everything we can on Hitchings from when he was at the orphanage to the moment he dropped out of sight. As for Franks, the minute we find out his address, we'll send a team to talk to him. If he's in the area, Katherine and Harrison, you'll take care of it. Harrison, in my office, please."

Harrison followed Malik to his office and took a seat. "Everything okay, Chief?" he asked apprehensively.

"More than okay," Malik confirmed. "We've been paying close attention to the work you've done on this case, even before it actually *was* one of our cases. You're still relatively new with the Bureau, but of course, you come with unusual abilities and background. Those have helped you to become an agent this office can be proud of. With the Boss's agreement, we're officially making you co-case agent on this one. I predict a lead in your near future."

"I . . . thank you sir," Harrison fumbled, clearing his throat. "But don't you think, well there are a few others on the team who've been here longer. They might—"

"They might want to stay in their lanes and let me do my job, which is making the best decisions possible for this task force. I just did that. And you're welcome."

"Thanks for your faith in me, Chief. I won't let you down."

"No, you won't," Malik assured him. He stood up, gave Harrison a pat on the back, and grabbed his jacket and briefcase. Confused, Harrison asked, "You're taking off, sir?"

"I wish I could. Phil is actually going to take off tonight. I'm going to run home, change clothes, and kiss my girl for the last time this marriage year. It's going to be a long night."

Harrison shook his head wistfully as they walked out of the office together and said, "Wow. Your relationship it's . . . it's kind of great to see, sir."

Malik stopped a moment. He glanced over at Kate and back again. "Son, work is important, but don't ever forget about your real life. Even with all that's going on here, tomorrow night, I'm taking off and celebrating the fact that I have her in my life. There'll always be more bad guys. You don't want them to be the stars of your personal show. Don't ever make it all about the job. You'll blink, and thirty-eight years will seem like thirty eight days, and all you'll have to show for it is some solved and some unsolved cases. Trust me, it won't be enough."

"Wait here just a minute, sir," Harrison said. He hurried to his desk and grabbed a wrapped package. "Since we probably won't be here when you get back, I have to give you this now. I have a little something for you and Sharon. I won't tell you what it is, but you have to take it with you to the restaurant and open it before dinner tomorrow night."

"Thanks, son," Malik said and gave Harrison a big hug. "You be careful looking for this Hitchings guy, and don't forget what I said."

"I won't, Chief. I won't."

Harrison watched as the elevator door closed on him.

Chapter 11

MONDAY – Morning: Washington, DC

Jameson crossed out yet another word, wrote in a substitute, crossed that out, but went with the original word. It had to be right. No, better than right. It had to be memorable. Historical. This had to be one of those speeches that deservedly garnered its own title: one that school kids would learn for speech class and competitions. He had to laugh at himself. *Calm down, little Jamie. You just have to do what you always do: give the best damned speech containing the most truth and information possible. Show them your vision, and they'll share it with you. That's all. Just do your best.* He went back to work, close reading and questioning every word, until he had what he wanted to say. Again he went back over it. The gentle knock on his door was a welcome relief.

He knew something was up when he saw the trepidation on Chen's usually stoic face. "What?" he asked. "What's happened, Nathan?"

Chen stood for a moment, clearly contemplating some major decision. He leaned toward the President, opened his mouth and closed it again, looked down, and shook his head.

"Nathan, what the hell is it? Some crisis? Something personal? What's going on?"

Finally, Chen squared his shoulders and looked him in the eyes. "Permission to speak freely, Mr. President."

Jameson sighed; glancing down at the speech in his hand. Then he beckoned him in and pointed to his sofa. "Have a seat, Nathan."

The President sat in his favorite chair; his knee almost touching Chen's and said, "Okay. It's only us here. Nathan and Jameson. What's up?"

Nathan nodded, took a deep breath, and said, "You can't do it. This drive? Respectfully sir, it's just this side of wacked-out crazy."

Jameson laughed. "Well *that* was certainly respectful."

"I'm serious, Jameson. We, along with the rest of Homeland, the FBI, and most of the country, can do everything in our power to protect you, and that one nutcase may still find a way to get to you. Especially once you do your announcement and they have time to prepare. Jameson, you have to listen to me. There may be whole groups working together to try and bring you down. People love you, but like Kennedy, not all people love you. Don't present your own head on a platter for them."

"Hmph. I guess your point refers to John the Baptist," Jameson said. "You know, he came first to prepare the way for someone who wanted some of the same things I want: peace, people loving and caring about one another, and I'll add prosperity to that list. I'm okay with being that person."

"No sir. That is not my point. My point is that you're practically begging for an assassination attempt and making it easier for potential assassins. It's my job to stop that from happening. Please don't do this, Mr. President."

"So now we're back to Mr. President."

"If that's what it takes to remind you of your responsibility to yourself and your country. You don't have the right to put yourself in this kind of danger. And I should add that it's not just about you. Your wife, any innocent citizens who get in the line of fire, and those who are sworn to protect you will all be put in harm's way on a whim."

Jameson's face hardened, and he stood up. "Thank you for your input, Chen. I will take it under advisement."

Nathan opened his mouth to say more, but Jameson knew his face was saying, *Not another word.*

Chen walked to the door and threw a quiet, "Thank you Mr. President," over his shoulder.

"Nathan," Jameson called before he walked out, "It's not a whim. You know I've been planning this for ages. It's not frivolous. It's symbolic. It means so much more than . . . Wait until you hear my speech. I think, well I hope anyway, that after that, you'll understand. I trust you guys and the FBI. I know this drive is going to go well. It's going to be a turning point in our country. You'll see."

"Thank you, sir. We'll do our best."

Jameson saw him shake his head sadly, just before the door closed behind him.

* * *

He had worked for another 45 minutes when his phone rang. He tried to keep the annoyance out of his voice. "Lila, I'm not done here yet. Is it urgent?" He decided to take it when she told him Phil Stanton was checking in.

"Mr. President," Phil said, "I know you have your speech coming up, but I wanted to update you as promised. We have some excellent leads. There was actual DNA left at one of the scenes, and it led us to a suspect who looks good for these crimes. He suffered grievous abuse in Catholic orphanages as a child and lost when he tried to sue them after he aged out."

"How could that be? His evidence must have been incredibly weak when the church was losing and settling all over the world."

"It was all about timing and intimidated and unwilling witnesses, sir. He lost his case before the "Spotlight" articles and the other events that broke the silence on a large scale."

"So, do you know where he is or how to find him?" Jameson asked.

"Not yet, sir, but we have a lead on his best friend from the orphanage. They may still be in touch. Two agents have been dispatched to his home to do some questioning and surveillance. No promises, but we're feeling pretty good about this. We may soon have pictures to share with the media. We'll get him, Mr. President."

"Thanks, Phil. That's great news."

* * *

When he went to their bedroom to get dressed for his speech, he was relieved to see Pat had not only put a suit and two ties on the bed for him, she'd also placed a dress right beside it for herself. He didn't miss, and knew many in the media (Well, at least any self-respecting fashion blogger) also wouldn't miss the fact that it was a black and white polka dot, reminiscent of some of Jackie Kennedy's outfits. Pat was on board. He chuckled and shook his head; she had put an arm of the suit around the dress like a caressing couple.

She came into the room, carrying some papers and wearing lacy blue panties and a bra that would have probably given Jackie O an attack of the vapors. He gave her a huge grin and a hug.

"What? No pillbox?"

"Ha ha. I thought maybe a tasteful little fascinator instead, your majesty."

"Oh yeah, that's all I'd need . . . you in one of those funny little duchess hats, looking like royalty. I can see the headlines now, accusing me of wanting to be king. But seriously, Pat. I couldn't do this without you. What made you change your mind?"

She held up the document she was carrying.

"My speech. You read it," he said.

She came close and looked up at him. "I still don't approve, my love, but I get it. I still think the ride is dangerous and crazy, but I believe your speech will resonate with millions of people. But Jameson Harold Mitchell, if you get shot, I swear I'll kill you."

He laughed, kissed her, and laughed again as he hugged her close.

* * *

It was his favorite kind of DC fall day: cool and breezy with enough sun to make it comfortable. He had a moment of nervous anticipation as he looked out on the crowd filled with reporters and supporters of course, and, per his request, some who weren't so supportive. He noted the presence of conservative journalist Ed Garry—definitely not on team Mitchell. It seemed no matter what he did, Garry was suspicious or at least disapproving about it, and he could be counted on to share that disapproval on all available platforms. But that was the main reason he wanted him here.

He saw Ed looking curiously around the Jacqueline Kennedy Garden, which he'd chosen for the announcement, then peering cynically up at him. He felt a pang of doubt, because he wasn't entirely sure about his choice. And once they understood the connection between what he planned to do and this particular location, some might find it incredibly cheesy and maybe disrespectful . . . but it was too late to change now. He felt Pat squeeze his hand once then hold it firmly, as she always did before a big speech, and as always, he felt the love and support center and calm him.

He almost didn't hear his introduction before he stepped up to the mic and began:

"My Fellow Americans. I come before you today to share a vision quest. We have come through a time of grievous loss and hardship and division. Many of us are still reeling from the loss of jobs, businesses, and homes. The great benefits that were supposedly coming from ignoring treaties and economic agreements with our allies and separating our country from the world never materialized. We learned there were no benefits to isolating our country from our friends and embracing despots.

Some of you have had treatable health challenges made exponentially worse because you had no health insurance. But even worse than all the economic issues has been the divisiveness between us. This was not the country we were striving to be.

You or your friends or relatives who are different, in some way, from the mainstream, have likely experienced bigotry, sometimes leading to violence, because the message came from the leadership of our country that that kind of behavior was acceptable.

I don't have to tell you about all this; you've lived it. But what I want to assure you of is this: those days are gone."

There was applause. So far, so good.

"We have been through the fire and come out on the other side, stronger than ever. But we can be even better. I'm like you: I want peace, prosperity, a good life for my family, especially my son. I want to do well at my job and be well thought of by the people I work for. And let me tell you, they can be very demanding."

He shook his head and sighed theatrically before joining the laughter.

"I have been called naïve, even foolish, because it appears that I'm not aware of the things that still separate us. But you put me in this office because I represent the things that bring us together. I see them so clearly; in my vision we all can get along. But I also know this, my fellow Americans: I am not the answer, I cannot do it alone. *We* are the answer. We aren't red *or* blue like two rival street gangs; our colors are red, white and blue. And, black, brown, red and yellow."

More applause and supportive comments after each color. Then with a straight face, he added, " . . . and a tasteful little sprinkling of lavender and hot fuchsia."

The crowd erupted with cheers and laughter, and he thought even Ed Garry looked amused.

"This is what I see in my vision quest: we are all the colors together. The beauty of a rainbow, the unity signified by e pluribus unum: out of many one. Let every force that has tried to divide us be banished into the dark pages of history. Let them stand there as a warning, a cautionary tale; a snapshot of a place we never want to return to.

Many of you know that our 35th President John Fitzgerald Kennedy is one of my heroes. He wasn't perfect, but for me, that humanity was part of what made him great.

We can seriously mess up and still be the impetus behind putting a man on the moon. We can be firmly stuck in the mud by our own clay feet and yet help bring equality to citizens who have been deprived of their rights and freedom for generations. Like Kennedy, we can make mistakes, but we can come back from them. We can put all the rage and rhetoric behind us now. Let it be done. That's what I see in my vision quest.

Let's bring back hope. Others have talked about 'Make American Great Again' as if there was one and only one time—somewhere in the dusty, distant past—when our country was great. We know the secret handshake that's encoded in that idea: a time where men—yes, usually white men—ran everything unopposed. A time where women and people of color and those durned foreigners knew their place and by God stayed in it.

I say they were wrong. I say, our country is great right now."

There were some cheers this time, and he glanced at Pat who was applauding.

"Still, I think we can do even better. We can do better here at home for ourselves, but also for the world. We can reach out again. We can turn terrorists into our tribe. We can show our haters that we are heroes. We can make racists our relatives because they probably already are!

I can see it. We will Make America Greater. M.A.G. MAGnificent! That's our country!"

He held for the applause, but then he quieted his voice.

"But the M, it also stands for Maturity. We will no longer fight and feud and name call and call out like petulant children. We're here to set an example . . . to guide and love and protect our children, not act like them on their worst days."

"Yes!" came from several people and did he hear "Preach!" from someone?

"And the A? That's also for Agape, the kind of unconditional love that God-fearing people know comes from their Creator, and the kind of love that all parents should have for their children. But it's not only about religion: this is the love that we, in this great country, can share with the world. And I have to stop a moment here and acknowledge the love of my life."

He turned toward her and was about to continue, when a chant of "Mom! Mom!" started, and she grinned and waved at the crowd.

"Exactly. Mom. Pat Mitchell showed me what that word agape means. She was a mom even before we had Aidan because she cares about children, any children, anywhere. And then there's Greatness.

Let us ask ourselves: Is our country greater because we exclude people who aren't white enough or rich enough or just because they aren't exactly like us? Is it greater because we don't care about any other country on Earth? My vision says no. It says we're better than that.

Some of you have heard the rumors, but now I can confirm that I am ready to take the first symbolic step toward a new unity, toward our MAGnificence. On Nov. 22nd, I propose to retake John F. Kennedy's historic ride through Dallas and, with the help of my fellow citizens, give it the ending it should have had."

As he'd anticipated, there were gasps and some cries of dismay from the gathered spectators. Garry was shaking his head slowly and giving him a look that clearly telegraphed, "You are an idiot." Jameson held up a hand to quiet them.

"I know. I know. This ride is dangerous, but I am protected by the full power of the Secret Service and the rest of Homeland Security along with the FBI and, of course local Dallas police officers, not to mention hundreds of thousands of loyal Americans. I am in no more danger than a black or Latino boy in our toughest ghettos. I'm safer than a wife who lives in fear of her abusive husband and puts herself between him and her children every day, or many forgotten inmates and their guards who are at the mercy of our broken penal system. I am safer than the least of these, but I am no more important."

"Yes you are, you are more important," came from several people. He shook his head and again held up his hands for silence.

"No, not me. The Presidency, yes: but no individual. I am one of you. No more, no less."

He allowed the warm applause to continue for a while.

"I'm not trying to be a martyr, but the situation we find ourselves in now needs heroes. Not mythical, superhuman types, but everyday people being heroic in small, everyday ways. Those everyday people are you, all of you . . . everyone within the sound of my voice. We can be better. We can do better. I think we as a country lost something that day in Dallas, but I believe we can get it back. We can be a little kinder to our neighbors, we can be a little more welcoming to strangers. All great religions teach us about helping and loving one another. Whether you're Christian, Jewish, Muslim, Buddhist or none of the above, you can be a part of our American family. Our Maturity and Agape will lead us to our Greatness. Together, we will Make America Greater than we ever imagined. That is my vision quest. My beloved fellow Americans, please, please join me."

When he was done, there was a heartbeat of silence, like they'd all taken a breath before releasing it in a collective roar of approval. Of course, he knew his many allies were certainly leading the cheering, but some of the faces he was looking at were not automatic supporters. If this group was a microcosm of the nation, maybe he had a few more people on board. That was the most he could hope for.

The questions started right away, and he was glad they were pretty much what he'd prepared for: what did the Kennedy family think? (They had been consulted and had no objections, though they would not be participating in any way). How much would it cost (Expensive, yes, but donations from several prominent business people and his own two-million-dollar donation would defray most of it.) Would they use the actual car? (No another 61 blue Lincoln). Would it be the same route exactly? (Up to Dealey Plaza, but new ending to be announced.) Was the Vice President going? (No. We thought it best that he not go, besides there's a rumor that Mrs. Williams is very happy about that.) And of course, there were some grassy knoll and book depository jokes. But all in all, it was going well.

Then his favorite question of the day from a CNN reporter, Troy Nathan, "Mr. President, your vision quest sounds very nice, but are you sure it's not vision impossible? Do you really believe we can somehow put all that's happened in the past few years behind us and start over with a clean slate? How do you clean a slate like that?"

He paused a moment. "Troy, I do believe it. I took the most challenging job on Earth because with every fiber of my being I believe we can achieve all the shining, golden ideals any of us ever heard or thought of. I believe we can actually be the country we told ourselves we were. We clean the slate by taking a page from our First Lady's book when she says, 'I refuse to judge. I refuse to hate. My heart is fixed on love.'"

There was more warm applause and a cheer. He looked over at Pat and was surprised to see tears in her eyes. He reached for her hand and held it high.

He basked for a moment, feeling a little pride and a whole lot of love, "Thank you everyone. Thank you."

They started to leave the stage, with a couple of people still calling out "Mr. Presidents", to which he waved and smiled, when a loud female voice cut through the noise. He didn't even know the young woman who asked it, but he wished she hadn't been invited to the party.

"Mr. President there's some speculation online that there may be a serial killer who's replicating famous murders in different parts of the country. Do you have any concerns about that? After all, what's a more famous murder than the assassination of JFK?"

Jameson felt his stomach tighten. *What the hell?* For a moment, he had second thoughts about his commitment to press freedom. Bring back the days when every question was checked and cleared beforehand.

He didn't know how long it was before he formed a reply, but it felt like an hour.

"Well, speculation online is that. Someone is guessing at something, trying to create a buzz to get more followers. We can't listen to every rumor we read or hear online, and we certainly don't want to put ideas in anyone's heads, do we?" He tried to keep his tone light as he pointed to another raised hand, but she wouldn't stop.

"But it's more than just a rumor, isn't it Mr. President? People are actually dying, and there's one particular blogger called MayHem who's hinting that the FBI believes the same thing. Isn't it worrisome to you or to the First Lady that law enforcement can't seem to—?"

"That's not what we're here to talk about," he snapped. He knew they were probably all getting close-ups on his tightening jaw. He forced a smile and said in a softer tone, "Those local murders, sensational as they may seem because they're more violent or gory than others or because they may in fact be reminiscent of past murders, are still local crimes being investigated in those local jurisdictions or by the FBI where appropriate. We don't do law enforcement any favors by trying to make the crimes seem more sensational than they are. Thank you everyone." He turned, leaving a chorus of "Mr. Presidents" trailing after him, took Pat's hand, and strode away.

Chapter 12

MONDAY – Afternoon: Los Angeles

As the man drove south, he shed "Christian" and "Matthew" and any and all others he had had to be over the past years. "Michael Hitchings" may have been a connection with his failed parents, but it was still who he was; it was a reminder of all he had been through, a reason to continue his mission. Beside him on the seat was a small, neatly wrapped package. A gift. He could have sent them something like a bomb, but this was going to be so much better than a bomb. This was going to tear them to pieces in ways they could not even imagine.

He had left the PCH, jumped on the 10 West, and in a few minutes was on Olympic Boulevard. He had taken this same route many times before—sitting, watching, looking for the person who, he knew, was the right one. He'd finally found him.

His time as an Army Reservist had helped in this immeasurably. He'd joined the Reserves originally thinking it would be a way to fight the bad guys. He quickly learned there were bad guys everywhere. Not everyone who joined the Reserves had the same noble intentions as he did. Some of them simply wanted to "blow shit up". The Reserves, for some, was a convenient outlet to exploit their violent tendencies. One particular fellow Reservist had nauseated and enraged him above the others. He was a fellow novice who was fond of drinking too much and blowing off his mouth. It was in one such drinking session he revealed, and with some pride, that he and his mates had "stuck it to some fat black bitch" who was still in high school. Hitchings knew what that meant. Rape. Pack rape. The very thing he'd joined the Reserves to escape, to fight against in some way. This piece of slim even laughed about how the bitch had been forced to carry his bastard child as a result. "The only good thing about her," he mocked luridly, "was the one piece of white on her nigger body and the one little white missile that found its mark in her torpedo tube . . . if you get my drift."

Hitchings hadn't bought into the conversation between this scumbag and his mates, but he had listened intently. Insights into human behavior, of all sorts, was of value to him. Apparently, their victim had a little heart-shaped birthmark on her neck. Incredibly, the self-confessed rapist seemed proud to claim it was his "missile" that found its mark, when in reality it could have been any of the rapists. It seemed to be a perverted badge of honor for him. In an ironic twist of fate, it was his bragging about his crime that had landed him in the Reserves. As it happened, Corporal Richards hailed from a wealthy and respected family. Unfortunately, his privileged upbringing had been his undoing. He was spoiled, lazy and considered himself entitled. The excessive drinking was most likely a result of boredom, the side effect being loose lips. When he shot his mouth off about his accomplishment within earshot of parents they were mortified. Nevertheless, even though they were enraged and outraged by their son's actions, he was still their son. They not only didn't want to see their baby boy wind up in jail, they also couldn't contemplate the shame this would bring upon their good family name.

The most logical solution his parents could come up with was to teach him a lesson, and simultaneously some discipline and some skills, by signing him up to the Weekend Warriors. At first he'd complained bitterly but once he discovered he could "blow shit up" he quite liked the idea. However, this was only part one of his parents' way of addressing the issue. Like Corporal Richards himself, they assumed their son was the one who had caused this poor young woman's unwanted pregnancy. Afterall, he was from superior stock and it was well-known that the strongest genetically coded sperm was always the one that fertilized the egg. It was that same level of arrogance which had filtered down into their offspring from their own genetic coding. This assumption, which was beyond doubt in their minds, meant that somewhere a half-cast baby carrying their lineage was going to be born. They could not have such a child raised in poverty and squalor. On the other hand, they could hardly claim the child as part of their family, nor would they want to. It was a quandary to be sure. Ultimately, they decided the most logical solution was to find the victim of their son's brutal assault, buy her silence and arrange for the child to raised in a "decent white family", whose silence they would also buy. The mother of the child would be offered a fully funded decent education to give her the best opportunity to make something of herself so long as she never spoke of the "incident" and never attempted to claim the child as her own in the future. For an unpriviledged black child with no other prospects, it was an easy sell.

Hitchings remembered it all. His time in the Reserves had served him well in many ways, even if he had been disgusted by his comrades. He had learned munitions training and how to command the respect and obedience of subordinates. In truth he had learned a good deal more.

He drove up Beloit Avenue—an odd, cramped little street that looked like it should be one-way. He went through a short tunnel created by overhanging trees, parked, and walked a while, approaching the underbelly of the highway where some of the more "fortunate" homeless lived in makeshift tents. He walked up to one that was made mostly of old clothing and plastic bags but was neatly bordered by rocks the occupant had collected. It even had a colorful weed garden on one side. The owner, in surprisingly neat camouflage fatigues, was sitting cross-legged at the entrance, appearing to be in a trance or perhaps deep meditation.

Michael crouched before him and said softly. "Marine."

The man's piercing blue eyes were instantly open. "Sir, yes sir," he said and saluted.

"Your mission, the one we talked about: it's time."

"Time, sir? We have our orders?" He pushed his dog tags inside his tee shirt, jumped to a crouching position, reached into his tent, pulled out a camo jacket and hat, and put them on.

"We do," Michael said. "You remember the plan? You remember what we talked about?"

"To save us all. For our country, for the children, for the world. To stop the aliens from taking our brains and changing us, like they did to you and me. I deliver a message to the generals. They'll understand and decode. I go dark after."

"Excellent. And the location?" Michael asked.

"FBI headquarters, across from my duty station. Where our fallen brothers live. Where I do recon and protection patrol every day, 0700 to 0900."

"This is the mission, Marine." Michael handed him the package. "You must make delivery at precisely 19:45 hours."

"Nineteen forty-five," the marine repeated.

"Tell them it is urgent for the man whose name is on the package to get it immediately."

"Yes, sir."

"And if they question you about me?"

"Protect the mission."

"Yes," Michael said. "That's right. Protect the mission."

Michael took out five one hundred-dollar bills, folded them in half, and pressed them into the man's palm.

He said, "Sir, my duty. I can't take this."

"Yes you can, Marine. Think of the good you can do. How many you can feed. Take it." He looked the man directly in the eyes and said, "For the ones who didn't make it."

"Sir, yes sir. Semper Fi. For the brothers."

"For the brothers," Michael echoed.

They both saluted and as they stood there, like a statue dedicated to fidelity and courage, Michael saw the clouds open and a warm beam of amber light caress them both. They were here with him, watching, blessing him. *This is our beloved Son in whom we are well pleased*, he heard his Voices say. There was no doubt: he was doing what he was supposed to be doing.

He turned to walk away but called back over his shoulder. "If I don't make it out, Marine, remember me."

"Never forget the ones who served sir. Never!" called a voice from behind him.

Before he turned the corner, he looked back, and the man was still standing, tall and erect, saluting him.

* * *

Malik hurriedly showered and changed to prepare for yet another late night. This was the part of his beloved job that he absolutely hated: leaving his girl alone in the evenings after not seeing her all day. Even after all these years, Sharon Daniels brought a light to his eyes and a nice warm feeling in his heart every time he looked at her. Hell, she *was* his heart. He didn't know what he would do without her. Sharon never complained, but he knew she didn't like it much either. But no worries: retirement was just around the corner. And anyhow, tonight wasn't quite as bad because Sharon was babysitting their adorable grandbaby Malia while Shayna and their son-in-law took in a movie.

Sharon came in the bedroom, and as always, he felt that "luckiest man alive" rush. Maybe life could be better, but not for him.

"Is she asleep?"

"Not yet, but it won't be long. She has that thousand-mile stare going."

"Speaking of sleep, looks like somebody had their beauty nap today."

"All right, old man," she said. "You keep looking at me like that, and you won't get out of here alive. Someone may have to do something really bad to you."

He hugged her close, and then stepped back, so she could help him with his tie.

"Thirty-eight years, can you believe it? It's like we blinked, and the time is gone."

"Not until tomorrow," she said. "And on that note, with this case heating up, should we postpone dinner? I don't mind."

"Nope, we are celebrating on the actual day. Phil and the team know what's up. I'm going to be with my girl. Phone off, full attention."

"So you're close to catching this monster? You're feeling confident?"

"We're pretty sure we actually know who he is. And with our boy on the case, we will find him."

"Harrison's coming to our party on Saturday, right? And Katherine?"

"All right matchmaker, back off. But yes, they'll both be there along with the rest of the task force."

"That gift he gave us: so beautifully wrapped. Wonder if Katherine helped him?"

He shook his head and laughed. "You can ask him yourself on Saturday."

"And one more question," she said, patting his tie and brushing his lapels. "Are you sure about Valentino's? I don't know if I can properly digest a $40 piece of chicken. Might upset my tummy."

"Okay. Get the veal, because we're going, we're splurging, and we aren't going to think twice about it. You're worth every penny. Besides, once I spend that much on you for one dinner, I'm gettin' me some booty."

"Boy, you need to stop," she laughed and planted a juicy kiss before he walked out the door.

* * *

Two hours later, Michael stood outside the Daniels home preparing himself for the beauty that was to come. He was preternaturally calm, his breath and heartbeat slow and contented. But earlier, when he'd seen Daniels arrive at home, he'd been terrified. How could this be happening? Was he wrong? What he was hearing from his Guides: was it possible it could be inaccurate? He didn't know what he would do if that were the case. Who was he if his entire reason for living wasn't what he thought it was? But within the hour, Daniels was hurrying out the door, not realizing what a help he was to Michael, who scurried through their automatic sliding gate before it closed. He silently thanked Daniels and his Guides for this definitive proof. He moved silently around the house he had become so familiar with, cut the wire to the land line, and, carefully avoiding the cameras whose locations he had memorized, proceeded to the back door with his tools.

* * *

Harrison and Kate were almost halfway through the two-hour drive to San Diego when Daniels called. "Chief," Harrison said, as the car's blue tooth put the call on speaker, "any word on the tap?"

"You have it, Harrison, but it's limited to his land line. I'll have Laurie text you the number we've identified. We can't find a cell phone listed to him and nothing on a computer as yet. We couldn't really find an online presence, and the judge wouldn't allow us to be too general. From the looks of it, this guy may not even use a computer."

"That's a start," Kate said. "Whether or not we get anything tonight, we'll pay him a visit first thing in the morning. If he has any info on Hitchings, we'll get it."

* * *

Malik hung up with Harrison and started to call Stanton with an update, when his office phone rang. He was surprised to see building security was calling. "Sorry to bother you Mr. Daniels," the man said, "but I have a package that was delivered by someone who is adamant that you and only you are to receive it. Those were instructions he was given by someone else."

Daniels sat up in his chair. Could this be Hitchings?

"Who is he? What does he look like?" he asked excitedly. "Hold him there until—"

"Hey, Hey!" he heard the guard yell. "Wait, come back here!"

He heard the phone bang to the counter or floor, and footsteps clattering across the marble. Moments later, the man picked up the phone and said breathlessly, "Damn, that sonofabitch could run! He ran right out into traffic across Wilshire toward Veterans. Didn't even stop."

"But you had a good look at him."

"And he's on camera," the man offered apologetically. "But I know who he is anyway. You know that homeless guy we call the Sentry?"

"Who?" Malik asked.

"He's in the cemetery patrolling every morning. Wears fatigues, salutes people who come in to visit. Even stands guard at funerals sometimes. It was him."

"So he should be easy to find. Now the package, what does it look like? Do you think it's suspicious or dangerous?"

"Maybe sir, but it's a little thing. Made it through the metal detector just fine. He held it in his bare hand; didn't seem to be worried about it at all. Not much bigger than a jewelry box. Light weight. Wrapped like a gift with your name on it."

"Okay, don't handle it any more. I'm calling the bomb techs."

* * *

Michael could hear the television from where he stood just inside the house. He couldn't tell where Sharon was, but he had to proceed as if she might be on the first floor. The lights were off in all but the kitchen and another room. It took only a moment to see she wasn't in the kitchen.

He could hear the tinkling of a nursery rhyme and the soft babbling of a baby coming from the other lighted room. She might be in there with the grandchild. He trod softly and cautiously down the hall the hall to the open door. When he peeked around the corner, he saw only an infant's crib where a baby was sitting and rocking to the music. As if she sensed his presence, she suddenly stopped, stared at the door, and pulled herself to her feet using the bed railings.

She was a cute little thing, light brown with a big halo of fluffy-looking dark hair and huge eyes like one of those dolls. She had on a tiny pink tee shirt with a picture of a badge that said "FBI Baby." He liked that.

They stared at each other.

She had a pacifier in her mouth, but when he took a step toward her, she opened her mouth and let it drop to the bed. She seemed to know exactly who he was.

I look like a giant to her, he thought. *Like Goliath. But you will not stop me, Little David. Go ahead, call your God. See what happens.*

She took a deep breath and began to wail like a siren.

He heard her grandmother calling down in a soothing voice from upstairs. "It's okay Gamma's baby. It's okay, I'm on the way. I'm coming. Why did you wake up? Did you have a bad dream? It's okay, Gamma's—"

When she reached the bottom step and turned the corner, he was waiting in the hall just outside of the bedroom.

He watched the emotions with pleasure and full understanding. *She's thinking about a telephone, about something she might be able to do. But she's also thinking about her granddaughter.*

She turned and started running back up the steps, but he said loudly and calmly, "I have your granddaughter, Sharon." His words jerked her backward like a dog on a choke chain. She spun around, jumped the last two steps and raced down the hall toward him. He disappeared into the bedroom, and when she reached the door, panting with fear, he was across the room holding baby Malia lovingly in his arms.

* * *

Malik and the team watched the screen nervously as the bomb tech, on camera down in the lobby, finally, painstakingly slowly, opened the small box. Malik knew how impatient they were, he felt the same. He told them, "I think we know exactly what this is." But still, he'd called in the Bomb Squad. And of course, they sent over the guy who used the first line of "Whistle While You Work" as his personal theme song while he was dealing with the package.

Years later, or so it felt, x-ray confirmed that all there was inside was something thin and folded, cloth or paper most likely.

When they heard the whistling part of the song coming over the walkie for the tenth time, Othello said, "I used to like that song."

Skip groaned and said, "Sir, you know I have experience. I could have done this. We wouldn't have had to take a trip to Disney-frackin-land while we waited."

"Skip, we had to wait," Malik said firmly.

"He doesn't want to blow us up, he wants to taunt us with how brilliant he is and how stupid we are," Skip replied.

"And we *would* be stupid if he put something toxic in that box or on the fabric that could kill all of us," Jeanne said.

"You mean like Ricin or something?" Othello asked.

"Exactly," Malik said.

"I was willing to take the chance," Skip sulked.

"It's okay, Robin. We know you're a hero," Jeanne said.

Skip snapped "Shut up," and Malik snapped even louder, "If you think that's helping, people, you are dead wrong. That's why it's going to end. Now."

There was quiet for a moment, before Jeanne said "Look, he's opened it."

They leaned into the screen and saw the bomb tech holding a piece of fabric up toward the camera.

"That's it, isn't it?" Skip asked excitedly.

"Is there anything else in there officer? A note?" Malik said into the walkie.

"No, that's it," the man said, shaking the wrappings for them to see. "But this piece of fabric has writing on it. It's brown. Looks like dried blood."

"Can you read it?" Malik asked.

"It's . . . uh . . . pretty tiny. Looks like "palm," maybe? Then some numbers: 45 colon 14." He looked toward the camera. "Mean anything?"

"Psalm 45:14," Malik said. "Thanks, you can wrap it up. Leave the fabric there."

He turned to the two of them. "Jeanne, go and get it, including the wrappings. Skip, find Fletch. I think he was trying to get some dinner. I'll update Phil. We need to find out what this means."

* * *

"Please, please don't hurt her," Sharon said, holding out her arms in entreaty. "If you just leave, I won't call anyone for an hour. Two hours. Give you time to get far away. I didn't see you. I don't even know what you look like."

"Sharon. Sweet rose of Sharon. They already know everything about me. You know that. Everything, that is, but what the apocalypse will really look like."

He shifted the baby to his right arm, so she could see what he was holding in his left hand. After that, she couldn't take her eyes off it.

"It's called a buck knife," he said flipping the blade open. "Hunters use them."

She drew in a deep breath to scream, and he instantly put the blade to her baby's throat. "You scream, she dies."

"I know who you are," she hissed at him.

"Of course you do. 'I'm the devil, and I'm here to do the devil's business.'"

He held out the baby toward her, the knife still gripped in his left hand. Sharon tentatively took a step toward him, searching his eyes, as if hoping for some kind of humanity, some kindred spirit. "Please, please. You don't have to do this. You've been hurt in your life, I know that. You don't have to hurt other people. Other innocent people. We've never done anything to you."

He smiled, shook his head gently and held out the baby toward her. When she clutched the child and tried to back away, his right arm was around her in a flash, gripping the three of them together.

"Not one of you is innocent. Not one."

He watched the tears form in her beautiful brown eyes and then flow down her face. He used the knife to ever so softly lift a tear from her cheek. He licked the blade with the tip of his tongue and said, "Jesus wept," before plunging the knife deep in her abdomen. He thought she said, "Malik," before he stabbed her four more times, but he couldn't be sure. Her cries and the baby's together made what sounded to him like an angel chorus, in praise of their God.

He watched the light fade in her eyes and admired how she tried to hold onto her grandbaby even as death embraced her. He had never known that kind of love. Michael let her clutch her precious little one until she was gone. He placed the bloodstained child in her crib. Despite the smell which must be filling her nostrils, she had cried herself out. She lay on her tummy and turned her face away from the bad man and went to sleep. The bad man went about his work.

* * *

"Did Skip brief you?" Malik asked Fletcher as the two walked in the conference room.

"Yes he did. Sounds like you guys waited till I was gone for the party to start. May I see it?" He turned the piece of shirt over and looked closely at it then thumbed through his much-used Bible.

"Forty-five is actually a song celebrating a royal wedding. It tells how handsome and brave the king is, how beautiful the bride is, and how happy they're going to be, that kind of thing. Now fourteen specifically says . . ." he ran his finger down one of the columns:

> 'In her colorful gown she is led to the king,
>
> followed by her bridesmaids,
>
> and they also are bought to him.'

"Obviously, on its face, a reference the wedding of a powerful man or couple."

"This one is an anomaly," Malik said.

"How so?" Fletcher asked.

"For the first time, he sent a Psalm, and as far as we know, there's no murder."

"Yeah, probably this one is some kind of clue," Skip said. "Son of a bitch loves his games."

"Right," Fletcher said staring from the Bible to the swatch of cloth. "You know . . . well this may be a crazy long shot but . . . Malik, Skip said it was addressed to you, that it had to be put in your hands and no other, right?"

"Yes, so?"

"Well, I don't want to think this but what if . . ."

"Fletch, for God's sake spit it out!"

"Your anniversary tomorrow: what if this guy knows somehow? What if the wedding and bridesmaids images and the king—your name, Malik, you know it means 'the king' . . . well, maybe you should call Sharon just in case and—"

"Oh shit!" Malik had his phone out and had hit the button for Sharon's cell before the man finished his sentence. "Laurie! Call my home number!" he yelled across the room. "If she answers, tell her to get the baby and get out of the house right now!"

Jeanne said, "Chief, do you want to go home? We'll take you." She glanced at Skip who grabbed his jacket.

"Yes. Yes I . . . dammit, voicemail!" He hit disconnect and tried again.

"I'll get the cops over there while we're on the way," Skip said. "Your address, sir?"

They hurried to the elevator as Malik kept trying his wife's phone and whispering to himself, "Please, please dear Jesus, please, please!"

* * *

There were already three black and whites with flashing lights sitting outside his house when they arrived. It looked like every light in the house was turned on.

"The gate's open. Why is the gate open?" Malik asked, trying unsuccessfully to stop his voice from shaking.

"Sir, we could be wrong. Maybe . . ." Jeanne started, but a look from him silenced her.

She pulled into his driveway but didn't have time to stop before Malik catapulted out of the car and sprinted toward his front door.

"Chief, wait! Don't—" Skip called out, but nothing could stop him.

Two officers, stationed at his front door, stepped out to bar the way. "This is my house, my wife's in there. Move goddamit!" he screamed at them, not slowing for a second. "Sharon! Sharon!" he yelled.

They tried to block him. He knocked the smaller one, who looked straight out of cadet school, to the ground and managed to drag the other one along with him hanging on like a determined Rottweiler. In seconds, he made it to his living room door.

He saw it all in flashes. Like a picture of a picture of something he once saw: blood on his floor, blood on the furniture, blood, "Death to Pigs" scrawled on his living room wall in blood and a body: a woman's mutilated body that someone had stabbed and stabbed and stabbed, with a rope around her neck.

He wasn't sure where he was after that. The room was moving. That much he knew.

There was a voice coming from behind him that sounded like someone calling out to him underwater in a swimming pool.

"Malik, don't go in there. Malik, Malik!" He felt strong hands grab both his arms. There were men on either side of him, dragging him from the room.

"Malik, come on out of here, man. You don't want to be in here."

In slow motion, he turned his head to one side and realized he was looking at Phil Stanton. He didn't remember him riding over with them. Maybe he had been there all along. He heard himself say in an odd little voice, "Oh, hi Phil."

"I'm so sorry. I'm so sorry. I was on my way home. Heard you guys on the radio. When I heard the address I—"

"The baby!" Malik said. "Where's my Grandbaby?"

"Chief, I'll find out right now," Jeanne raced into the house.

Malik could see the crowd gathered with their inevitable cell phones flashing and taking their stupid videos. He wondered if he should smile. He turned to Stanton and said, "Manson, right? Sharon and Sharon. Clever."

"I'm so sorry," Stanton said again, angrily wiping tears from his eyes. He turned to the officers and yelled, "Get the goddamned neighbors out of here. If they keep taking pictures, confiscate their phones for evidence."

It felt like a lifetime had passed when Malik remembered something. "Sharon Tate," he said. "They killed her baby. Do you think he—? What's taking her so long? Oh please, don't tell me. Please God."

Jeanne appeared in the doorway at that moment. She was holding a little bundle swaddled in white towels. Her face was grim. Whatever she was holding wasn't moving.

If he took her too, I'm dead was all his mind could manage. *If she's gone too, I'm already dead.*

Jeanne came closer, and it seemed to him the whole world held its breath. He suddenly couldn't hear anything—not the crowd, not the cops and their radios, nothing.

Then the silence was broken by an infant's angry wail. A little fist punched the air, and tiny feet began kicking in protest. *She is alive. Malia is alive!*

"Sorry, Chief," Jeanne said, handing him the bundle. "Had to clean her up a little bit, but she's fine."

He pressed his beloved baby against his chest, kissed her damp head, and rocked her until her cries stopped.

"Let's get back to the office," Stanton said. "We'll get you both together with your daughter and son-in-law and decide where you're going to go."

"Go?" Malik asked.

"Malik, I don't want you to have to think about this right now, but we're going to have to proceed as if all of us and all of our families are in danger. This can't be a coincidence: if he knew who you were and where to find you, somehow he's getting information about who's on the team."

"Oh great, look," Skip said, pointing down the street. A news van was rolling slowly up the street, trying to maneuver around the cars and onlookers.

"We have to get out of here," Stanton said. "Malik, you're riding with me. Jeanne and Skip, go and grab her car seat and get clothes for Malik and baby gear. Hurry with the seat, and whoever drove here, follow in your car with the rest. The other one, stay here and coordinate with the police."

The baby was strapped in, and Phil was hurrying around to get in the car when Malik looked out the passenger window at an eager looking reporter who rushed up and planted herself just outside the security gate. She scanned each face coming and going, and when her gaze lighted on Stanton's, the recognition was immediate.

"Director Stanton," she called, "What happened here?"

"No comment."

"Why was the FBI called? There's speculation it's a murder."

"No comment," Phil repeated.

He opened the door and started to get in when she said, "Is this connected to the Psalm serial killings that are happening all over the country?"

"What did you say?" He straightened up and looked down at her threateningly.

Undaunted, she stepped closer. "There's a lot of online chatter about it. Any comment? Is this the Psalm killer?" She thrust her mike toward him.

He stood staring at her for a moment, as she continued to pepper him with unanswered questions, "No comment," and escaped into the car.

"Why did she ask that? How does she know that?" Malik asked.

"I don't know," Stanton said. "But we're sure as hell going to find out."

Chapter 13

TUESDAY – Morning: San Diego

Harrison was studying Kate's sleeping face in the dappled morning light when she opened her eyes and looked right into his. Embarrassed, he quickly averted his attention to one of the cups of coffee in the holder between them. "Here, I uh bought these a little while ago at a little place called Heartsleeves. I think you'd like it. I got some muffins too. I knew you were tired, so I . . ."

"Thanks," Kate smiled at him and took a careful swallow. "Mmm, still hot. Thanks," she said again.

She seemed to be waiting for him to say something, which made him even more uncomfortable. Finally he said, "This is Franks' place."

Kate sat up straight and looked around the property. "Section 8 I'm guessing," she said as she surveyed the place.

Their parking space, which was one of six or seven in front of a low hill of dirt and scrubby weeds jammed between two sets of concrete stairs, faced a light gray, two-story stucco apartment building. Its monochromatic blandness was broken only by slightly darker gray doors. Here and there, a tenant had put up curtains in a feeble attempt at color or style, but even those had faded to just another shade of gray.

"All that trouble to get a warrant and this guy is a hermit," Kate said.

"You'd think at least a telemarketing call would come through. And who only has a land line?"

"Don't tell me," Harrison chuckled. "You were hoping Michael Hitchings himself would give a call and turn up at the front door, right on cue."

"Well, a girl can dream."

They left the car and walked up the stairs, avoiding the cracks. It was only a few feet to a ground level apartment.

Kate knocked. After a long wait, she knocked again harder.

"Maybe he's out," Harrison said.

"I'd be out too. This place is so depressing."

Harrison frowned and looked around. "Is it? I would have said neat and, I don't know, minimal?"

Kate squinted at him and gave him a wry smile. "Yes, that fetching gray on gray on gray. I suppose there's something to be said for that."

"It's . . . orderly," he replied. "I like that."

"I guess we're looking at different things," she said, turning to look around once again. "Well, as they say, beauty's in the eye of the beholder."

"Yes," he said, looking at her, "it is." He took a nervous breath and said, "Kate, would you ever—"

"I hear something. I think someone's coming," she said, cutting him off. And immediately after, they heard a lock clicking open, a pause, another and another.

The door opened a crack, and a gravelly voice wheezed, "What is it?" took a gasping breath and continued, "Whaddaya want?"

Kate held her badge at eye level and said, "Mr. George Franks? I'm Special Agent Katherine Fleming, and this is Special Agent Harrison Carter from the FBI."

The door opened an inch farther, and they could now see a suspicious brown eye below a shock of dingy-looking brown hair.

"Can't see him," the man said, opening the door a little wider. Harrison stepped to Kate's left, and the man raised his arm suddenly. He was holding something, and both agents stepped back reflexively, fearing a weapon. But it was an oxygen mask that he put over his mouth and inhaled from deeply. He took it down, looking from one of them to the other and said drily, "Ha ha. Gotcha."

"Mr. Franks, we'd like to talk with you about a man you know, a Michael Hitchings," Harrison said, ignoring the jab.

Franks nodded, turned, and walked away, leaving the door open behind him. "Come in. I have to sit down now. That was my exercise for the day. Not that I don't love a good, brisk walk." He inched slowly back to his couch, dragging the oxygen tank behind him.

They stepped inside, blinking as their eyes became accustomed to the dimness.

"Oh," was all Kate could manage as their senses were assaulted by the place. "Not so spare. Or neat," she whispered to Harrison.

"You can sit," the man said, indicating two frayed, once-yellow upholstered armchairs. "Just move that stuff." He felt beside himself for his cane then grabbed the remote and muted the TV, placing it on his dusty coffee table.

As the smell hit Harrison's nose, he, for some reason, flashed back to a wine tasting his father had hosted once. The sommelier had gushed about the fruits and woodsy notes and hints of honey and smoke. He'd blathered on and on about the 360° sensual experience from the sound of the liquid swishing around the glass to the colors, the fragrances, the textures on the tongue, and finally, the tastes. It had made him appreciate and relate to wine in a whole different way.

What was happening to him now was like the evil twin of that experience. There was stuff everywhere; every surface had something on it. There were papers, books, dirty clothes, bric-a-brac, and things he didn't want to get close enough to, to identify. On a small table next to the sofa where the man now sat was what looked like the remains of at least five meals, and from the smell, some clearly weren't from today or even this week.

"You'll have to excuse the mess," Franks said, "I have a debilitating illness which leaves me with little strength to clean. I have a lady that comes and helps out when I can afford to pay her."

From the looks of things, Franks hadn't been able to pay the lady for quite some time. Kate stepped carefully to one of the chairs, making sure her feet were on the stained carpet, not something unidentifiable, and cleared the items off before sitting down. Harrison was still standing near the door, trying to convince himself to walk the rest of the way, even as his nose told him he was smelling notes of dead rodent, rotting vegetable, and a hint of something very, very sick, like vomitus from extremely cheap wine.

"Harrison," Kate said, "you okay?"

"Sure, fine," was all he could manage. This wasn't threatening like a criminal firing rounds at him or anything like an open chest or gut with blood everywhere at the hospital, but there, it was sterile. Here was . . . He almost wished he had a hazmat suit.

He looked around the room and paused when he spotted one small, spotlessly clean area on a wall across from the sofa. There were neatly arranged pictures on the wall and a little cleared space in front with an umbrella stand containing a stage-prop looking sword and a couple of canes and a table with some papers on it.

Franks saw him looking and smiled bitterly. "Hmm. My little shrine to what used to be. I deserve a little beauty in my life, right?"

Harrison noticed the papers arranged in a fan shape were programs from various plays. "You're a theater fan," he said as he finally went to the seat and cautiously sat down.

"Well, not only a fan," Franks said proudly. "I was in all those plays. Not a pro or anything. Amazing the talents and skills that can come out through the impetus of sheer terror. You should have seen me in *Forum*. I killed. The audience was screaming laughing."

"That's uh . . ." Harrison looked at Kate for help.

"The musical? A FUNNY THING HAPPENED......?" Franks said hopefully, "Never mind. You're not interested in the history of some never-was actor. But so you know, I wasn't always this dried up piece of shit you're looking at now. My life wasn't always this way." He waved a hand indicating the mess he was surrounded by.

Franks took a few more breaths from his mask before pulling it down around his neck. "So what is it you want to know about Michael?"

"You are still in contact with him, is that correct?" Kate asked.

"So what if I am? Is that a crime?" Franks asked.

"Of course not, Mr. Franks," Harrison said, "but it's very important that we contact him. Would you know an address?"

"No. He stops by now and then, but he doesn't come in. We usually talk outside. Not sure why," he said, smiling slyly at Harrison.

"We understand you both were together at a Catholic orphanage as boys. Can you tell us anything about that?" Harrison asked.

"What about it?" Franks looked suspiciously from one to the other over the top of his mask. "What do you want to know?"

Kate pushed aside a rotting banana peel and put a small digital recorder on top of the table. "Do you mind if we record our conversation?

We just want to get an understanding of how things were there. We're told there was a court case."

Franks shrugged, and she clicked the recorder on. "What was the case about? Were you a part of it?"

"Why are you playing games with me? If you know there was a case, you know it was about the abuse." He sighed and bowed his head, and began speaking as if to himself, his focus still on the floor.

"I was six or seven when they brought Michael in. He was a small kid and was actually bullied sometimes because of it. I guess you could say he was cute. Looked like the kind of kid who'd be picked for modeling or commercials or something. And he was picked all right. The priests definitely thought he was cute. The first day he got there, they took him up to the office. We all knew what that meant, what was going to happen to him."

"You mean all of you had been exposed to some kind of sexual assault by the priests?"

"All of us were exposed, yes, but not necessarily in the same ways. Everybody knew what was happening, even if later on they denied or pretended they didn't. Some were only touched and groped, some had to watch, some were raped occasionally, and some, like Michael, well they were the 'special ones.' They called them 'The Chosen.'"

He looked up suddenly and saw how they were reacting before letting out a humorless, "Ha." He continued, his voice completely emotionless, as if he were reciting a laundry list. "They had it all worked out, like a catechism, like it was the real reason they and we were there. They were like a secret sect; some of them even came from other churches and parishes around the area. There were rituals and rules and right and wrong ways to do what they wanted. They would first groom the boys they wanted, before making them do what they'd decided they'd be best at. Me, for example, they never touched me for the first five or so months after I arrived. But I could tell what was coming. They would tell us about our place in God's work, how Baby Jesus would be so proud of us for doing our duty, how blessed we were to be chosen."

"Mr. Franks, if you don't want to—" Kate began.

"Oh, too much for you, is it? You wanted to know, so now you're going to know. Do you think those bastards are still affecting me? Running my life?" He sat up straight and leaned toward them, his eyes burning, "I'll never forget when my time came. Father Simmons was the one who called me into the office. There were six of them standing there without their robes on. But it's okay, you see, they were praying. They all had their crucifixes in their hands. They made me comfortable in a chair against the wall. He made me open my mouth, and one by one they came over and gave me a taste of what was to come. So to speak," he said ironically and laughed bitterly until he began to cough and grabbed for his mask.

"You know what's funny?" He paused and looked at them expectantly as if they might actually have an answer. "We never talked about it. Never. We all knew, but somehow, we knew we shouldn't ever, ever talk about it. Some of us never did."

"And Michael?" Harrison prodded gently.

"That first day, one of the boys said, 'We have another fish.' That's what we called the new boys, like in prison: 'fresh fish.' I'm pretty sure they didn't rape him that soon, they didn't want the little ones to end up in the hospital, I guess. But I'll never forget when he came back. I was lying in the bed reading when I heard his footsteps. The ones who were still awake started shaking the others. He looked like most new kids did after the first time: like they'd been hit by a truck but were somehow able to get up and walk around."

"What happened then?" Kate asked. The look on his face showed he was back there, going through it once again.

He roused himself, grabbed a glass of water on a tray next to him, and downed the remainder of it.

"Not much more to tell. He became their number one toy boy. Something about him seemed to turn all of them on. They would have parties, I guess you could call them, with sacramental wine and other drinks and food, and boys on the side. We'd know what was coming when we were ordered to go and 'clean the office.' Funny, to this day, if I hear someone talking about cleaning an office, I get a really bad feeling." He tried to laugh again, but he gave up, shook his head, and looked at the floor.

"Tell me, Mr. Franks, did Michael ever talk to you about getting some sort of revenge on the priests that he claimed had raped him?" Harrison asked.

"The lawsuit—that was going to be our revenge. We started talking about it in our teens. We wrote to each other after I left there. We knew he'd be free in a few years, and our plan was to out them, humiliate them in court and maybe even walk away with enough to give us a start in life. But it didn't work out that way. The cops didn't try very hard to get enough evidence for a criminal case, so we found a useless little legal aid guy who agreed to help. It was a circus, and our lawyer was the clown."

"What do you mean?" Harrison asked.

"They had hot and cold running lawyers, clerks, assistants, everything. Even investigators. There was this one fat one we called the Sacred Cow. Every time she lumbered into the courtroom and whispered to them; it became worse. They would hand our pathetic, outgunned loser-at-law a piece of paper before starting on another, even more damaging, line of questioning."

"So you lost," Kate said, nodding.

Franks paused a moment and looked at her like she'd just cartwheeled through his living room.

"Yes, Special Agent. We lost." He closed his eyes for a moment, and Harrison saw a tear fall down his cheek.

He quickly took another hit of oxygen, managing to wipe his face as he took it down. "The priests always said no one would ever believe some dirty little bastards who nobody wanted, and they were right."

"But weren't there other witnesses? Other boys willing to speak out?" Harrison asked.

"Apparently you've never been raped," Franks snapped back. "These days boys act like they're proud to talk about some guy doing that to them, but it was different back then. We found as many of them as we could who hadn't overdosed or committed suicide, and once we ruled out the ones who were prostituting or on drugs and the ones who flat out said nothing happened, the church terrorized or bought out the rest. You'd be surprised what tens of thousands of dollars, plus a fear of burning in hell, will do to a young man's memory. It came down to Michael."

"Down to Michael? Not down to the two of you?" Harrison asked, watching him closely.

Franks was twisting his hands as if his palms were sweaty. He suddenly burst out, "Michael, that idiot!" before grabbing his hair and shaking his fists in frustration.

The two agents made eye contact briefly.

"It was his own fault. I told him and told him. I knew we weren't going to win. After Billy, I knew we'd never win no matter what."

"Billy?" Kate asked.

"He was only four when he came. Michael tried to protect him, like he did with all of us. He was Billy's big brother. They would come for him, and Mike tried to stop them. Sometimes he'd even pretend he wanted it, wanted them, so they would take him instead. But one time, after a few years, there was a day he couldn't be there. Michael was at the doctor's, and they came for him, for Billy, and he just couldn't take it anymore. They ordered him to come to clean the office, and he screamed and kicked and cried, but Father Simmons grabbed him by the arm and dragged him up there. He was calling out for Michael the whole way. Then it was quiet."

He stopped, staring into the distance, his face, looking years older, was a tragic mask. "About five minutes later, we heard the priests yelling, and there was this sort of thud, a sound like . . . well," he took a breath, smiled defiantly, and recovered his composure. "I guess it sounded like a body crunching on concrete, since that's what it was. We all ran outside, and there was Billy, face down on the driveway, and a lot of blood. I remember this little black kid, Freddie, kept saying over and over, 'He crunched. Did you hear it? He crunched.' They ordered us in while Fathers Simmons and O'Brien tried to revive him, but he died, right there in front of us."

"Oh," Kate said, "That's . . . that's horrible." Harrison reached over and squeezed her arm without thinking, and she nodded to show she was okay.

"Michael must have been really upset," Harrison said.

"He wanted to kill Simmons. He lunged at him in front of the police, but they stopped him. And before you ask, nothing happened to them. Those priests. Nobody charged, no real investigation. They had information from their own doctors and counselors to show both

Billy and Mike were mentally unstable. Billy was written down as a suicide, and Michael was ignored. He was never the same."

"But he was still determined to get some kind of revenge," Kate said.

"That was never going to happen. I knew and they knew they were going to win. They offered him a settlement right along with the others, but only if he kept quiet. I told him to just take the money, but no, he had to be some kind of superhero. He was going to save people. He was going to get justice," he scoffed. "Well, he found out, it's 'Just Us.' Amen, praise Baby Jesus. And the irony is, a few years after, the truth started coming out about pedophile priests all over the world. But it was too late for us, for Mike and his case. He never was the same. It crushed him."

Harrison leaned forward. "Mr. Franks, were there any prayers or parts of the Bible Michael cared about or recited often?"

"What?" Franks looked from one to the other, confused. "It was a Catholic orphanage. We all said prayers and read the Bible six days a week and all-day Sunday."

"Do you think Michael ever showed signs of mental or emotional problems after he lost the—"

"Mental or emotional? Are you fucking crazy?" Franks tried to jump up, using his cane for support, but fell back to his seat, his whole body shaking with rage, his breathing ragged and wheezing. "What are you asking me? We little kids got screwed by grown men representing the church . . . from God!! Didn't you hear me? Don't you see what . . ." he stopped and slumped over, gasping for breath. He jammed the oxygen on his face. "Sorry," his muffled voice came through the mask. "I'm so sorry."

He rested his arms on his thighs, nodded, and looked up resolutely. "I took the money. I was one of them." He stared at them unblinking for a moment, the only sound, the stuttered rasping of his breathing, in an alternating chorus with the hissing of the oxygen. "Yeah, I know," he said as the two exchanged a glance, "but Mike promised he'd show us the way. He would win, so we could win too. But it didn't happen. It couldn't. We begged, we pleaded for help. We even asked the FBI, but you people were like God, all much too busy and too important for us mere mortals. Some kind of good had to come out of it for me, for us, I mean, right?"

"That's not for us to say, Mr. Franks," Harrison responded.

"Well, he forgave me. Mike forgave me. But I guess God didn't," he laughed bitterly, tapped the tank, and took another hit of oxygen.

"Mr. Franks, we appreciate all the information, and you've helped us to understand Michael better, but we must find him. He may be involved in some very serious crimes, and anyone who tries to shield him will be instrumental and may be considered an accessory in whatever he does next. Anything you can tell us might save an innocent victim from being hurt," Kate said.

"I don't know any more," Franks said, struggling to his feet. "I don't know where he lives or a phone number." As he began inching toward the door, even more achingly slowly than when they arrived, the two reluctantly followed him.

Kate picked up her recorder and glanced at the silenced television.

"All I can say to the both of you is to look deeper into what unfolded at court. Who knows? Maybe you'll find what you're looking for there."

Suddenly Kate screamed out, "Harrison, oh my God, Harrison look at this!" she grabbed the remote and hit the volume button.

Harrison, almost at the front door behind Franks, jerked around and ran the few steps to her, almost tripping over a broken table leg.

The banner beside the field reporter on the screen said "Murder in Brentwood," and the crawl at the bottom repeated, "Breaking News."

She was standing outside a house they both recognized. "...been confirmed that the victim found stabbed to death inside this Brentwood home, not far from the site of Nicole Brown Simpson's murder decades ago, was Sharon Daniels, the wife of FBI Los Angeles Criminal Division Head, Malik Daniels. Information we have received indicates police were dispatched to the home after someone who may have been the killer contacted Agent Daniels directly. We will keep this story updated as we get more information."

The two continued to stare at the TV for a moment. "It's him. He did this," Kate whispered.

"Oh my God, Sharon!" Harrison answered. "Let's go."

They hurried to the front door, which Franks was holding open.

"Someone you know?" he looked intently at their faces and nodded. "Yes, she is. She was. Yeah, I'll bet the Bureau will move right along on this one, won't you?"

"Thank you for your time, Mr. Franks," Harrison said, holding out his card. "We may have to speak with you again, so if you happen to hear anything from Michael please call us"

"He's not a bad person. He's a victim," Franks said, taking his and Kate's cards and placing both in his shirt pocket.

"He's dangerous, Mr. Franks," Kate said. "He's probably a vicious killer, and you'd be wise not to forget that."

They stepped outside, and he stood watching them. "You enjoy it, don't you?" he called after them, gripping the doorknob to steady himself.

"What? What are you talking about, Mr. Franks?" Kate turned and asked impatiently.

"Being you. Being healthy and strong and in love. Being normal humans, with a future."

"Oh, in love? Oh no, Mr. Franks, we're not—" Kate began. "We're just partners, sir, and—" Harrison said, the two of them vocally stumbling over each other.

"And," Harrison continued, clearing his throat and not looking at Kate, "and we are sorry about your situation."

"Course you are," Franks said bitterly as he began to close the door. "Every goddamn body is sorry."

He slammed the door shut, and they stood a moment, not looking at each other. "Come on," Harrison said, "We have to get to Malik." In the car they didn't speak another word and sped north toward Los Angeles.

Chapter 14

TUESDAY – Afternoon: Washington, DC

The midday Dupont Circle area was choked with traffic even worse than usual. Commuters, who were probably annoyed with the delays, had only to glance at all the limos around and near the Washington Hilton to figure out something fancy, political, and ridiculously expensive was going on. At least, that's the way the President thought of such occasions. He knew how necessary they were, but thousands for a plate of food, even if the money was going to a good cause, seemed almost criminal to him. *Am I becoming my mother?* he laughed inwardly, remembering all those, "Children-are-starving-and-these-richass-sonzabitches-are-throwing-away-money-on-lobster-and-designer-gowns-and-patting-themselves-on-the-back-about-throwing-a-few-dimes-at-the-poor" rants she would go into every now and then. If he ever reminded her that their family wasn't exactly poor, she made sure to impress on him that he was making her point: it wasn't about having so much money; it was about how you spent it. They had a responsibility, nay, an obligation.

He had to admit, looking out from the dais over the glittering crowd of ladies who lunch and movers and shakers who hoped to catch his or his wife's attention for future gain, there was a lot of money on people's tables and on their backs. Here was another reason he was so proud of his wife: she was wearing her favorite blue Christian Siriano dress. He knew the media buzz tomorrow, especially fashion blogs, would be about how she'd worn it before and "Oh my god what is she thinking?!" and "Can't the President afford to get her something new?"

She couldn't have cared less; her goal, as always, was to help as many people as she could in whatever way worked. And if food and the chance to rub elbows with the First Lady would bring in a million here and there for her two passions—homeless children and groups supporting people identifying as LGBTQIA—she would put on the dress and put up with the BS. She felt the first group was the most vulnerable and neglected and the second the most rejected and misunderstood. And she was making it her life mission to help them as much as she possibly could.

He watched her going from table to table, meeting people, thanking them, stooping to chat with awestruck children, and couldn't help thinking, *My hero.*

"Looks like you really like that lady," a gravelly male voice said. "I could introduce you."

He turned to reporter Ed Garry, seated on his left and smiled, "No need, I hear she's taken."

The two contemplated each other for a beat before the President turned forward again and continued checking out the crowd, occasionally waving or throwing a kiss at an older attendee. He knew Garry was still watching him.

"So, Mr. President. Thank you for the invitation. Why am I here?"

"Now Ed," Jameson said, "you like a delicious brunch as well as the next man. Don't you enjoy a chance to get out of the office and hang with people who, shall we say, think differently from those you spend most of your time with?"

"Contrary to popular opinion, President Mitchell, my readers and supporters run the gamut. And some of them may be here. Even the ones you wouldn't think of as being conservative."

Ed looked around the room at the attendees and allowed his attention to rest on three tables featuring a crowd of ultra-feminine, flamboyantly dressed trans women and men with some tending more toward traditionally male garb, and some dressed somewhere in between.

"Even those you think of as being automatically left wing and liberal might surprise you if you could follow them into the voting booth. But my question wasn't about the crowd; it was about you. Why did you invite me?"

Jameson turned to him. "You don't like me very much, do you Ed?"

"With respect, Mr. President, I don't really know you. I know about things you've said and some things you've done, but I don't know you. I feel like, well . . ." He stopped himself and shrugged.

"It's ok, go ahead and speak freely," Jameson leaned closer, watching him intently.

"Fine. I feel like you're perhaps too slippery to hold onto sometimes. You're neither here nor there."

"You mean neither Republican nor Democrat. The fact that I'm an Independent is not new information for you. After all, I'm—"

"Yes I know," Garry waved a hand impatiently. "We all know: the first independent-on-election president since Washington, 'The Great Unifier'."

Jameson could almost hear the air quotes.

"But," Garry continued, "that doesn't mean you have to pretend to be in the middle of the road on all policies and issues. Some of us feel you're going wherever the wind blows to maintain popularity. You're working so hard to separate yourself from the old two-party system. It appears you'll say almost anything to prove you're not, and sometimes it just seems like you're trying to be Clark Kent."

"I'm no Clark Kent because I'm no Superman, but is it wrong to try to be the best possible person, the best possible president I can be? Does even the attempt make me look like a phony? How jaded and cynical we've become if that's our truth."

"Recent history says trust is much overrated, Mr. President. And this Dallas drive thing . . . Well you said speak freely so, speaking once again of heroes, are we supposed to now think you're the resurrection of Kennedy, absent the amazing hair? Is that what it means? Are you saying to the American people we are back in those Camelot days? Forget how bad things are, and all pretend ourselves back into the past, and we'll be there?"

Jameson knew how he could, and perhaps should, react, but that wouldn't get him what he wanted: a fair shot with this man and his millions of fans and followers.

He looked unwaveringly into Garry's eyes. "Ed, that's not true anymore than the idea of 'Make American Great Again,' was true. You and I both know the problem with trying to take us all back to a former era. Some things during those times were really, really bad for some of our people." He ran his hand through his hair and frowned, choosing his words carefully. "I know you and many others think I'm insincere or phony, and trust me, I've been hearing that all my life, so it's not an issue. What's so sad to me, though, is people always say it when I'm trying my hardest to do my very best." He saw the corner of Ed's mouth twitch and nodded. "See? Even if I talk about trying to do the right thing, it's received that way. All I can tell you is, what I'm trying to say, to evoke, with the Dallas Ride is we can do better; we can change the outcome. If we can take that moment, that tragic time, and turn it around and make it come out okay, we can change anything. We can all get along. And I don't care what anybody says or thinks, Pat and I believe it, and we won't stop trying to prove it, no matter what."

Garry stared at him again, searching his face. "Hmmph," he said, and took a long sip from his untouched Jack Daniels, "I almost believe you."

"It's okay, Ed, I'll take that," Jameson said, smiling. "Don't trust me, test me. And feel free to call me and let me know what you think and what you're hearing from your readers. They'll share things with you. So maybe you can help that wind to blow their way a little."

He put out a hand, and Garry looked down at it for a moment before shaking it and his head and muttering, "Sure, why not."

Jameson grinned, put his other hand on top and said, "You'll see. Just wait."

They were interrupted by a woman's voice crying, "Oh my goodness. Please don't hurt me!" Two Secret Service men appeared in front of Jameson, and the two behind him stepped closer.

"What is it? What's happening?" The President asked.

"Not sure, sir," the closest agent replied, "but the First Lady . . ."

Jameson looked past him and realized something was going on near Pat. He couldn't tell what from where he was, but there were two agents holding the arms of an elegantly dressed woman who appeared to be in her fifties. Jameson was up immediately and started towards them. The agent to his right said, "Mr. President, sir, please don't—"

"Move!" Jameson barked at him and strode toward his wife. At her side, he could see the woman. She was one of attendees at the LGBTQIA table, and clearly fell in the "T" category. Despite the hints here and there that she was most likely born male, she was clearly feminine and extremely soft spoken and right now, frightened out of her wits.

"Oh my goodness gracious. Oh my goodness gracious! Miss Pat," she sobbed, "I'm so sorry, I'm so sorry! I only wanted to say hello. I wasn't trying to--oh my goodness. My name is Elizabeth Cash, and I was trying to—"

"Cash? Elizabeth Cash?" Pat said. "Wait a moment. Aren't you the person who bought three tables and gave them back so people who weren't able to, could come?"

"Well. Yes, yes. Just doing my little part, but I'm, I'm so embarrassed! I didn't mean to cause any problems. I was only trying to . . . I wanted to meet you. I'm so sorry."

"Guys, thank you, thank you," Pat said to the agents. "But please. It's all right."

The two Secret Service men who were holding Elizabeth looked at the President who repeated, "Thank you, guys, she's fine."

One of the agents picked up her cane, which she'd dropped, and handed it to her before the two stepped away. Elizabeth pulled a lace handkerchief out and dabbed her eyes. As if actually seeing the Mitchells for the first time, she looked from one of them to the other and said with star struck reverence, "Oh my goodness gracious. Oh my stars and all the planets in the galaxy! Miss Pat Mitchell and the President of the United States. Well, I think someone has to die now, and I think it could just be me!" And now her tears were clearly happy ones.

Everyone within hearing distance laughed, and she looked around, clueless as to what was so funny.

She dabbed her eyes again and grimaced at the mascara on her handkerchief. "Finally I get to meet you, and I look a perfect wreck."

Jameson took her hand and said, "You look very fine . . . a beautiful dress you have on, and that's one snappy cane."

Elizabeth did a little half turn, modeling her shimmery silver dress and showing off her wolf's head topped cane. "You don't think it's too much? I wanted it to be special for today."

"It's just right," Jameson said.

"Stop flirting, Jameson," Pat said fake sternly. "And you, young lady," she continued. "He's taken."

Elizabeth giggled, covering her mouth with a gloved hand. She looked back at the people at her table while pointing gleefully at the First Couple, and they cheered and applauded. Finally, she drew a courageous breath. "Miss Pat, in my entire life, I never ever, ever thought a moment like this would come. Especially after the way things have gone in the past few years. All the hate and bigotry. All the struggle. A lot of people wouldn't even want children in the same room with us, because they think they need to be protected from us, like who we are is some contagious disease they can catch. You have helped to make this country a place where people like me finally feel at home; you have no clue what meeting you means in my life."

"If by people like you, you mean citizens of the United States, well people like you *should* feel at home, period. This is our country. Yours and mine," Pat said.

"Your saying," Elizabeth said, "is carved across my heart: 'I refuse to judge. I refuse to hate. My heart is fixed on love.' We know that's you and what you stand for."

"That's right!" someone from a nearby table said, and everyone cheered. Pat and Jameson waved to the crowd, and they turned to walk back to their table. Jameson looked back to throw a kiss to Elizabeth and saw Chen touch his earpiece, step to the side of the room and motion two other agents to accompany them. Chen talked briefly but showed no emotion except for the slight widening of his eyes before he turned and looked at the President, raised an eyebrow, and nodded slightly. Jameson knew he wasn't going to be finishing his lunch just now. As he expected, the agent standing to his right stepped up and said blandly, "Mr. President, if you wouldn't mind, Agent Chen would like a word?"

Jameson held Pat's chair and leaned down to kiss her on the cheek and whispered. "Don't know what's up," he whispered, "but I can see you're going to have to make my excuses. Take care of Garry for me."

Her disappointed frown lasted only seconds before she said a resigned, "Okay," and moved to her husband's seat.

He shook Garry's hand, gently rebuffing the journalist's attempts to get information, and waved to the crowd as he walked off the dais. When he stepped into a much smaller dining room off to the side of the banquet hall secured by the Secret Service, Chen was waiting there for him.

"Chen, what's up?" Jameson said.

"Sir, we've had a call from A.D. Stanton's office in LA. Sharon Daniels, the wife of his Chief of Staff Malik Daniels has been murdered. They're sure it's the serial killer, the one they're calling the Psalm Killer. This time, they say it looks like a copycat of the Charles Manson murders. It's pretty brutal."

"Oh my God. Oh my God," Jameson said, trying not to imagine what the crime scene must look like. "Did they catch him, at least?"

"No sir, but they said they have a suspect who looks good for the crime. They can place him with one of the other victims."

"Let's go home. Don't tell Pat anything. I'll let her know later."

Chapter 15

TUESDAY – Afternoon: San Francisco

MayHem was loving life. Since the President's Dallas drive press conference, hits on her site had increased by hundreds of thousands. On any given day, she could count on seeing someone in one of her tees or carrying a canvas shopping bag with her logo. Sometimes she had to sign autographs on the street. And she would be happy to sign all day long if necessary. Finally, she was getting closer to where she was meant to be!

Her next goal was to hire an assistant. She could barely keep up with the merch sales. But she was going to murder two crows with this one stone: her plan was to get Christian to take the assistant job. She knew he was just as attracted as she was, and this would be the perfect opportunity to have him close by more often, not merely dropping into Farley's every now and then or messaging through the site. He didn't know it, but she was already grooming him, giving him insider info and sharing ideas in a way she wouldn't think of doing with anyone else.

The very next time she saw him, she was going to make sure to get his digits and let him have hers. It might be hard to overcome his shyness, but she knew she could take care of that in no time. Her life was going exactly as she'd planned, except so, so much better.

"Slammin' shirt, MayHem," a girl with fiery red, bushy hair and two nose rings said as she tucked her autographed napkin in her bag. "One of yours?"

"No, this is from one of my favorite bands, a New York group called Black Table." She leaned back so the girl could get a better view and pointed to the illustration of a glittery-eyed Grim Reaper on his deathly horse. "You should hear them. The lead singer, Mers, she gets it. When she screams, we have to be aware that death is around us all the time. If we're smart, it teaches us how to live life more intensely, to stay on the edge. I'm going to put a picture of me in this one on the site. If my Baby Blackbirds really like it, I'll see if Black Table wants me to carry it. Keep checking, it may be available soon."

"I will," the girl said, glancing down at her phone. "Oh no, late for class! But it was worth it to meet you. Bye, see you on BKA." She hurried out the door and down the street as MayHem watched, laughing.

And there he was once again. But something was different: she was surprised by how resolutely Christian was striding up the street. She frowned slightly and watched him closely, thinking. *What's happened? His energy has shifted. It's almost like he's another person. New job or something? New woman?*

He stopped abruptly outside, staring at her through the window. His look was so blatantly sensual that she couldn't help wondering. *Has he had sex since I saw him last?* He trotted up the steps, came right to her table, and sat down without asking, leaving her open-mouthed for a moment before she regained control.

"Well, Christian, my darling," she said, studying his face and clothes, which no longer looked slightly nerdy and old school, "have we had a makeover?"

"I guess I needed one," he said, and looked slowly from her face down to her waist, "unlike some of us."

His eyes came back to her face, and once again, her mouth was stuck on open. She smiled. "Well, well. Whoever you are? The person who almost looks like Christian is welcome."

He laughed briefly, but this wasn't a shy, embarrassed laugh. It was the kind of laugh confident, handsome men do when they know they're impressing. She wasn't sure she liked it.

"You asked about me. You wanted to know more about me," he said.

"Well yes, I—"

"There isn't much time," he said tersely. "I want you to know. I'm not a bad person."

"What?"

"Listen. At the orphanage, it was bad. Really bad. I won't go into details, but after all the reports in the news over these years, you can imagine. I left there and went to a couple of foster homes. Some were almost as bad as the orphanage, but one was really great. It was with a family in Wisconsin. They treated me like a son. It was the closest thing to normal I had ever known. I even had an older sister, Dominique. We were besties. I could talk to her. I couldn't tell her everything, of course; I wouldn't have. But she was always willing to listen. And she would talk to me, too. She had a jerk boyfriend who didn't know how to treat her, but she loved him. One night, when the parents were out, I passed her room, and I could hear her crying and begging someone to stop. I burst in the room, and he had forced her down on the bed and was tearing at her clothes. She was clawing and pushing at him, but I know she didn't want to scream and get him in trouble." He stopped, out of breath, looked down and shook his head as if to empty it of the picture he was seeing. He looked like a sad little boy.

"What happened, Christian? What did you do?"

He looked up at her. That other Christian returned. All she could think of was a cobra. She had seen that hooded, venomous look on killers she'd visited in the past, but only on the worst of them, only on the ones that should be kept away from living things. Those were the rare times when she was grateful for the thick glass between them. But there was no glass between her and Christian.

"I pulled him off," he said, smiling. "I was only 14 and not that big, and he was 17 and an athlete, but I was driven by rage and hatred. I gave him the beating I'd been saving up for those priests and everybody else who let them get away with it."

"Get away with what?" she asked, not sure she wanted to hear the answer.

"I hit him and hit him and hit him. I punched him until my own hand was sore and bleeding and Dommie was pulling at me and screaming at me to stop, but I couldn't. When I did, I was pretty sure I'd killed him. But that didn't bother me. What bothered me was how she looked at me and how she yelled at me to get out of her house. She called me a monster. I don't think I've ever felt so alone."

"And you left?" MayHem asked.

"That same night. And I never went back. I called later though. Waited until she was on the phone and asked about him. Turns out he survived just fine, but he dumped Dommie, and later that year he was charged with the rape of one of her school friends. He did it while they were still together. She forgave me and told me to keep safe. She said the cops came to the house and asked about me, but once he was charged with the rape they dropped off, knowing it was self-defense."

"Did you feel good or, I guess, better about it after you found out about the other girl? He may have attacked a lot of innocent girls. He deserved a good ass beating."

He looked at her thoughtfully for a moment. "Actually, no. I never wanted to be like them . . . inflicting pain on people. I never wanted to hurt anyone, even bad guys. I saw myself as a helper, you know, a hero type. But there was a devil inside, I guess, and for Dommie, it was released. Everything changed. Sometimes, heroes have to punish bad guys."

"Have you punished any other bad guys?"

"I do what I can," he said.

"And are there more punishments to come?"

He looked at her shirt (*or at my breasts?* she wondered) and said, "The Grim Reaper: He comes when it's time. He takes whoever he has to take. There's no judgment, only justice. By the time Mitchell rides through Dallas, the torture will be ending. All these years of torture and injustice will be over."

"Christian, I don't understand you. What are you talking about? What does the President have to do with your redemption or feeling better?"

"I've told you all I can. You'll know the rest in the fullness of time."

"The fullness of . . . ?"

"'Society wants to believe it can identify evil people, or bad or harmful people, but it's not practical. There are no stereotypes.'"

"Ted Bundy. Why are you quoting Ted Bundy?"

Suddenly, he reached out and grabbed her hand, leaving her speechless. "You'll remember me, won't you? No matter what, you'll remember me."

She tried to pull her hand away, but he wasn't letting go. "Christian, Christian! Let go! It hurts," she said quietly but intensely enough so a couple of people in the café began paying attention.

He loosened his grip some but held on, gunmetal gray eyes focusing on her like a laser. "Promise you'll remember me."

"What do you mean? What's going to happen? Remember you after what?"

Christian looked deeply into her eyes then down at their hands, stroking hers gently. He said softly, "Beautiful." Then, he released her.

He sighed and stood up, took a step toward the door. Suddenly he turned back to lean down and kiss her gently on the lips. "Goodbye, May," he said before walking away for what she somehow knew was the last time.

Chapter 16

TUESDAY – Afternoon: Los Angeles

Harrison didn't know what they'd find back to the office, but it was even worse than he had thought.

"It's like a funeral parlor," he whispered to Kate.

People were working, but there were also moments when someone would just stop where they were as if hypnotized, the horror of it rendering them immobile.

Kate touched his arm and pointed at Othello. He was sitting in front of his computer screen, but his focus was somewhere down on his desk, near his unmoving fingers. His eyes were swollen and red, like he'd been crying for hours.

Confused, Harrison said, "He never met her, right?"

"But he's heard about her. He was going to their anniversary party. Plus, he's seen pictures of how vibrant and pretty she was before. And now, he's probably seen the after," Kate said.

The cheerful puppy of a guy they had met not so long ago was now gone. Harrison wondered if this was still "hashtag dream job."

Jeanne was standing next to him with a hand on his shoulder. In stark contrast to Othello, she looked like she'd like to punch a hole in the wall. She looked up and she and Kate made eye contact, but there was no playful "S'up." It was almost as if even this small greeting was too much levity.

"Where's the Chief?" Kate asked.

"He's in the director's office," Jeanne replied. "He said to send you two in there as soon as you arrive."

"How's he doing?" Harrison asked, feeling incredibly stupid the moment he said it.

The looks Jeanne and Othello gave him made him feel even worse. How the hell would he be doing? Sharon was gone. The love of his life was gone.

They knocked softly and entered Stanton's office, and once again, Harrison couldn't help feeling like the funeral was taking place right here, and they were visiting to comfort the bereaved.

Malik didn't even look up from where he sat like a statue of grief on Stanton's sofa.

"Sir, Malik . . . I . . ." was all Harrison could manage. He and Kate sat on either side of Malik. Harrison put his arm around him, and Kate took his hand.

"I loved her so much," Malik whispered.

"I know. Me too," Harrison said.

Malik squeezed Kate's hand, nodded his thanks to both of them, and took a couple of huge breaths. "Okay, let's, um . . . let's . . . Why don't we update them?"

Stanton nodded and said, "Well, first, the courier or possibly accomplice we still don't know. All we're really sure about is he's that homeless guy they call the Sentry—"

"From the cemetery?" Harrison asked.

"The same. We've looked everywhere in the area, and LAPD is on it too, but he's a ghost. It could mean anything: he's a part of it, he's being manipulated, he was only a messenger earning a few dollars, we just don't know. But here's one thing we found out from questioning some of the homeless who are familiar with him: he's an orphan, and he grew up either in an orphanage or in foster care. He was never adopted before going into the military."

"So he may have grown up with Michael and Franks," Kate said.

"A distinct possibility," Stanton answered.

"If he was from the orphanage, do you think there may be more of them helping Michael?" Harrison said. "All those boys for all those years."

"But remember, when they had the chance to help him, in the court case, they didn't," Stanton said. "But we're going to keep that on the table. And, Hitchings sent the shirt swatch and—" He stopped himself and looked at Malik.

"It's okay. Doesn't matter now," Malik said. He went to a small credenza and poured himself some water from a pitcher Stanton had there. "He wrote the next Psalm on the swatch. The verse was about brides and weddings. We figured out the verse was related to my anniversary, but I guess it was a little too late."

The other three stared helplessly at each other, and finally Stanton said, "We have one more piece of news: we've talked it over, and Katherine, you're going to take over as interim while Malik's out."

"I . . . what?" she managed.

"You know you're ready, and we have every confidence in you."

"Wow, I'm very grateful, sir. Thanks. To both of you." She looked at Malik, and Harrison saw the tears forming before they fell. "But the way this has happened, I just can't—"

"You can and you will," Malik said and hugged her. He stepped back and held her shoulders. "Get him. Get him for me."

She nodded, wiping her tears.

He turned to Stanton. "I'm going to go now. Your house still available? We'll get a car for you. Shayna and your son-in-law will be there within the hour. I'll have the agent bring Malia out. She's napping peacefully."

"Good, that's good," Malik said. Stanton picked up the phone, and Malik watched him for a moment. He added, almost offhandedly, "She'll never know her grandmother though."

Harrison looked at the old, sad, defeated creature who had replaced his dear friend: his Malik was never coming back.

The Chief opened the door then turned back.

"Harrison, your gift; what was it?"

"Oh, sir. It was nothing, just—"

"Doesn't matter," Malik said. "I'm never going to open it."

After a long pause, Harrison said, "Champagne glasses. Your names were on them and your wedding date."

Malik nodded. "Thanks. So thoughtful. She would have loved them." He closed the door gently behind him.

* * *

When Stanton made the announcement about Kate taking over in Malik's absence, Harrison noticed two things: Jeanne was happy for her, as expected, but the sudden tightening of Skip's jaw and the mottled red traveling up the back of his neck and suffusing his ears. That, he didn't expect. He glanced down in time to see Skip relax his right hand from a fist.

He thought it would be him. He thought this was *his* opportunity. So maybe he didn't care about Kate as much as Harrison thought he did. Good. He tried not to smile, but he felt it on his face. *Jerk.* All about himself; did he even care how this particular opportunity came about? No one had really congratulated Kate because it might have looked like they were being insensitive about Sharon.

And Kate, always a class act, didn't seem to mind at all. She was straight to work, checking on everyone's progress and making new assignments.

He sat at his desk watching her make the rounds, encouraging and listening to each person. She was going to make a great leader when an actual promotion came along.

He kept thinking about the things Franks had said to them, especially about "looking deeper." *Whatever did he mean?* He may have been jerking them around, but suppose he wasn't? Suppose he, like Michael, was dropping hints, pieces of the puzzle, for them to figure out? He decided to go back over the abuse trial transcripts and available evidence. Maybe there actually was something there.

He had been hard at work for a couple of hours when his phone rang. He picked it up absently, keeping his focus on the line-by-line perusal of the court documents.

"Special Agent Harrison—" was all he was able to get out before a male voice, deep like his own, said, "Agent Carter. Let me finish."

"Who's calling?" Harrison asked. But somehow, he already knew. "Michael. It's you, isn't it?" He looked around to see if anyone was looking in his direction and stood up, waving his arm to catch the attention of anyone who might see him.

Skip looked at him, frowned, looked away, but finally he couldn't resist looking back again. Harrison beckoned to him, and he took his time walking closer.

"What, Carter? What are you—" Harrison held a finger to his lips to quiet him. He wrote on a pad in huge letters "HITCHINGS! TRACE!"

Skip, galvanized into action, ran over to Othello, talked to him briefly, then hurried back to his own desk and picked up his phone.

"Harrison, Harrison," the caller said in a patient, gentle voice. "Why are you searching for me? Know you not that I am about my fathers' business? All of my fathers. They loved me so. Really, really looooved me."

He laughed in a sexy, creepy way chilling Harrison to the core. But he had to keep Michael on the phone as long as possible.

"Michael, you know that's not what that verse means. Those priests did horrible things to you. What they did wasn't love."

"They said it was. They taught me, 'there's nothing like a father's love.' You know what I mean, don't you Harrison? Or maybe you don't. Bet you aren't as close to your father as I was to all of mine. And how is your brilliant, celebrity father? Love his books, by the way."

"What?"

He saw Kate burst out of Malik's office, look in his direction, and went to stand over Othello's shoulder. Othello looked up at her and shook his head.

"He must have been so disappointed when you left his profession to become a glorified policeman," Michael said.

"Why are you talking about my father?"

"Oh Harrison, one good thing about those priests, they were always teaching. Always. I can build things, handle languages, find out anything about anybody. I used to win prizes for my research papers. They loved rewarding me. Want me to tell you about it? I could show you some tricks with a whip that you haven't even seen at a rodeo . . . have you calling out for God, Harrison."

"Michael, why don't you—"

"Your father's a medical man. He might be interested in how they rewarded me. The things they did to my body. Should we call him?"

"I swear to God, Michael. If you touch my family I won't stop until I find you. And when I do I will k—"

"—kill me? Well look who's the dangerous murderer now. You see? Anyone will kill if they have the right incentive. You're like me. If someone hurt your family, it would turn you into a killer. Well someone's hurt my family."

"But the people you've killed, Michael. They have nothing to do with the crimes done to you." He looked inquiringly at Othello and at Kate, who kept glancing back at him, but clearly they hadn't found anything yet.

"You still don't have the slightest, fucking clue what's going on, do you? The end is near, Agent Carter, and you may as well let me finish because you will not be able to stop me. We look and think we see so clearly, but now you see through a glass, darkly."

Kate wrote something and hurried over to him. Her note said, "Burner, can't locate. Still trying."

"People aren't always who they seem to be," Michael continued, "but soon it will all come face to face. You know only in part, Harrison. The time will come when you will know even as I am known. And by the way, I'm sure you're trying to trace this call, so you know by now this sweet little prepaid I will leave for you should you get any closer. I already have another one. Let me finish, Harrison."

"Michael, Michael!" Harrison shouted. But the line was dead.

Chapter 17

TUESDAY – Afternoon: San Francisco

Only a couple of hours later and Harrison was in San Francisco, studying the outside of a café called Farley's. They could barely believe their luck when Laurie told them they had a tip from someone who was pretty sure a guy she knew had just made a threat against the President, and whatever he was going to do would most likely take place during the Dallas drive.

"This witness? Do we think it's valid information?" Kate asked.

"Well how about this?" Laurie said. "That blogger who seems to know so much about our cases, tied them together just like Harrison did—MayHem, right?—that's who the caller is."

"But why did she call our office? Why not her local police or FBI?" Harrison asked.

"I don't know. I didn't ask. I do have an address where she's agreed to meet someone. She told me to text her the time and who she'll be meeting with. Should I contact San Francisco and have them interview her?"

"No," Kate said. "Arrange next available transport for Harrison. You can let the locals know what's going on. There's a reason why she called us and a reason why she seems to have an inside track on this investigation. Let's find out what that is."

Harrison paused for a moment before walking up the steps of Farley's. There was an incredible looking black woman sitting in profile at the window table. She was so still, he wondered for a moment if she was a sculpture. But she turned her head in extra slow motion and looked directly at him. It almost felt like she knew he was standing there. She smiled coyly at him and turned away. He recognized her: it was MayHem. But the pictures he'd seen online didn't even begin to do justice to the real thing.

"Agent Carter. Please, sit down," she said when he walked in the door. She held out her hand like a queen bestowing a favor.

"You're Ms. MayHem, correct?" he asked.

She tilted her head and gave him a wry smiled. She was acting like an A level star with a huge ego. *You know who I am, why are you asking?"* her expression seemed to say. "Just MayHem. That's enough, don't you think?" She pointed to the seat next to her, but he opted for the one across the table.

She had on a black turtleneck top which went from her chin to her wrists, but that didn't mean anything. The part that should have covered her breasts featured see-through mesh curving in a long, waggly, meandering V from her shoulders down and around toward her right side.

There were things to see from her clavicle to her navel, and probably more around the back where the third point of the triangle ended. But he wasn't going to check.

"I like this one too," she said.

"Uh, sorry?"

"This bodysuit. It's comfortable and pretty at the same time, you know?" She paused, appearing to measure his reaction, before continuing, "And it eliminates the need for underwear. Another plus, don't you think?"

She's playing games with me was what he thought. But why? For fun? Or was there something else?

"Thank you for calling us, Ms.—"

"MayHem."

"Ms. MayHem." He wasn't going to be drawn in. "Could I ask, though, what made you decide to call LA instead of a closer office, or even local police?"

A small twitch at the corner of her mouth showed him she was surprised by his question.

"Oh, is there a local San Francisco office? I thought the FBI was sort of regional, so of course, LA would be my closest really large western city."

She's lying he knew instantly.

"So you weren't aware there's a team in our office working on some cases that may involve the man you know as Christian Hayes? Funny, MAYHEM—your blog—would indicate otherwise."

"But my darling," she purred, "you're not here to investigate my sources, am I right? I'm giving you information which may have some bearing on our President's safety. Shouldn't we focus on that?"

He wrote "avoiding some questions" in his notebook, and then looked up quickly enough to see that she was trying to read it.

"Christian Hayes: how did you two meet?"

He pulled out four of the age-advanced pictures Othello had come up with and placed them on the table in front of her.

"He's a fan," she said. "One of my Murder of Crows. You've studied my site, you know who we are, who I am. My baby blackbirds sometimes find me. Christian did. Then, he came back. And came back again. People do."

She looked closely at each picture before she looked up. Without looking down again, she put a finger on one of the clean-shaven examples and stared into his eyes long enough for him to get very uncomfortable.

She put her elbow on the table and rested her face gently on her hand. Starting at his forehead, her gaze went slowly downward while she talked, until she had perused all of the visible parts of him.

"This is the closest, but it looks too old. I know he's in his thirties, but he looks at least ten years younger than this. To tell you the truth, he could easily be your younger brother. Not age wise as I'm sure you're quite young. Just appearance-wise. You and he could almost be brothers. He's intense, strong, innocent in a strange way yet maybe a little dangerous. He's bee-yootiful."

The way she said it bothered him; it was like she was caressing him with her words. *Watch out She's trying to distract you.* He forced himself back to attention.

"At these visits and meetings where he came back, what did you two talk about?"

"Anything . . . and everything. His childhood as an orphan some. Not his favorite topic. His work."

"Which was?"

"First rehabbing vintage cars and motorcycles, and then rehabbing homes. He gave me the feeling he could make or fix almost anything. Kind of a MacGyver type."

"Did he say where any of these homes were located?"

"No, and I didn't ask. Not interesting. We talked about literature and history and music and art. He's very well educated, you know. I think they call what he experienced a 'good Catholic education.' We talked about life. And of course, death."

He saw the way she studied his face after that last word. What was she waiting for? What was she trying to say? Or not say?

"What about death, MayHem? Before what he said about the President, did he give you any indication he might try to harm other people?"

"Of course not," she said indignantly, "or you would have heard from me before. But if I'd known they would send you, Agent, I might have had to think up a reason to call."

"Do you have a phone number for him?"

"No, no phone number."

"And your relationship, was it romantic?"

"Romantic. You are so cute. I wouldn't characterize it, but then, I don't do romance. There was an attraction, a dedication if you will. He did keep coming back."

"So you're pretty sure you'll see him again?"

"Before we talked last, I would have said of course. But no, I don't think so. He definitely said goodbye."

"I see," Harrison closed his notebook. "Well, thank you for the information, MayHem. It may help us to stop a dangerous killer. Please don't hesitate to contact us again if you think of anything else."

"Oh, I won't," she said with an odd smirk.

He stood up, wondering again what her game was. What was she hiding? She chuckled, and for a moment, he wished he could grab her by the mesh and shake that annoying grin off her face.

"My goodness, Agent Carter, what a grim look! Maybe we can turn that frown upside down. Perhaps his address would help?"

"His . . ." He stared at her incredulously. Was she joking? But the casually amused way she leaned back and contemplated him gave him his answer.

"You've known where he lives all this time and not said anything?"

"Harrison," she said his name like she could taste it, leaning toward him so her breasts strained against the mesh, "why would I do something that would give us less time together?"

He felt like she was trying to hypnotize him, like she was leaning in for a kiss.

"One of the times I saw him here, he left so abruptly and mysteriously, I wondered if he might be hiding something, like a wife. Or a husband. So I followed him to his car. It wasn't hard to find out whom it belonged to, but as it turned out, it was an older couple. And since he'd already told me he was renting space from surrogate mom and dad types, I let it go. It checked out so . . ." She shrugged.

Harrison's patience was at an end. "MayHem," he snapped, "are you covering for him? Giving him time to escape? I need that address right now!"

"Of course," At a maddeningly leisurely pace, she looked up the information on her phone, glancing up occasionally to watch him watching her. She took out a black business card and a gold gel ink pen and wrote on the back.

For the first time, she spoke in a serious tone. "Despite what you might assume from my site or my activities or my persona, I do not condone murder or support murderers. I called you because I really do want to stop whatever it is Christian is planning."

She handed her card to him, and the temptress was back. "That's my number at the top. You may have more questions for me. Call me. Any time."

He took the card and stood up. "Thank you, I'll . . . the Bureau will get in touch if we need any additional information," he said as formally as he could.

He was at the door but he couldn't stop himself from glancing back. She flashed a smile at him and leaned back, her hands behind her head. The way she was looking at him, her eyes half closed and her lips parted, it was so sensual, he was lost for a moment. He recovered but he was annoyed with himself.

"You know," she said without a trace of irony, "something about you reminds me of Christian . . . Michael. Not just your looks, something . . . else."

He didn't want to know what she meant. After a pause he said. "We'll send someone from the local office for any updates or additional—"

"Why Harrison," she interrupted, "you're so cold and indifferent to me. One would almost think your focus was elsewhere." She looked at her phone and dismissed him.

He opened the door, determined not to look back again. Unexpectedly an odd thing: from behind him he heard her sing, almost under her breath, a few words from an old WWI song, "K-K-K-Katy, Beautiful Katy." He spun around, but she appeared to be engrossed in whatever was on her screen.

"Why did you sing that?" he demanded.

"Was I singing? Sorry, I wasn't aware. I do that sometimes."

She knew about Kate. Someone on the inside was talking to her. Did she also know about Sharon Daniels? Did she give Michael the team information, or was he feeding it to her? Was calling the FBI just part of Michael's game plan? But he couldn't stay to question her anymore. He had to get Michael's address information to the Bureau and get a team out to pick him up. Maybe, before MayHem's connection even mattered, they would have Michael Hitchings in custody.

He didn't look back when he heard, floating behind him: "Bye Harrison. Say hello to everyone in LA for me."

Chapter 18

TUESDAY – Afternoon: Los Angeles

Even though Katherine knew she was the most experienced agent and the logical one to take over under the circumstances, she didn't like it. This wasn't the way she wanted her promotion to happen. She wanted her next step to be clearly because she deserved it and it was time to move up, not because of the horrible act of a madman.

She thought the team was okay with the choice. Of course Jeanne was glad. When the Director made the announcement, she saw Jeanne do a silent *yes!* and fist pump the air. That was expected. The surprise was Skip. She watched his face morph in a heartbeat from surprise to anger to a begrudging smile as he joined the others' muted applause. *Well, so much for this crush he's supposed to have on me* she'd thought with some satisfaction. He doesn't even think I deserve this temporary command. Or maybe he thinks it should be him. That would be vintage Skip.

But no matter what, she was ready. She was going to do everything in her power to make sure no matter what Michael Hitchings did, it wasn't going to demoralize them nor derail their hunt.

It felt strange that after only a couple of hours, people were already treating her differently. It was subtle, but she couldn't help but notice.

Othello said, "Sure Chief" to her once, and she put a restraining hand on his arm and shook her head. He blushed and said a quiet "Sorry." That was all right. But later Skip, in front of everyone, said the same thing, and whether he intended it or not, she felt a sarcastic edge under his smiling compliment.

She just said, "The Chief's not here," in a way she hoped sounded professional and not as annoyed as she felt.

"Anything else from your Tulsa research?" she continued without a beat.

"There's not much helpful there," Skip said. "We did find out three of the guys knew each other, apparently hung out together when they weren't working the streets. Five of the seven had moved there from somewhere else. Nothing unusual for young hookers. We did find two guys who he'd approached who didn't go with him. Something made them suspicious. Their description matches what we know about Hitchings, but here's something: they were both positive he was gay. No doubt at all."

"And we have the agents in Little Rock who profiled a pedophile who loved little girls, and Mary in New York who thinks she's met the man of her dreams," Kate said. "This is a different kind of animal."

"Unless you count chameleons," Jeanne said.

"Yeah. Who is he going to be next, and why? We haven't heard any more from Davi, so Jeanne, why don't you check in with him in case there's some new info, and—" Her phone rang. She checked the display and clicked on immediately. "It's Harrison."

She walked away from the group, knowing all eyes were on her. "Hi. Anything?"

"The boss still there?" Harrison asked.

"Yes, on my way to his office right now." She doubled her pace as he filled her in.

"What's going on?"

"We have an address," he said.

"What? Where is he? Close?"

"Kind of. Pescadero to be specific, but not sure he's actually there. I'm on my way now to coordinate with the locals. We'll get a team ready as soon as we can. I think we have to deal with the Pescadero Sheriff's Department and the San Francisco Bureau. Any help the Director can give to move things along will be good."

"How did you find it?"

"MayHem. She knew it all along and just wanted to play some kind of cat and mouse game. I'm sure it'll go viral when she tells the story on her site, probably in a new see-through top for the occasion."

She stopped, "What? What did you say?"

"Nothing. It seemed like maybe she and Michael Hitchings, well Christian to her, had more than a fan/follower relationship."

"She told you that?"

"Not exactly."

She waited, but he didn't say any more. She continued to the boss' office, knocked on the door, and quickly entered.

It only took a few minutes for Harrison to tell them what he'd found out. She waited while Stanton called the Pescadero Sherriff and the local FBI office before she went out to update the team.

It was exactly the opposite feeling of the announcement about her taking over because of Malik. There were a few cheers and some excited chatter. And of course, both Jeanne and Skip wanted to hop on planes and get there immediately.

But that wasn't happening. "By the time any of us could get there, it'll all be over, one way or the other," she told them. "Right now, it's just an address. We hope he's there, but we don't even know as yet. For now, everyone get back to the tasks at hand. If there's anything else, I'll update you."

An energized team went back to work, and she felt a bit more hopeful. There was one other thing Harrison had said that she wasn't going to announce to everyone. She went to Othello's desk and sat down facing him. She saw him tense and his eyes widen, and she sighed inwardly. *Was everybody going to start reacting like she was coming for them, now that she was in charge?*

"Sorry, did I startle you? I know you're concentrating," she said.

"No, I'm . . . It's okay. Do you need me?"

"Only checking in with you. How are you holding up? There are a lot of tasks getting thrown at you all at once. It's a lot of pressure. And the brutality of these murders . . . well, it never gets easier. Especially when it hits so close to home."

"Yeah, Mrs. Daniels," he said, looking downward. "I didn't get to really meet her, but the way people talked about her. I don't know, it almost seemed like I actually knew her."

"She was that kind of person. You would have loved her." He looked even sadder and she told herself this was not doing him any good. "But we're going to get the guy who did this, and you're helping. Remember that."

"I will," he said and attempted a smile.

"Ok and you can always come to me and talk if you need to, including when Malik comes back."

"Thanks," he said, and this time his smile was genuine.

"Oh, and by the way, everything good with that girlfriend?" As expected, he blushed until his freckles danced before replying uncomfortably, "Good. It's good."

"Great." Kate said. She looked around to make sure everyone else was otherwise engaged. "Now, I need you to do another task for me, and it's strictly between us."

He seemed to relax, and he leaned forward and whispered, "Ok."

"I don't think we have to whisper," she whispered back at him. "Do you think you can hack into MayHem's followers list?"

"Uh . . ." he began, and then asked carefully, "We, well, we have a warrant for that?"

"Not officially. Not yet." She watched him as he began to work it out. Now, he was the one who looked furtively around the room.

"There's a reason why you don't want it to be, well, known by the other team members." When she didn't say anything, he continued. "You think somebody from here might be telling her things?"

"Or she might be telling them. We can't be sure as yet."

"But I might be getting somebody on the team in some real trouble, right?" She could see how much this bothered him.

"Maybe, maybe not, Othello. But it will help us with the case. You can do it, right?"

"Yeah, sure, I'll get on it."

She stood up. "Now don't worry Othello. It's probably not a team member, but if there's a leak or if she's more involved with Hitchings than she's admitting, this is our way to find out." He still looked pretty miserable about it. Poor kid. She knew ratting out a team member was probably very low on his things to do list.

The boss came out a while later, and they all turned toward him, expectantly.

"Nothing to share," he said. "Except as you know, it takes a while to assemble a team for an operation of this kind. We're going in like he's actually there, and he might be expecting us. We also have to be careful about stepping on local toes. Everyone has to work together and not feel encroached on or passed over. In addition to the ground squad, Harrison is going to arrange for a helicopter, so this is going to take a minute. We may only have this one shot to catch him off guard right in his home. We want to get it right."

"But here's what I've come to say: I know you're all waiting to find out what's going down in Pescadero, but it's been a long day for all of us. The minute we get an update from Harrison and his team, I'll let everyone know. Meanwhile, you should all go home. Be with your families or friends and take a short break from all this. And I strongly suggest that if you live alone, you team up, maybe stay with someone. We know he seems to have information about us. You're doing great work, people. I'll see you first thing tomorrow. Me, I'm going to go and check on Malik. He's going to want to hear this news."

She saw a few people start to gather their things, but when she went back to her desk and sat down, most of them did the same.

A short time later, Stanton came out of his office, looked around, and walked to Kate's desk.

"Katherine, you're getting ready to leave?"

"Well, no Boss. I thought I would just—"

"Listen," he said quietly, leaning close to her. "They're taking their cue from you. There's nothing wrong with being dedicated, but you're tired, and so are they. Give yourself and everyone else a break. Sometimes leadership means going home and going to bed. Harrison is a phone call away, and there's nothing we can do about anything until we hear from him."

She looked around the room, stood up and said, "Okay everyone. The boss is right. Time to go."

Jeanne came over while she was getting ready and said, "Want to get a drink or something?"

"No, maybe not."

"Do you want me to stay over? You know I always keep stuff in my bag."

Kate thought a minute. "No, thanks friend. I think I'll actually try to tuck in early tonight. This command stuff is wearing."

"Please. You know you'll be up with the phone in your hand waiting for a call from Harrison."

"What's that supposed to mean?"

"For a case update. What did you think I meant?" Jeanne grinned at her.

Kate shook her head, grabbed her things, and said her goodnights.

* * *

In the ladies room a short time later, she stared at her reflection in the mirror and frowned. Even to herself, she looked tired and stressed. She wet a paper towel and pressed its coolness to her eyes. The boss was right: she did need a break.

When she came out and was about to turn the corner to walk to the elevators, she heard an argument going on and hung back to listen. It was Jeanne and Skip.

She peeked around the corner and saw Jeanne smirking up at Skip.

"Why you catching an attitude with me? It's not my fault you didn't get picked," Jeanne said. She added with a huge fake sob, "Always Robin, never the Batman."

"Aw shut up, lesbo bitch," Skip growled.

"I got your bitch right here Boy Blunder," she fired back at him, laughing and grabbing her crotch.

"Grabbing what you don't have doesn't make you a man."

"That's the best you got, 'roid rage? Come on, don't hate 'cause my dick is bigger than yours."

Skip took a step toward her, and Jeanne lowered her chin and stared straight up at him, wolf style, opening her arms wide. "Go 'head. Step to me so you can get your ass kicked twice in one day."

"Jeanne!" Kate snapped, as she stepped around the corner. "May I have a word? Skip, excuse us please."

He started to say something, but the look on her face convinced him to just walk away.

"Doh! You're using your school teacher voice. I'm going to detention, aren't I?"

Kate sighed. She loved her friend, but sometimes . . .

"Why do you antagonize him? You know how sensitive he is."

"Well maybe Susie Snowflake should get over it." Jeanne replied.

"Friend, you know we need everybody working together on this thing. It's hard enough taking over for Malik, but I can't also have team members at each other's throats. Now when it's done, if you to want to get in the cage and go medieval on each other, fine and dandy. But if we're gonna catch this guy, we need all heads in the game."

She grabbed her friend's shoulder and said, "Jeannie, I need your support."

"Ok, sorry. I was only messing with him. You know he'll get over it. He always does. Sure you don't want me to stay over? I'm almost ready to go. I just have to get my bag."

"No, that's okay. I need to go home and detox a little. I'll call you if I hear anything."

* * *

Her head was swirling as she left the elevator in the garage and walked toward her car.

What if they got him? What if Harrison and the San Francisco crew actually nabbed Hitchings? Or worse, what if he knew they were coming and he slipped away before they could get to him? Could there be a leak coming from their team or elsewhere in the FBI?

And MayHem? She wondered if it might have been helpful if she'd been there in the interview with Harrison. What did he mean about the see-through outfit? For some reason, she had a bad feeling—*Stop it!* She chided herself. *You should be worrying about the case, not Harrison's reaction to . . . whoever . . . some random witness.*

And this new command. She knew she could handle it, but so many moving parts! Her head was actually starting to hurt. There was something to be said for not having to deal with personnel and their personality conflicts. Especially since, like with Jeanne and Skip, there sometimes didn't seem to be a way to solve the issues.

And thinking of "solving" brought her back to the case. She wouldn't let Malik down, of course, but only in her own head would she admit she almost hoped they wouldn't get Michael yet, not until she was there. She could practically taste him trying to fight back, so she could put one right between his eyes.

"All right killer, dial it down a notch," she murmured to herself. If she somehow was lucky enough to be there when they caught him, she would handle it like a professional. She hoped. Her mind looped back to Hitchings and the possible leak. Once she had the info from Othello, she would have an idea what to do next. She sincerely hoped it wouldn't point to a team member.

She was concentrating so hard that she was already a few feet from her car door when she noticed the footsteps. Someone was behind her.

She clicked the remote at the same moment she felt a powerful grip on her left arm.

She spun around, jerking her arm away and clawing a handful of shirt as she swung her right fist, reinforced by keys, toward his eye. It was Skip.

"Goddamn Katey! What the hell!" he yelled as he ducked and grabbed her wrist just in time. "Didn't you hear me calling you?"

"No, sorry I . . . a lot on my mind."

"Yeah, this command thing can be hard the first time out." He grinned and squeezed her arm. "Don't worry, you'll do fine. You know I have your back." He dropped the cheesy grin and moved a little closer to her. "You let me know if you need me, Katey."

"You know, I never said anything," she took a step back, "but I really don't like 'Katey.' Katherine is good."

"Oh, sorry," Skip said. "But Dale always—"

"Yes," she cut him off right there, "he did."

"I guess you still miss him, huh?"

So annoying! Why did he have to keep bringing Dale up?

"What did you want to say, Skip? Something about Jeanne? The case? Something bothering you?"

"Yeah. Something's bothering me."

She looked up at Skip, hard core man's man Skip, and watched his chiseled face change into something soft, vulnerable. All she could think was, *Oh no!*

"I asked you about Dale," he said. "We haven't had a chance to talk with so much going on."

"Uh, Skip. I'm not sure what it is you—"

"I always felt like you didn't like me much," Skip said.

"Didn't like you? That's not true. I just felt like maybe you were jealous. Like—"

"I was," he interrupted.

"Like," she continued, "you were deliberately trying to keep us apart, to keep him away from me. I was probably wrong, but it felt—"

"No, you weren't wrong. I did try to get him to stay out sometimes, to work longer or hang out longer. Like you said, to keep him away from you. But it wasn't because of him. I was jealous of him, not you. You had to know how I felt about you, Katherine."

Kate had a dozen responses warring in her mind, trying to fight their way out, but all she heard herself say was a weak, "No . . . I . . . No."

"Look, let's go to your place and talk about it. The boss said we should probably be extra careful, maybe not be alone."

"No, that's not . . ." she opened her car door and tossed her purse and bag in. "Thanks, but that's not necessary. I'll be fine."

"Kate--Katherine," he said stepping closer, "you really need somebody with you tonight. Let it be me. Give me a chance to tell you how I feel."

"I don't want to know how you feel," she snapped.

He grabbed her arm and said, "Listen, Katey. I want us—"

"Hey Kate," she heard from behind her, "you ready to go? Why don't you drive? I'll leave my car here tonight."

My friend. Right on time, Kate thought.

Jeanne went to the passenger side, shot Skip a smirk, and jumped in. He released Kate's arm and stepped back. "We'll talk later," he said.

"No. We won't," Kate replied and slammed her door.

Chapter 19

TUESDAY – Evening: Los Angeles

Later, the two lounged side by side on Kate's sofa, shoes off, with a bowl of popcorn between them and the remaining half bottle of Sofia red wine on the coffee table.

"Smart to redo your sofa this color," Jeanne said, rubbing the burgundy cushion next to her.

"What? Why?"

"If we spill, won't even show," she said in a too-cheerful voice.

"Oh, right," Kate tried and failed to smile. Instead, she sighed and drank more wine.

They were silent for a while, but Kate couldn't help saying one more time what she'd said several times in the car: "Sharon. I still can't believe it."

"I know," Jeanne said. "We should have been there. Somebody should have been there."

Kate squeezed her arm and said, "But we couldn't be. We couldn't know."

"How does he know?" Jeanne wondered. "How does he know who we are?"

"I don't . . ." Kate turned up her palms and shook her head. "This, all of it. The meticulous planning. He had to know where they lived and matching that Psalm to Malik's name and the anniversary. I've only read about this kind of mind. It's another thing to actually encounter one. And speaking of another kind of mind and knowing too much: MayHem. Harrison thinks someone may be telling her things."

"'Someone.' You mean like somebody on the team?"

"He didn't say that exactly, but at least someone on the inside with access." She thought a moment then said, "Funny—" but abruptly stopped herself.

"What's funny?" Jeanne squinted at her through her empty glass and allowed Kate to pour her some more.

"Off the subject. Nothing . . . just . . . He sounded so odd when he talked about her."

"And?"

"And nothing." Kate knew Jeanne was waiting, so she finally said. "Well, you've see her picture."

"Yep. She'd be on my hot tamale train." She paused. She stared at Kate. "So, you're thinking . . . Ooooh."

"Don't 'oooh' me. Drink your wine," Kate said.

"Good idea," Jeanne chuckled. "You better be nice to me or I'll rat you out to Skip. Some people get all the boys. Hashtag threesome."

"Oh shut up. And don't get me started with Skip. I can't even."

"Why are you acting so surprised about Skip? You had to notice he had feelings for you, 'Katey'," Jeanne said.

"Well yeah, kinda. Now. But all that time? With Dale right there? What kind of friend is that?" She mimicked him in a whiney, hurt voice. "'Oh, I miss him too you know.' Dick."

Jeanne held up her glass for a toast. "To dicks everywhere."

"I'll drink to that. To big dicks everywhere."

"Ugh," Jeanne said. "Drown that thought." She took a big swig, shivered, and said, "Ooo that's better. Sterilized out of my head."

She wagged a finger at her friend. "See, that's what happens when you 'give a poor guy a break.' He tries to move into your damned house. You believe that? He was actually going to make me let him come home with me? To protect me? From what? From him?" She knew her voice was getting higher as the level of wine in the bottle was getting lower.

"Oops," Jeanne hooted, "A brother didn't know he was messing with the president of the Take-No-Shit Club. It kills me how these men think because you look like Brunette Barbie and you try to be nice and professional in the office, you won't kick their asses. They don't know I have to be your friend because I'm scared of you."

"Oh zip it, Muscle Mama. I can't beat you arm wrestling. Yet."

Jeanne snorted and said, "I'll be waiting right here, Cinderella." She checked her watch. "I'm starving. What's taking Pizza Crek so long? Don't they have a guaranteed time thing?"

"They'll be here. Chill out. Have some more popcorn."

"Popcorn isn't food," Jeanne said, grabbing a handful. "He better hurry or I'm going to get hangry. You wouldn't like me when I'm hangry." Jeanne did an Incredible Hulk pose, roared, laughed and repeated her joke a few times.

"You are so not as funny as you think," Kate said, laughing despite herself.

She sighed and tossed a kernel of popcorn into the air, catching it in her mouth. "It's going to be hella awkward with Skip from now on."

"Poor little Robin. What's a baby bird to do?"

"Well, he's not exactly little," Kate said.

"You know, thinking of all that working out and gettin' swole. I wonder what he's compensating for. Bet he's got a little tweet-tweet, tweet-tweet."

"OMG, that silly song. You need to stay off the internet."

"And stunt my educational growth? How else would I learn about the mating habits of SIS males?"

"Yeah, that's info you couldn't live without."

"Speaking of," Jeanne said. "Ok, full confession; I never liked Batman."

"You think I don't know?"

"Harrison. You know he's the one, right?"

"You think so? I don't know. The way he's dedicated to this job. The focus. That doesn't remind you of Da—"

"No! Ugh," Jeanne said, waving the thought away. "Batman was selfish and self-centered. It was always about him, and you know it. I won't talk about your birthday, and on Valentine's Day when I had to be your date. And how many dinners did he blow off? I even remember one night a bunch of us were out, and his phone kept ringing until he muted it. I found out the next day that was you."

"You never told me."

"Course I didn't." She tilted her head and smiled slightly. "I didn't have to, did I, friend?"

Kate shrugged and toasted her. "Well, you were a very good date."

"Yeah. Uh huh. But no happy ending."

They giggled, and Jeanne finished her glass and poured them both more.

"Besides," Jeanne continued, "that jerk—may he rest in peace—wasn't smart enough to know what he had. He always acted like, 'Yeah, whatever,' about you. Harrison looks at you like . . . like you're the answer."

"'The Answer,'" Kate mused. "I like that. Wonder if he has any answers for me?"

"Yeah," Jeanne said. "Like how big is his—" A pillow whacking her in the face stifled the part Kate didn't want to hear. She jumped up to avoid the return fire pillow Jeanne lobbed at her and ducked just in time, then swiftly traversed the room, grabbing every pillow in sight and launching them at her opponent. Jeanne batted a couple away and ducked to the side, knocking the popcorn over in the process, then threw her arms up in surrender.

"Ok, ok you win, vicious, mean lady." Jeanne collapsed on the sofa laughing. She looked thoughtfully up at Kate's loft-level balustrade. "I love this place. It's so you." She groped around her for some of the spilled popcorn, picked up a few kernels, and popped them into her mouth.

"What do you mean?" Kate looked up at the dark wood railings contrasting with the pale yellow of her walls. "Like some kind of corny light and darkness personality psychobabble?"

"I meant like sleek and beautiful and . . ." Jeanne began to writhe on the sofa and caress her body, "all open and warm and like, ready for love. And your balcony's all ready for a Romeo and Juliet scene. Romeo, Romeo. Where fart out? Thou Romeo."

Kate laughed, shook her head, and began picking up popcorn. She leaned over and kissed her friend on the forehead.

"What was that for?" Jeanne asked.

"For the best, stoopid funny, make-you-laugh-at-the-worst-time friend anyone ever had."

"And that's a reason to slop lipstick on my head?" She rubbed her forehead and grimaced at her fingers. "Definitely not my shade."

"You're welcome. How about another one to match?" Kate poked out her lips making kissy noises and approaching Jeanne.

"Back off, I'm warning you!" Both were laughing hysterically when a sudden pounding on the door froze them in place.

"Pizzacwuhdeyivwybesgwihpeetsinehway!" a muffled male voice called through the door.

"What? What did he say?" Jeanne asked.

"It's Pizza Crek." Kate grabbed her credit card off the counter and walked toward the door. "I think he's saying, 'best Greek pizza in LA'."

Again there was insistent pounding and, "Pizzacwuhdeyivwy besgwihpeetsinehway!"

"Okay, okay. Coming!"

"They have to say the whole thing every time?"

"Well mostly they don't, but sometimes they hire delivery people with challenges, so no cracks!"

Kate opened the door and peeked out to see a guy with shoulder length blonde hair and thick-lensed glasses in an ill-fitting Pizza Crek uniform. He was holding two large bags in his right arm and had his left fist up, poised to knock yet again. She was about to say hi but was met by, "Pizza Cwek deyivwy best Gweek pizza in Ehway. Am I yate? I'm twying to not be yate. I cannot be yate any more times."

Ok, a little autism or something happening here, Kate thought.

"No, no, you're not ya-, uh, *late*. You're right on time."

She turned to give Jeanne a don't-you-dare warning look, and her friend, biting her lip, pointed toward the bathroom and retreated down the hall.

"I bwought the Cweks for you. Mozzawella and kielbasa and chicken—"

"Ok, that's—" Kate began, reaching for the bags.

"And magawita and supweme and—" the delivery man continued.

"Great, thanks, you're, that's uh, thank you." She took the bags, thinking it was good of Pizza Crek to give people with disabilities opportunities, but they should also give them uniforms that fit.

She turned away to place the bags on the counter. When she turned back to hand the man her credit card, there was a gun pointed at her face. It kind of looked like a .22, but something had been done to alter it. Something on the business end looked like a homemade silencer.

"One word from you, and she dies the minute she comes out. Hands up." Kate nodded and did as she was told.

The man took off his thick glasses and tossed them aside. "Those aren't mine, neither is this stupid shirt, but it's okay. The owner won't be needing them anymore. And this," he pulled off a wig and put it near the bags. "Like it? Didn't even know if I'd need it tonight, but I'm always prepared. Like a good scout or choirboy. Ready for whatever comes up." He chuckled drily.

"Sit," he commanded, indicating one of her dining room chairs. He pulled heavy duty zip ties from one of his pockets, handed her one and said, "Right wrist."

It was already threaded, and the moment she looped it around her wrist and the chair arm, he pulled it tight before moving behind her to repeat the action on her left side. She felt the silencer pressing against her head the whole time.

She heard the toilet flush, the door open, and Jeanne chuckling as she walked down the hall. "Okay, weady for some of that Pizza Cwek. Hope we're not too yate to—"

She stopped, staring at the man who was holding a gun to her friend's temple.

"Looks like you're definitely vewy, vewy yate," the man said.

"Who the hell are—?"

"I think you know the answer to that, Jeanne is it? I'll need you to take a seat right over there. I wasn't expecting you to be here, like I wasn't expecting to deliver Pizza Crek, but I like surprises. Keeps one on one's toes, don't you think?"

Jeanne sat down, never taking her eyes off him.

"You'll please put this around your right wrist and secure it to the arm of the chair. I'll be right there to help you out with the other hand."

He tossed her a zip tie, which she caught and put around her wrist.

"Tighter Jeanne. Wouldn't want those feminine little hands slipping out, now would we?"

He pulled out another cable tie, knelt beside Kate, and grabbed her right ankle, pushing her leg against the chair leg. He kept his eyes glued to hers but glanced at Jeanne now and then.

They would have a moment, Kate thought, just a moment when he would have to put the gun down to put the plastic tie around her ankle and tighten it.

"Why are you here?" Jeanne asked. "To stop us from looking for you? We'll never stop."

He smiled and poked the gun barrel into Kate's temple a couple of times.

"Explain it to her, Katherine. Apparently, she doesn't understand."

"Michael you don't have to do this. Let us help you," Kate said, her voice neutral.

"Help me? Help me what? You gonna save me FBI? You didn't when we called and begged for your help. Where were you when a bunch of little orphans were suffering all those years? It's too late now. We don't need your help anymore."

Kate leaned as close to Michael as possible, so her face was inches from his. She knew Jeanne was on alert.

"Michael," she said softly. He wouldn't respond, but she saw his breathing quicken. "Michael, please don't hurt us."

He recoiled and averted his eyes.

"All of us can come out of this alive," Kate said. "Maybe we can't help you, but you can help us. Please, help us to survive. Please Michael, I—"

"Shut up!" he jammed the muzzle of the gun right between her eyes. "Shut. Up!"

She squeezed her eyes shut and drew a quick breath as if she were terrified and began sobbing gently. When the first tears came, she gazed at him in silent entreaty, then hung her head in defeat.

Finally, he put the gun down on the floor beside him and focused on securing her ankle to the chair leg.

"Now you cry. Now all of you cry. For yourselves. Well you're going to be crying a lot more for a much greater reason than you could ever imagine, for I will punish the proud and mighty and bring down everything that is exalted."

He pulled her ankle tie tight. *Now! Before he reaches for his gun!* She flicked a glance at Jeanne and screamed, "Ow! Ow!! That hurts! You evil bastard!! No wonder nobody wanted you! You filthy little whore!"

Michael looked up in hurt surprise, and Jeanne launched across the room toward him, her chair still attached at one wrist. But she was only able to run two steps before Michael, still on his knees, grabbed his gun and pointed it at her. She froze like she'd slammed into a wall.

Kate used her free left leg to push herself over on him, chair and all, but she only threw him a little off balance. He lashed out at her with his left arm, and she felt something crunch as his fist connected with her left eye. She screamed in agony and tumbled to the floor, ending up on her right side.

Jeanne yelled, "Bitch, I will kill you!" and lunged toward him, grabbing for the gun with her free hand.

Kate felt her face swelling and a stinging liquid rolled across the bridge of her nose and into her right eye. She blinked repeatedly, struggling with her bonds and trying to see what was going on.

Like a view through a shimmery pink curtain, she could see their blurry feet struggling back and forth, inches from her face. Their collective bumping and rumbling sounded to her like an approaching earthquake. She heard Jeanne straining and grunting like she did during her workouts, but not a sound from Michael.

Kate twisted and pulled, rocking the chair and straining at the serrated ties cutting into her flesh. Finally, she managed to pull out her left arm, scraping the skin off her wrist and hand. She didn't know if her friend could see her free arm, but she waved it and yelled, "Jeanne!"

Kate saw Jeanne's feet dig in and push Michael closer, so she grabbed for him. All she could catch was a handful of pants fabric. She yanked as hard as she could, pulling his leg from under him.

Michael lost his balance. And for a moment, Kate thought they'd won. She thought they still had a chance. But his momentum backward also threw Jeanne off balance. Kate never knew how it happened—at that moment; she heard two unmistakable sounds so close together they seemed like a single voice saying a single, strange word "pyoongpyoong." His silenced gun had fired twice. Jeanne yelled "Ahhh!" and Kate knew her girl was hit. It felt like a lifetime before she crumpled to the floor, still holding onto Michael. Her eyes were closed, and she wasn't moving.

Michael rolled away from her. Panting, he hopped to his feet. "Well thank you, Katherine," he said and nudged Jeanne a couple of times with his foot. When there was no response, he re-secured Kate's left hand and moved to where she couldn't see him.

"Jeanne, Jeeaannne," she whispered.

"Too late, I'm afraid," she heard from across the room. "Everything you needed to say to your friend should have already been said."

He knelt beside her again, and she heard the sound of paper tearing.

"They will find you, Michael. Adding the deaths of two agents to the others will—"

"Two agents, Katherine? You think I'm going to shoot you, don't you?"

He fumbled with something, out of her line of sight, and she smelled a strange, pungent chemical odor.

"That would mean nothing, and your death shall not be meaningless. You are a part of the plan—a piece of the puzzle. Your role is so much greater than you know."

She could see he had a white cloth in one hand and a bottle of something in the other. He poured a few drops on the cloth and in a swift move, put it over her nose and mouth while pressing the back of her head.

She tried to hold her breath, squirmed and struggled to free her head, but it was useless. She began to feel woozy. She was almost out when she heard a weak, "Kate" from behind him. Jeanne was reaching a hand toward her. It was red with blood from her abdomen.

Before she lost consciousness, Kate clearly saw her dear friend reach out to her one last time through the red mist and say, "Katey. Love you."

"Jeannie, don't try to—" Kate began, but Michael had picked up his gun. He shook his head and said gently, "Stop," before putting a final bullet in her head. Jeanne's face exploded.

He turned back to finish his business with Kate.

Chapter 20

TUESDAY – Night: Pescadero

They were ready to go. Finally. Harrison complimented himself yet again on the way he was showing (outward) patience and being a team player. He fought the urge to bellow and curse and throw things every time another roadblock appeared, or another self-important asshole decided he wasn't being properly respected or had to inject himself into the case. But he held back. He saw Malik and Sharon's faces. He saw those of the other victims as well, before him. This was no time to alienate and annoy people. The goal here was to put this team together, get all the resources they needed, ascertain who in which agency would do what, and get the hell out to that house and nab Michael Hitchings.

Thanks to the Director smoothing the way, the team from the San Francisco FBI (which covered San Mateo County where Pescadero was located, he'd discovered) was deferring to him. He still had to remain aware that he couldn't just start ordering the San Mateo Sheriff's Department around. As luck would have it, he didn't have to; Sheriff Camilo Begay was a dream to work with. He was strong and in charge in an effortless way that Harrison hoped he could achieve one day.

The man reminded him of Malik. He was younger and looked nothing like him (Harrison thought maybe he was Native American), but he had a direct way of looking at people and an easy, warm smile that almost made Harrison want to cry. Was Malik ever going to smile like that again?

In a much shorter time than Harrison would have thought, Begay had deputies from their Homeland Security, including a SWAT team, ready to go. Harrison knew the Sheriff could probably tell he hadn't run an operation like this before, but like the way Malik might have, he got Harrison's input about decisions and made suggestions helping to guide him to the right choices.

So now, there was a squad surrounding the guest house, another around the main house, and one in the woods flanking the property. They even had an FBI helicopter and two canine units standing by.

If Michael Hitchings was home, he wasn't getting away from them. Not alive.

Begay sent deputies to all the closest homes on both sides to make sure no one came outside or placed a call to Hitchings or the owners.

And now they were ready to go. He and Camilo stood just out of sight at the foot of the driveway.

Harrison pressed the button on his walkie. "Beta team leader, anything back there?"

"Nothing, sir," the officer answered. "Guest house completely dark. The car is here, but the white van isn't parked back here."

"Perimeter team leader?"

"Nothing here, sir," she said. "No way he could make it through these woods without a light source."

"Alpha?"

"We can see the couple sitting at their table talking, but there's no sign of anybody else. Table only set for two."

Harrison looked at Camilo and nodded. "Let's go in."

They raced up to the front door accompanied by an officer with a battering ram and a team of eight mixed SWAT and FBI agents, weapons drawn.

Harrison banged on the door and shouted, "FBI! Open Up!"

He gestured to the officer with the enforcer who stepped up ready to breach the front door, when the Alpha leader said, "The old man is walking to the door, no weapons visible."

Harrison knocked again, and a frightened man in his late sixties opened the door. Harrison could see he was flanked by a woman who was peeking around his shoulder. Both looked terrified, and the woman's red eyes said she'd been crying for a long time.

"FBI. Step aside please!" Harrison said as the team stormed in past him. "Harold Sebring?" he demanded loudly, but the panicked man could hardly hear him as he focused on the black-uniformed team thundering through his home.

They heard "Clear!" "Clear!" echoing from all over the house.

"Oh no, what are they doing?" the woman wailed. "What are you looking for?" She clutched her husband.

"Are you Harold and Doris Sebring?" Harrison demanded again.

The man's attention snapped back to Harrison, "Yes, yes," he said, rapidly nodding his head as he watched the officers.

"Is anyone else here?" Camilo asked.

"No."

"Does anyone else live here?"

"Yes, well, actually no, not anymore." Sebring looked at his wife who hung her head and began to cry again.

"Who are you talking about?" Harrison asked.

"Our, well, kind-of foster son, Christian. He's gone now." He put his arm around his wife who pressed close to him.

"When is he coming back?" Harrison asked. He felt frustration rising. They can't be this close and have Hitchings slip away.

"He's not," the woman said and sobbed. "He's left us for good. I don't understand it. He was making plans, talking about settling down. There was even a new girlfriend. We thought . . ." She shrugged her shoulders and dabbed at her eyes.

"Please sit down," he said. "I'm Special Agent Harrison Carter of the FBI, LA office. This is Sheriff Camilo Begay."

"From right here in San Mateo," Begay said.

"Sure, we've seen you on TV. My wife is always talking about your nice smile," Harry said, making a feeble attempt to smile himself.

Harrison pulled out the photos of Michael and laid them on the table. "Do these look familiar at all?"

They looked at the pictures and then each other. Finally Harry gave an almost imperceptible nod and Doris said, "That's our boy. That's Christian."

"Why are you looking for him?" Harry asked.

"He's a suspect in multiple m—" Harrison began, but Camilo cut him off.

"Very serious crimes," he finished the sentence. "We can tell this is someone you care about very deeply, but he may not be who you think he is."

Harrison knew why Begay had stopped him. He was going to slap them with the news about Michael and gauge their reactions to see what came of it, but Camilo clearly could tell what this news was doing to them. Harrison could tell too, but they had a job to do. And yet, he somehow knew they were not involved. They probably were as clueless about Michael as the woman in New York.

"Of course he's who we think he is. You have the wrong person," Doris said firmly.

"I'm sorry to tell you, but we don't have the wrong person," Harrison said.

"But what's he done? Did he rob a bank or something?" Harry asked.

"Harry that's silly," Doris said to her husband. "He works very hard all the time, you know. Bank robber!"

"We know Christian by his real name, which is Michael Hitchings. You're going to be seeing his picture on TV as well as hearing his name," Camilo said. "You'd better prepare yourselves."

"Well, it's not a crime to change your name. A lot of people do. Besides, he grew up in foster care and orphanages, so if he wanted to be someone else, what's wrong with that?"

"That's not why we're looking for him," Harrison said. "Why do you think he's not coming back?"

"We're not really sure," Harry said. "He said it was best for us. We would know the truth. All would be revealed . . ." He stopped, and the couple locked eyes until Doris shook her head and looked away, ". . . in the fullness of time," he finished. Then it was his time to look away.

He rubbed at an invisible spot of something on the table and said softly but resolutely, "What do you think he did? We're prepared now, tell us. What do you think he did?"

Harrison said, "Have you heard anything in the news about the killings happening in different parts of the country? Copycats of other infamous murders?"

"You mean like the woman who was killed in New York, and that little girl?"

"And there was another one in LA, right?" Doris asked.

"Correct. And that's not all. There are more than those," Harrison said.

"But what do those have to do with Christian . . . with Michael?"

"Mrs. Sebring, I'm sorry to say Michael is our prime suspect in all those cases."

"Outrageous!" The woman jumped to her feet. "You are—no. NO! He did not do any such thing, not our Christian. No. He's the sweetest, kindest, most loving . . . He's the kind of boy we wish we could have found and adopted when he was little. We would have been proud to have him as our son. He's in our wills. He did not do this!"

"Honey, honey," Mr. Sebring joined her and put his arms around her. "Calm down." He looked around at their grim faces then down at her. Harrison didn't see tears, but he heard them in the man's voice. "Honey, sweetheart. Listen to me. They must have some kind of evidence. The FBI and the Sheriffs, they wouldn't come here for nothing. And well, we know he told us he was doing those rehab jobs, but we can't be sure of what he was really doing. We never saw any of the homes."

"Nonono, it just can't—no!" She stopped and hung her head, still shaking it from side to side trying to hold back the truth.

Her husband released her and looked at each of their faces. He sighed and let his shoulders slump. "I . . . I suppose you want to see where he actually was living."

"Yes. Yes sir," Harrison said. "Thank you."

"Okay." He walked them out to the guest house, his eyes downcast, appearing to barely notice the teams of heavily armed deputies and agents milling around.

Something about the way the man shuffled across the yard reminded Harrison of the change in Malik, once he knew he'd lost his wife. This man too had lost someone he loved dearly. What kind of creature was this Michael Hitchings? It almost seemed like they were dealing with more than one person. How could this monster inspire this kind of love and devotion and trust?

When they reached the padlocked door, Sebring turned to them and said. "Oh, we don't actually have keys anymore. Christian . . . Michael changed the locks."

Camilo said, "With your permission, we can get it open, no problem." He turned to one of his deputies, but Sebring said, "That won't be necessary. I'll take care of it for you." He walked to his toolshed to the right of the guest house and pulled out a sledgehammer.

He stalked back, his eye fixed on the door like it was some dangerous beast he had to dispatch. He clenched his teeth, lifted the hammer high, and swung it, striking the lock so hard he damaged the door behind. Harrison heard the CRUNCH at the same time Sebring let out a pained "Ahh!" And then, it seemed, a demon was let loose inside of him. He slammed and slammed at the lock and the door, demolishing it almost to kindling, until Harrison said, "Sir! Sir! Mr. Sebring! Stop! Stop!!"

But he kept going until the door was in slivers. Camilo grabbed him from behind, and Harrison took the sledgehammer from his hands.

The man crumpled to his knees, and all Harrison heard was a single sob and the name, "Christian."

* * *

When Harrison stepped inside, he knew immediately: this was Michael. He tried to stem of the wave of comfort or satisfaction rolling over him when he saw how ordered, how regimented, the place was. He would not allow himself to think *we could have been friends,* but on some level, someplace deep inside, he knew they had more in common than he would ever want to admit to himself or reveal to anyone else.

He turned slowly, looking around the room, his vision sweeping back and forth like a lighthouse. Camilo watched him for a while, "According to what you've told me, he doesn't really leave much evidence. This place would definitely be a poster child for surgical level cleaning. Nothing in here looks like someone lived here."

"There has to be something more," Harrison said.

"More?" Camilo looked around the small room. "Where?"

"There has to be something more."

He walked around the room again waiting for the missing piece—not knowing what he was looking for but knowing it was there. He turned to a couple of the agents and said, "Check all the furniture. There's something more, there's something else."

They moved books from bookshelves, took off his sheets, sliced open his mattress and pillow.

One of the agents shook a few books and started to move on, and Harrison said, "No, open everyone. Look carefully."

In a very short time, they had run out of places to look. Camilo said, "I think this maybe it, my friend. If there was anything useful, he probably took it with him. We've searched every place but the roof, and we can see from outside there's nothing . . ." He stopped, staring at Harrison, who was staring at the floor.

"Harrison?"

"The roof," Harrison said. "What about a basement? This place was probably a barn before it was a garage, right?"

"Yeah," Camilo looked speculatively at the floor. "This guest house is definitely a conversion. It could have had a root cellar or some kind of storage area at one time. People usually seal them up when they do renos."

"And Michael could have unsealed it. Let's check this floor."

It took only a few minutes before they'd moved and checked under everything including the small chest at the back of the apartment.

"Here, this area here," Harrison said, fingering the corner of one of the floorboards. "The wood is a little different." He pressed and pulled, until he discovered a latch concealed in the pattern of the wood.

All weapons were drawn as he slowly lifted the trap door. The lights in the underground area flashed on automatically, and they all recoiled, ready to blast Michael if necessary. "He's not down there," Harrison said and proceeded to the ladder.

"Careful, there may be booby traps," Camilo said.

"No," Harrison replied without hesitation, "you don't understand. He wants us to find this. He wants us to see it."

He climbed to the bottom and walked around the room, going from display to display. That was how he thought of it: a series of displays, a murder museum. If the upstairs was the outer façade of Michael Hitchings, this was his core: the part he held close and secret, revealed only to him. *And to me* Harrison thought.

It felt like the man had carved himself down the middle and turned himself inside out so the world could see what was truly going on. His heroes: Jeffrey Dahmer, Ted Bundy, Dennis Rader, Jack the Ripper, the Zodiac, Golden State—all here. Each one had a dedicated area with text and pictures and related items. He could tell without even close inspections which were done, and which had not yet been completed.

This was not merely a museum: it was a shrine, a sacred place.

He'd seen things like this in ancient Catholic churches where there would be areas dedicated to specific saints. There was always a statue or painting and artifacts or some supposedly holy, magical relics relating to that particular saint. Did he think these things gave him power? Somehow, they made him blessed or divine?

Then he saw it: Manson.

He felt a wave of rage wash over him. He knelt before the Manson shrine. Michael might have knelt right here, in the same way, before he went after Sharon.

He looked at the pictures and details of the case he knew so well, but there was something extra here: he picked up a small piece of pink cloth with splotches of dried blood and an FBI badge logo on it. He knew it was Malia's, and he knew Michael had left it for him. "Bastard," he hissed.

He stood up still holding the bit of tee shirt.

"Harrison?" He turned and saw the concerned expression on Camilo's face. "Why don't you take a break? We'll secure this area and finish with the Sebring's. Maybe dinner?"

"I guess I'll call the Director and update him," Harrison said. "Yeah, maybe dinner."

He walked back toward the house and stopped when he saw Doris leaning against the side of her open back door as though she couldn't stand up by herself. She stared at him, expressionless.

Harrison stepped closer to her and said words that surprised even him, "Was Christian your . . . only child?"

She looked at him at if she wasn't sure whether or not he was being sarcastic.

"No," she said softly. "We had a daughter, Naomi. We lost her too. We used to tell each other God sent us a son in her place."

Harrison nodded and said, "I'm . . . very sorry for your loss. Losses."

She squinted up at him looking from one eye to the other, searching for the truth, he thought, and she put her hand on his heart and said, "You've lost someone too, haven't you?"

He nodded.

"So," she said, "you understand. You're a good man, and I . . . I believe you. Oh God. I believe you."

Her husband put his arm around her; she closed her eyes and rested her head on his chest as if it were simply too heavy to hold up on her own.

The man looked at Harrison and nodded, and he left them there.

As he walked toward the car, his phone buzzed with an incoming text: it was from Kate. He stared in confusion at the words "Bye Thy Katherine."

Chapter 21

TUESDAY – Night: Los Angeles

When Kate came to, she was sitting upright. She tried to move, but both her hands and ankles were tightly secured to the chair. And something was around her neck, holding her head in place. She was able to look downward out of her one good eye far enough to see the plastic ties had been replaced by what looked like pantyhose.

She had been moved across the room, and she stared groggily at the place where Jeanne had landed. She could only see part of her on the other side of the chair she was still attached to, but there was no movement, only a bloody mess where her face used to be. It was true: Jeanne was gone.

Kate looked around the room, searching for Michael, then, "Hello, you're baaaack," came from directly behind her.

He walked around in front of her, and she blinked and blinked again, not sure if she was seeing clearly. He had taken off his pants and was wearing a pair of her panties. The pink ones. Her favorites. And he was holding the end of a rope snaking up behind her somewhere. She couldn't see where it went (*maybe looped through the balustrade?*), but she knew the other end was around her neck.

"You like?" he asked striking a pose. "This is just for you. No one else will ever know." He smiled at her, looking, she thought, more like a shark than a human man. He put his pants back on and watched her, waiting.

It came to her in a flash: chloroform, pantyhose, and the rope. It was Dennis Rader, the Bind Torture Kill murderer, better known as BTK.

Michael was nodding. "Yes, you know now."

"Michael, listen. You are not Dennis Rader or Jack the Ripper or any of them. You are Michael Hitchings, a real person who has had real world, unfair, unforgivable things happen to you. You can't get vengeance for those horrible, criminal acts by hurting innocent people. Jeanne never—"

"Innocent? Innocent! None of you are innocent." He jerked the rope, and her head snapped backward.

"Ah! Michael, please think about it. Listen, please. Jocelyn Simmons, she couldn't have done anything to you. She was just a little girl. A sweet little—"

"Whore! A whore of Babylon, teasing and strutting her way around public stages. Tempting grown men and boys alike. She had a father, this whore, and the father of the whore had a brother. He used to live in Little Rock too, but he loved boys too much when he was young and kept loving them as a man. So he ran away and joined the circus. The Catholic circus, that is."

"So her uncle . . . her uncle was Father Simmons. Franks told us about him. And you found her."

"Yes, I found the little beauty and ended her reign. God save the queen."

"But the others," Kate said, "they couldn't have all been related to priests. The Lyft driver, Fred—"

"Freddy. Little Freddy. Two wives and a baby mama and still couldn't make life work. He never would have. He was never right after he saw Billy splatter to the pavement in front of him. But he's free now. And soon, I'll be free too."

"What does that mean, Michael? What will free you? At least let me understand. You're in charge here. You could show a little mercy."

He jerked the rope again, harder this time, and she gagged as her air was cut off. She felt the chair rise a little from the floor.

"No," he hissed, "no, I couldn't. No one ever showed me mercy. And you're right, I am in charge now. This is my party, but there's a guest missing."

She began to see spots dancing before her eyes, and he released the rope, letting her chair bump to the floor. She gratefully sucked in a breath and held it a few seconds. Michael walked out of her line of sight and came back holding her phone.

"Let's call Harrison."

She shook her head like a stubborn child.

"We don't have to, of course. If you'd rather die without ever talking to him again, that's fine with me, but I have it on good authority that you two kids have quite the bond."

He pulled out a business card and shoved it inches from her eyes. It was Harrison's.

"Franks," she hissed, and her voice sounded like she was just getting over a sore throat.

"Oh, I wouldn't be quite so sure about my sources," he said smugly. "I probably have more connections than you realize. Your code please."

Kate couldn't think of another way out. She knew calling Harrison was what this psycho wanted, so he could gloat and prove to Harrison how he was outsmarting them, but if she could alert Harrison to where she was, maybe . . .

He wound the end of the rope around his hands, preparing to make a massive jerk.

"Ok! Ok!" she said, sounding panicked. It's FBI*KT, all caps."

"O-K-K-K-Kay," he said, laughing as he punched in the code.

She saw him sweep the screen, and looking at the card, he punched in Harrison's number. He was texting something.

"He'll love this," he simpered, making a kissy face at her before hitting send.

Moments later, her phone rang, and he hit the speaker button.

"Kate, it's me," she heard Harrison say. "What was that text? What did it mean?"

"I'm so sorry, Special Agent Carter, but Katherine is somewhat tied up right now. Hold please."

He snapped a close-up picture of her and sent it to Harrison, humming while he waited for it to arrive.

Kate could hear Harrison's gasp from where she sat.

"Michael, you son of a bitch, you'd better not—"

"What, Harrison? Better not what? Did you love my message? Clever, don't you think? Tell you what, you like puzzles; if you figure it out, I might let her live."

In the few moments' silence on their side, Kate could hear voices, activity; they must be clearing out the scene at Michael's house.

"Can you give me a hint? Something to work with?" Harrison said.

He's trying to buy some time, Kate thought. *He's already done something to alert people. I have to try to—*

"Aaargh!" she screamed as Hitchings yanked the rope again. Her neck felt like he'd wrapped a coil of molten metal around it.

"Was that a good hint, Special Agent? Did you get it? Need another one?"

"No! No! Stop!" Harrison yelled. "'Bye Thy Katherine.' It's . . . it's goodbye to her and stands for BTK at the same time. Dennis Rader. Please, Michael, please, don't hurt her. Kate! Kate! Say something!"

She could only cough and sputter for a moment, but she knew he could hear her.

"Okay," she finally choked out.

"Feel better now?" Michael said, dripping with fake sympathy. "Oh, that question was to both of you." And he bellowed with laughter. "And by the way, Harrison, you're right!"

One more chance, just one more chance. Kate drew in a breath, burning her throat the whole way, and choked out, "Get out of my goddamned house you impotent son of a bitch!"

Michael roared and backhanded her, knocking her over again. She screamed with pain, but it was worth it: Harrison knew where she was now. She had to stay alive a little longer.

But she felt the rope tighten once again as Michael used it to hoist her back to an upright position. She made as much noise as she could so Harrison would know she was still fighting. She heard him screaming her name and cursing at and pleading with Michael.

She'd started to lose consciousness when he stopped and let the rope go slack. He gently and sensuously massaged her neck, staring into her eyes the whole time. He leaned forward and breathed deeply like a lover taking in her scent. Nauseated and repulsed, she squirmed at her bonds, but it was hopeless.

"Agent Carter," Michael said, still staring into her eyes, "You guessed correctly, but I lied. I'm not going to let my little project live. She's hoping and praying for help, like we used to, but it's not coming. It's never going to come."

He stroked her face. "You can't help your lady Harrison, but maybe you can help someone else. Look deeper my son. Receive my words. Incline thine ear unto wisdom. If thou criest after knowledge and understanding, you must search for them as for hid treasures. Search, find it. Then shalt you understand righteousness and judgment. If it were not so, would I have told you?"

He kissed her gently on the forehead.

"Now, listen, Harrison. Listen to your lady die."

He tugged the rope until she gagged, let her loose and stared into her eyes, and whispered, "'Rage, rage against the dying of the light.'" He yanked the rope again, loosened it, and did it again. And again. Until he didn't stop pulling. She wanted to struggle, but she couldn't. Her neck burned, and her eyes felt like they were going to explode.

That was Harrison screaming at Michael calling her name over and over again. And then the pain stopped, and the room began to darken. She was glad to hear Harrison's voice.

She wondered if Jeanne would be waiting for her.

* * *

"Harrison. Harrison!" he heard someone say.

"Harrison, what is it? Did they get there? Did they get there in time?"

He shook his head and handed Camilo the phone.

Camilo grabbed the phone from him, put it to his ear, and hit the speaker button. Both of them listened intently and Camilo said "Hello! Hello Agent Katherine. Are you there? You okay?"

Harrison felt the silence screaming in his ear.

Camilo looked helplessly at him, and both their expressions said the same thing: *Too late.*

Camilo leaned toward the phone. "Wait," he said, "I hear sirens."

Moments later, Harrison heard what sounded like an army pounding into Kate's house.

"They're there!" Camilo yelled. "Hello! Hello?"

A man's voice came on the line and said, "Who is this?"

"I'm Sheriff Camilo Bergay here in Pescadero with Agent Harrison Carter of the LA FBI."

Harrison grabbed the phone. "Kate, my partner, is she . . .?"

"I'm Officer Cutler, LAPD. The EMT's are here. They're checking them out right now."

Them? Harrison wondered. Could he mean Kate and Hitchings? Maybe Kate was able to--

He heard a woman's voice say, "Nothing we can do here. Obviously, she's gone."

Gone? GONE?!?

"Harrison! Harrison!" he heard from far away. He didn't realize he was on his knees until he had to look up to find where Camilo's voice was coming from.

A male voice said, "This one's alive. Get that damned rope from around her neck."

When he heard those words, he felt like a rope was being released from his own neck. He could breathe again.

"Kate? Is it Kate?"

He heard a familiar, authoritative voice come on the line. "Harrison? You okay there?" It was Stanton.

"Yes, Boss, it's me. Is she—?"

"She's breathing. That's the important thing. We'll hold on to that for now. You finish up what you're doing there, and you can come on back."

"Yes sir, yes sir I will," he said, trying to regain his composure. He clicked off the call and turned, looking into Camilo's questioning eyes.

"So . . . your partner?" he asked, looking at him speculatively.

"Yeah. She's . . . she's my partner."

"I see," Camilo said, his eyes full of understanding.

"I, um, I need to, we need to . . ." Harrison said, willing his heart and breathing to slow to normal.

"No worries about what's going on here. We and your San Francisco team, I think we have this under control," Camilo said.

"Thank you," Harrison said, "I need to get back."

"I can tell you do," Camilo said with a little smile. "We'll get you on a plane. Next thing smokin' partner."

Chapter 22

TUESDAY – Night: Los Angeles

Harrison had already started walking to his car when his phone rang, and Stanton's name showed on the display.

"Boss, is she—"

"She's okay, Harrison. No voice, but—"

"I'm just leaving the airport lot, I'll be right there," Harrison said, jamming the phone in his pocket. He broke into a run, jumped in the car, and raced toward Cedars. He hardly remembered the ride there and the breathless run through the quiet halls of the sleeping hospital, where he flashed his badge at anyone who looked curious or even thought about slowing him down. He was past the last nurses' station and then stopped in the hallway outside Kate's room to mop his damp forehead and dial down the stress. She was alive. And awake. He could breathe now. He knew there might be other problems, but he refused to think about them right now. As he leaned against the wall, eyes closed for a moment, he heard a heavy, determined tread coming toward him.

He looked up and into his father's eyes.

"Harrison? What are you doing here, son? Are you okay?"

"Dad!" Harrison quickly stood up straight, adjusted his jacket, and regained his composure. "Fine, I'm fine. Um . . . I'm actually visiting a colleague who's here in the hospital."

"A colleague?" his father asked, peering past him at the door of Kate's room.

"Well, actually, my partner," Harrison said.

"Oh, your partner. Did he get shot? Is it bad?"

"She was attacked by a suspect, and it didn't go well."

"Your partner . . . she," his father said. "Sorry to hear that son. You seem to be really distressed." He paused a moment. "The prognosis isn't good?"

"No, I um, I think she's going to be all right, actually."

"This partner son," Dr. Carter said, scanning his son's face, "she's very important to you."

"Well yeah, Dad," Harrison said warily. "She's my partner, so, she's important to me, of course."

"How long have you been together?"

"Partners, Dad. We've been partners for a couple of years." He tried, unsuccessfully, to keep the defensive tone out of his voice. He wasn't accustomed to his father taking this kind of interest.

"I . . . I suppose there are a lot of things about your current life that I, that we, are unaware of," Dr. Carter said. "I guess we don't know much about . . . what's going on. If you like, son, I could drop in, check on her while she's here."

"She's not my pers-- um, yeah Dad, sure. I would appreciate that. But listen, there's something I need to tell you. I was going to call, but since we're both here—"

Harrison was interrupted by a resolute tap-tapping behind him oddly like the contralto version of his father's unyielding tread.

Dr. Carter looked past him, and Harrison turned to find a sharp-featured, petite woman in a voluminous lab coat approaching. She was staring up at his father.

"Well, Dr. Cartaire," she said, her slight French accent doing nothing to soften her tone. She pointed to the door of Kate's room. "Are you trying to steal my patient again, Chief?" She was smiling, but Harrison could tell his father was not her favorite person: not even close.

"Only in the best interests of the patient, Dr. Brouillard, but no, not this time. This is my son, Special Agent Harrison Carter, Jr."

"Ah," she said scanning both their faces, "of course. So you are the partner?"

"Yes, Dr. Brouillard I am. How is she?"

"Agent Katherine is an amazing and resilient woman. It is incredible she survived. As far as her voice, we'll have to see. There is some damage to her larynx, but we'll know more once the swelling goes down. I think with plenty of rest, she's going to be fine."

"That's wonderful. Thank you, doctor."

"You're welcome. You may see her now if you like. I believe your other colleague is still in there. But limit two visitors, and don't stay long." She glanced up at his father and threw a dismissive, "Dr. Cartaire," in his direction before tap-tapping down the hall.

Harrison, Sr. watched her walk away, "Women like that, brittle and competitive, all hard edges! They make me grateful for your mother. I know it's not PC to say or even to think, but sometimes, a man needs a soft place, someone who's nothing like him. Someone who keeps him balanced. I hope you find someone son."

Harrison was starting to wonder if an alien had taken over his father's body.

"Dad, I think maybe you've misunderstood—"

"Fine, son. I'm sure I have. Maybe your mother and I can meet your partner when she's feeling better?"

"Sure. Fine. But Dad, what I was trying to tell you earlier . . ." He looked around to make sure there was no one near.

"Did you see the news about the director's wife being murdered in Brentwood?"

"The Daniels murder. Yes, of course. I saw something about it."

"The suspect is someone I've been tracking for almost a year. Dad, he's done some very horrific things. This person, he called me at work."

"What?"

"He knows who I am, and he seems to know quite a bit about the team working to find him. And since the wife of one of our team was killed, we have to assume that all of our families could be in danger. And," he spoke even more quietly, "The word isn't out yet, but he's killed another team member."

"I see," Harrison, Sr. said. He nodded. "So he's the one who went after your partner?" When Harrison nodded, his father said, "We're in real danger, aren't we?"

"I can't know for sure, but we have to err on the side of safety. I need you to take Mom someplace safe just in case anything . . . well, just in case. It'll probably only be for a few days. We're close behind him. But we can't take any chances."

"I see."

"And Dad, could you do me one more favor?"

"Yes?"

"Please don't tell her what's happening. I'm all right, and I don't want her to worry."

He waited, unsure what his father might say and whether he even respected him enough to listen. "Of course, son. I'll do both those things. I'm . . . I'm glad you told me. Glad I saw you today. Call me on my cell and ask me how the vacation is going if she should pick up. I'll thank you for the . . . early anniversary surprise, how about that? And you'd better hurry up and catch him. The longer we're away, the more suspicious your mother will become. You know her."

"Yeah Dad, I do. Thank you." He turned to enter Kate's room.

"Harrison," he heard from behind him.

"Yes, Dad?" He waited, unable to read the expression on his father's face . . . afraid of what might come next.

"I love you, son," his father said.

There was a long silence, as Harrison tried to remember the last time he'd heard those words from him.

Finally he was able to say, "I love you too, Dad."

Dr. Carter cleared his throat and used his Chief of Surgery giving-orders voice, "Now be careful. Be safe. Tell Katherine we'll meet her soon. And go and make us proud, son."

Harrison watched his father stride away and wiped his eyes, surprised to find there were tears there. Had he misunderstood him all these years? Was there really a loving, beating heart under the harsh, "it's all about how it looks to those who matter" exterior, he wondered. Moreover, did "I love you" really mean "I'm proud of you, son"? It was too much for his brain to process at that moment.

* * *

He walked to Kate's bed and stood a moment looking down at her while she smiled crookedly, wincing through a bruised and swollen lip. In his head were all the words he needed to say. He saw himself wrapping his arms around her, holding her for the rest of the night and into tomorrow, but he was aware of Director Stanton staring at them, and all he could do was look at her.

In a husky whisper, Kate said "Hi."

"Don't try to talk, Katherine," Stanton said. "You know what the doctor told you."

Stanton cleared his throat and looked at Harrison. "Now that you're here, we should talk to Katherine about . . ." He stopped and looked down at her.

She looked from one to the other and nodded.

"You know?" Harrison asked.

She nodded again and closed her eyes. He watched the tears begin to slide down her cheeks. She whispered, "Jeanne."

She reached for Harrison's hand, and he grasped it in both of his, not caring about Stanton's presence. "I'm sorry partner, I should have been there for you. I should have been there."

She shook her head and beckoned him closer. He leaned down to her, and she reached up and gently touched his cheek, rasping out a weak, "Not your fault."

"Katherine," Stanton's voice came from behind him. "Do you remember anything? Did he say anything useful to us?"

She shrugged her shoulders, tried to say something and stopped, clearly in pain. She pulled her hand from Harrison's and mimed writing.

Moments later she had scrawled "Says we don't understand true meaning of Psalm."

"This is all he said?" Harrison asked. "No clue about his next victim?"

She shook her head slowly and wrote, "Knows too much—leak?"

"We're wondering that too," Stanton said.

She closed her eyes again, clearly exhausted.

"Harrison, we'd better let her rest now. Let's get back to the office. Please contact Laurie, and tell her to make sure the whole team is in. There's something we're missing. We have to figure this out."

"I'll be right behind you, sir. I only need a moment with Kate."

"Very well, I'll see you shortly."

Harrison turned back to her. He could see she was struggling to stay awake, as she looked up at him. "Kate, I . . ." and he stopped himself, as he had so many times. He thought *I love you. I love you and I should have told you before now. But if I say it now, you'll think it's just because I almost lost you.* So instead he said, "I'll get him. I'll get that bastard, I promise you."

She smiled and shook her head, gestured for the pad, which he held for her. Summoning her waning strength, she shakily wrote "COWARD," let the pen drop, and closed her eyes.

Chapter 23

TUESDAY – Late Night: Los Angeles

Back to the office, Harrison found most of the team was in. The buzz of activity was almost equal to the middle of a normal day. He sat at his desk, unable to focus at first, but he marshalled his forces from inside. *This was it, no more time.* He had to figure out Michael's maddening clues. The man said five different ways that he could save lives if he looked closer or paid more attention, so there was something, some obvious piece or part, there for them to find, if they only could.

His desk was covered with pages and pages of information from the murders, but somehow, he didn't think the answer was there; some of the murders hadn't happened yet when Franks said almost the same thing about looking deeper. It had to be something about the trial—some bit of testimony, something—they'd missed.

After a fruitless hour or more, he stood to stretch but kept his search going by walking to the evidence wall. As he'd done with the paperwork, he began to peruse each case, item by item.

He didn't even hear Skip when he walked up beside him.

"Carter," he said in a voice so subdued Harrison could hardly recognize it.

Harrison turned toward him, and instead of the hard-headed jerk he was accustomed to, he saw a guy, just a regular guy, whose eyes were full of pain.

"How is she?" he asked.

"Not bad, considering," Harrison told him. "They're not so sure about her voice, but it looks like she's going to be okay."

"I wanted to go and see her, but the boss said we should wait for a couple of days. So maybe, when you go, you can tell her . . ."

And Harrison saw in his eyes that this wasn't merely a crush or a rivalry: he loved her too. Skip loved her just as he did.

"Sure I . . . sure. My Dad's going to check on her too. I'll keep you updated."

Skip nodded. "The last time I saw Jeanne, we had words. I was a jerk. We did that sometimes, you know. Had little stupid dustups over nothing. But it would be okay later. Except this time . . ."

"Hey, you can't go there. She loved screwing with you. She would joke about it. She never took that shit seriously for a moment."

"Yeah, guess you're right." Skip said. "Sometimes I thought she did it only to get my reaction. Hey, maybe she had a secret crush on me."

"Maybe." Harrison tried to smile, as did Skip—but they both gave up.

"So what are you looking at," Skip asked. "Any progress?"

"I don't know," Harrison said, turning his attention back to the evidence wall. "Hitchings and his friend Franks too, he keeps hinting at something more, something else—quoting Bible verses about searching for hidden treasure and giving me wisdom. Both of them made it sound like it's right here—whatever it is—if we search carefully. I've gone over and over every line of the court records, the testimony, but so far, nothing helpful."

"Well what about the President?" Skip said. "He didn't expect us to find that out, right? Couldn't that be the big secret, the hidden treasure?"

"Maybe but . . . It just doesn't feel right." He looked at Jennings expecting the usual snarky crack, but Skip just nodded and said, "Your gut. I get it. I trust mine too."

Harrison walked past the cases, looking briefly at each one. "I don't think it's any one of these. Some of them weren't done yet when Franks said something about looking closer. Whatever it is predates the actual murders, even if it's connected."

He stopped in front of a section which they'd added after finding out about Michael. "I can't help but think it's the trial. That's when he really found out he wasn't ever going to get justice. Even his homie for life Franks sold him out. This whole insane plan started around there somewhere."

Skip stood beside him, looking at the trial-related pictures and documents Othello had posted. "Not a lot of witnesses," he said. "You'd think more of them would have come forward."

"I don't know," Harrison said. "At the time, the way victims were treated . . . It's pretty humiliating for a man to admit he couldn't protect himself, even if it happened to his much younger self. Would you want to get on a witness stand and admit something like that?"

"Hell no," Skip said then touched another picture, *to change the subject* Harrison thought. "This PR shot from the press conference; you identify all these guys?"

"The priests' legal team taking their victory lap. That's Patrick Chambers right there next to Jonas Barnes, heads of the firm." He touched each image as he spoke, "This man was the church spokesman for the area at the time. I understand he was promoted to Rome after their triumph. A couple of law clerks back here."

"Look at them," Skip sneered, "Just bustin' their buttons with pride at what they did to those kids."

"Yeah. You'd think they could at least be a little ashamed."

"Who's that?" Skip asked, pointing to a figure in the background.

"Oh, her," Harrison said. "We don't know. Probably some minor clerk or assistant. All they could tell us was she no longer works there, and no one really remembers her."

"Now she looks like she doesn't want to be on camera anywhere. Like she's actually hiding. Or maybe it's her weight; she seems like a hefty babe from the part of her you can see."

Harrison looked closer. "Franks talked about a woman they called 'The Sacred Cow.' He said every time she came in the courtroom they knew it would get worse for them. I wonder . . ." He leaned even closer.

"Explains why she's trying to hide. Maybe one person close enough to a normal human to feel a little shame."

Harrison barely heard him; there was something about that blurred image . . . Then it hit him.

He snatched the picture from the wall, grabbed a file from his desk, and rushed toward Malik's office.

"Carter? What the hell? What is it?"

"Have to make a call. I can't . . . I have to make this call."

He knew Skip and a couple of others were staring at him like he was having a psychotic break, but he didn't care; a whole handful of puzzle pieces were going to snap into place.

He wasn't sure. He thought he was right—and if he wasn't there'd be hell to pay—but unless his eyes were deceiving him, unless desperation was completely screwing with his perception, the Sacred Cow, that partially-hidden, blurry woman in the background—that woman was First Lady, Pat Mitchell.

Chapter 24

TUESDAY – Late Night: Los Angeles

Harrison paced as he waited for someone to pick up the phone. It had already rung four times when he growled, "Come on!" hit the disconnect, and dialed again. He knew it was ridiculously early (or crazy late) in Southampton, New York, but he didn't care. He needed the answers to his questions now so waking a fat ass, billionaire lawyer out of a sound sleep, was just too damned bad.

Finally, on the eighth ring, a soft male voice with a slight Spanish accent whispered, "The Chambers residence. Who is calling?"

"This is Special Agent Harrison Carter with the FBI in Los Angeles. Is this Attorney Chambers?"

"This is Alvaro, Mr. Chambers' butler," he replied. "Mr. Chambers is sound asleep. Most people are at one in the morning. You need to call back at a later time. Good—"

"Don't you hang up that phone!" Harrison ordered. "This is an urgent federal matter: a matter of life and death. Now you're going to go and rouse him and get him on the phone, or I'll have the Southampton police do it in person. And Alvaro, I'll make sure their sirens are blasting your sleeping neighbors out of their designer pajamas on the way. Now put me on hold, if you need to, and get him the hell on this phone."

Harrison heard a click before silence. While he waited, doubts began to circle in his head. He was still unsure: was that really Pat Mitchell? He thought so, but why would she not have made her background in law public? Why did she want to look so markedly different? Most people knew her as an organizer and advocate for underserved communities. He didn't remember ever having heard of her as a former lawyer.

A few minutes later, the phone clicked back on, and a steely, peremptory voice came on the line. "Agent, this had better be, as you say, urgent. I don't take kindly to being jerked out of sleep in this way. You said your name is Harrison Carter, correct?"

"Agent Harrison Carter, yes,"

"So that would make you a junior, right?"

Harrison sighed, reminding himself what this call meant and inwardly ordering himself to *be patient*. "That's right, sir. But I have some—"

"Only reason I decided to take the call. I know your father, and it's only out of respect for him that I—"

"Mr. Chambers, I need to know if the First Lady, Pat Mitchell, ever worked at your legal firm and whether you remember her working on a case involving three priests who were accused of sexually assaulting a man named Michael Hitchings when he was a boy?"

The sharp intake of breath on the other side was enough to let Harrison know he was on the right track. He could almost hear the gears in Chambers' brain ticking.

Finally, the man cleared his throat, took another deep breath, and began speaking. "Agent Carter, if I give you this information, you need to promise me that it can never be made public. Once Patricia-Sue made it to the White House, it was made clear to us that we had to seal the information about which cases she worked on, and not share it with anyone, or things would go very badly for our firm. We have many powerful clients who would not look too kindly on any embarrassing information about the First Lady."

"Did you say, Patricia-Sue?"

"Well yes, that's her name, or was her name: Patricia-Sue Alison Lee. I don't know why she changed it, she was pretty darned proud of it at the time. She would introduce herself using the whole thing, like anyone cared. She was continually trying to put on airs like having a lot of names and holding her chin ridiculously high while shaking hands gave her some sort of status. But she was just a fat country girl who lucked her way into law school. If you wanted to really get her panties in a bunch, simply call her 'Patty-Sue' with a hillbilly accent and stand back 'cause she was guaranteed to blow."

"And she was a lawyer for your firm?"

"Well not exactly," Chambers said. Harrison could hear the slightly disgusted sneer in his voice. He may as well have said, *We don't hire fat girls.*

"She might have become one of our regular staff attorneys had she stayed, but everyone doesn't gain status right away. We're very selective. She wasn't the elegant First Lady you're seeing now. She did well for herself, though. She shrunk and so did her name. Now, she is the beloved Pat Mitchell."

"So if she wasn't a lawyer, what exactly did she do for you?"

"She was the best damned investigator we ever had. She was brilliant, could get any information we needed from almost anyone. She was no beauty queen, well not at that time, but somehow she had this knack for fitting in and making people tell her what she wanted to know. And speaking of beauty queens: talk about extreme makeovers! She didn't realize that no one had to tell us not to say anything. She looked so markedly different, we didn't even know who she was. I'm still not sure I would have known if we hadn't received the keep quiet call."

"And who was it who asked you not to say anything? Did that come from the White House?"

"Not exactly. It was someone from her office, but it didn't sound like it was from the President. Maybe he didn't even know about it, who knows?"

"And of the investigations she did, were any of them for the Hitchings case against the priests?" Again, there was silence.

"Mr. Chambers, I didn't wake you up at one in the morning to ask a few routine questions. I said it was urgent, and I meant it. This may be a matter of national security."

"National Security? Is the President in danger, or is Patricia?" Chambers asked. "Is Patricia-Sue in danger?"

Finally, the man was sounding like he was talking about something other than his grocery list or a bit of neighborhood gossip.

"All right, um yes. She was on that case," he said. "And I have to say, information and the things she found out for us, well, I doubt we would have won the case without her."

"What kinds of things?" Harrison asked.

"You've studied the case, otherwise you wouldn't be calling me," the lawyer said. "So you know about the alleged abuse and so on. She found out Hitchings had a violent past. He went into foster care, and he beat up the boyfriend of one of his foster sisters in what may have been a jealous rage."

"Yes, I read the transcript," Harrison said. "So you're saying Pat, Patricia-Sue? That was how you found out about that?"

"That was how we found out about almost everything which helped us to win."

"But he was still only a juvenile when that beating happened, wasn't he?"

"I know what you mean: sealed records. But Patricia-Sue had a way about her. She could convince anyone to tell her anything. For example, Hitchings acted like he was such a victim, but she discovered, from one of the boys I guess, that he wasn't always so unwilling. Sometimes, he initiated sex. It was something he wanted to do."

"You're saying this child asked for sex? And that made it all right for the adults, priests to do it?" Harrison felt his anger rising and warned himself to keep control. He wouldn't get another word if he exploded on this asshole.

"I'm saying, without violating attorney client privilege, there was enough there that the case against the priests was dismissed. I'm saying the boy was conflicted and confused, and who knows if he even made the whole thing up?"

"If he was initiating sex then that means it was taking place. So he was telling the truth?"

"Truth?" Chambers spat out derisively. "What the hell is that? Deciding on the truth is not my job. Again, you read the case. Some other boys did get on the stand. You saw their testimony. It was in favor of our clients."

"Young boys who were afraid and young men who were too embarrassed or paid too much to speak up," Harrison said. "That doesn't mean it didn't happen."

"Well, there were many, many other boys at that institution over the years. If all of these things happened, where were the others to testify? I think you'll find they were missing. I don't have to defend myself for giving my clients a good defense. That is my job. If the other side lost, it's because they didn't give their clients a good enough defense. They didn't do their job as well as I did mine."

Before Harrison could stop himself, he said, "You really don't have a conscience, do you?"

"Agent, I'm not sure it's your job to judge me. It certainly isn't part of mine to judge my clients. And I'll tell you this: Michael Hitchings lost that case, but considering his background, considering everything, he did okay."

"It seems like you feel he somehow had a good result or found something positive out of this?" Harrison asked, genuinely confused.

"He left that place with an excellent education, a trade, and a prodigious knowledge of Christianity and the Bible. Some people might think that was a good thing. If you think I'm shameless about winning, well yes, I'm a person who's proud to do the job he's supposed to do and unashamed of doing it well. I'm probably like you in that regard, correct?"

Harrison drew a deep breath, ready to blast the soulless jerk, but instead he said, "Thank you for your help, sir. The Bureau deeply appreciates it." He knew Chambers could probably hear the sarcasm dripping from each word, but he didn't care.

"Of course, Agent. Any time," the man said. And Harrison could have sworn he heard him chuckle.

Chapter 25

FBI Office – Los Angeles

"What's going on?" Stanton asked as Harrison rushed into the Boss' office.

"Sir, I've just been on the phone with Patrick Chambers, head of the law firm that represented the priests in the Hitchings case. He's confirmed the First Lady worked there some years ago as an investigator."

"What? Pat Mitchell? Why haven't we heard this before?"

"Believe it or not, he didn't recognize her at first, and later, he wasn't allowed to reveal the information because of pressure from the White House."

"You mean somebody on the President's staff?" Stanton's doubt showed on his face.

"No. Actually it was the First Lady's office, and maybe Mitchell didn't even know. But get this—the Hitchings case was one of the last she worked on for them, and Chambers believed the information she was able to discover made the difference between winning and losing the case. When we talked to George Franks, he described an overweight woman they nicknamed the Sacred Cow who would come in the courtroom and bring information which damaged their case."

"Overweight? Cow? But Pat Mitchell—"

"Look." Harrison put the picture on Stanton's desk and pointed her out. Stanton squinted and shook his head.

"You continually amaze me, Harrison. I never would have recognized her. Still can't."

"I know, sir. But she didn't only change her appearance. She was using her birth name back then. Patricia-Sue Alison Lee. She dropped everything but Pat Lee and later married Mitchell."

And suddenly, when Harrison heard himself say her name out loud, the pieces of the puzzle he had been trying to solve stopped swirling and snapped into place.

"That would be a pretty long name," Stanton said drily. "So you're thinking maybe Hitchings knew this and blamed her? Like . . . I don't know, she's the highest profile representative of the church and the government, the two organizations that he couldn't beat? A good reason I suppose, but, Harrison, don't you think that's a little . . ." he finally stopped. Harrison was frozen in place, his eyes darting about like he was seeing a waking dream.

"Harrison, are you with me? Harrison!"

"That's what he meant! That's what Franks and Hitchings were taunting us with. It's been right in front of us, staring at us all the time. That's the answer."

"The answer to what? What are you talking about? Harrison!!" Stanton barked.

"Her name. Don't you see?" Harrison grabbed a notepad and pen from the desk, quickly wrote on it, and held it up for Stanton to see. "Her name after she married became Patricia-Sue Alison Lee Mitchell making her initials P-S-A-L-M. Psalm. She's Psalm. She is PSALM. It was never about the Bible or religion or the President. Those were merely decoys to get us to look the other way. He was trying to goad us and make us look like idiots, like the Zodiac or Jack the Ripper would do. It was her. It was always about her. Michael Hitchings wants to murder the First Lady."

They stared at each other as Stanton took the information in. He shook his head. For a moment, Harrison was afraid he still wouldn't believe it.

"Unbelievable," Stanton said, "And crazy. But I think you're absolutely right." He hit the intercom button on his phone and said, "Laurie, get me Secret Service Agent Nathan Chen. Tell him I know how late it is, and I know what I'm asking, but I have to speak with both the President and the First Lady right away. He'll need to be there too. Tell him it will impact on the ride tomorrow. He has to get them up."

He leaned back and looked up at Harrison. "You better be right about this, my friend. Or we're both about to start very long vacations."

* * *

Harrison paced most of the ten or so minutes they had to wait. The moment his phone rang, Stanton snatched it up. "Okay, put him through," he said, hitting the speaker button. "Nathan, you're on speaker, and Agent Harrison Carter is with me."

"Phil, I woke them up only because it's you, but it better be as important as you say. I'm outside their suite now, and I'll wait a bit and give you just enough time to decide if you want me to tell them go back to bed, false alarm, or if I should continue."

"I wish we were wrong, Nathan. Go ahead, I'll explain when you're all together."

After a moment, they heard a light tap on a door which was opened immediately.

"Sir, Ma'am," Chen said, "I have Assistant Director Philip Stanton and Special Agent Harrison Carter, both FBI, on speaker."

"Phil, I can only imagine how grave this must be, so please, go ahead," the President said.

"Thank you, Mr. President, Mrs. Mitchell. I'm sorry for the hour, but I'll get right to it. As you probably know, we've been looking into several murders in the country that seem to be connected to one killer, possibly trying to replicate other famous murders. One fact we've not shared with the public, though apparently it leaked to some people online, was that the killer left a verse from the Book of Psalms at every crime scene. We knew it was a test or code, and we've been searching for answers, and now we have one. I'll let Agent Carter fill you in with what he discovered." He beckoned to Harrison who stepped closer.

"President Mitchell, Ma'am . . ." he stopped and looked at Stanton. He was talking to the President of the United States after disturbing his and his wife's sleep. What if he was wrong? What if he was about to humiliate himself and the Bureau in front of the most important man on Earth? He could only imagine what his father would have to say about it. He felt his palms grow moist.

"Agent Carter, we're waiting," the President said. "Whatever it is, if it's this important, we need to know sooner rather than later."

"Go ahead, Harrison," Stanton whispered. He held up the pad that Harrison had written on and tapped it. "You're right."

Harrison took a deep breath and continued, shakily. "Sorry, sir. The individual we're hunting for was in a Catholic orphanage as a child and says he was molested by the priests there. He tried to sue them when he was older, but he lost the case. I . . . we, that is, discovered through our investigations that the First Lady used to work at the law firm which defended the priests and the church. They're called Chambers, Barnes,

Shepherd. I spoke with Patrick Chambers earlier, and it seems, well, from what he told me, her work as an investigator helped them to win the case. We think he shifted all his anger onto her once she became so high profile. His name is Michael Hitchings, and we think his revenge will be trying to assassinate the First Lady."

"Oh my God!" they heard Pat Mitchell exclaim.

"Uh . . ." was all the President could manage. They could tell he had turned away from the phone. "Pat? What is this? Law firm? Defending molesters? What the hell are they talking about? You know this guy, this Hitchings?"

They could hear the tension in her shaky voice. "He . . . yes. Well, I don't know him, but I know who he is. Or was. I did work for the law firm they're talking about."

The President's voice became louder, but now there was a different, harder note in it.

"Why do you think he's after my wife? She wasn't the only one working there, obviously. Why her?"

"Well, those Psalms, sir," Harrison continued. "As Director Stanton said, we knew they were a code. When we spoke with Chambers and learned Mrs. Mitchell's maiden name, I—"

"Which is?" the President said coldly.

There was complete silence. Harrison and Stanton stared at the phone and each other. They could almost hear the tension on the other side. Finally, Harrison pointed at himself and mouthed *Me?* Stanton nodded and waved his hand in a rapid circle to get Harrison to hurry and fill the silence.

"That's uh, Patricia-Sue Alison Lee, sir. So once you two were married and the Mitchell was added, her initials spelled out PSALM.

We think he was teasing us with the religious aspect, and she was the answer to the cipher all along."

"Mr. President and Agent Chen," Stanton said, "We're reasonably sure Hitchings is already in Dallas. He probably has a plan of some kind in place. He may not be working alone. As you can see, for your own safety and that of the First Lady, the drive through Dallas should probably be canceled. We're coming there now, and we'll of course have local law enforcement helping, and I know Chen will get the Secret Service on it, but we don't know where he is. I'm not trying to make him seem like some kind of mastermind, but this man is unbalanced and focused, and we already know he's a multiple murderer. I'm sure Chen will have more to say on it, but sir, we don't want a repeat of what happened all those years ago. I have to appeal to you to cancel."

He stopped, and the two looked at each other once again. Stanton shrugged, and they both waited.

Finally, the President said brusquely, "Thank you both for your time and work. We'll get back to you later." He clicked off the call before they had time to respond.

"He didn't know. Any of it. Not even her name before," Harrison said, wondering if what came next would be his fault.

"No," Stanton said, staring at the phone, "He didn't."

"So, what do we do now?" Harrison asked.

"Not much else we can do," Stanton replied. "We wait."

Chapter 26

Night – Dallas, Texas

The President sat staring at his wife as if she were an exhibit in a museum. And she may as well have been. All he could hear in his head were the words, *I thought I knew her. I thought I knew my wife. I thought I could trust her. I thought I knew her.* He hated the way she was standing before him, her arms folded protectively across her body, her head down like a prisoner expecting torture.

"You worked for a law firm?"

"Yes," she whispered.

"As what? A lawyer or clerk or . . . what?"

"No. I was an investigator. At least, that's how they used me. And it's true, I helped them to win that case."

"And your first name. It's Patricia hyphen Sue? Or is the Sue a middle name, or maybe it's all one long name. So many possibilities."

She didn't move.

Chen, stone-faced, had backed up to the wall, but finally, pointing toward the door he said softly, "Sir, maybe I should—"

"You stay right there, Nathan. You know you have to be close to me when there are strangers around." Chen moved his focus to the floor and became part of the wallpaper.

"Speaking of," the President said sarcastically, as he stood up and thrust out his hand for her to shake. "How do you do, I'm Jameson Mitchell. Apparently, we haven't met. But please, fill me in. I love a good origin story. You are?"

She sobbed, "I couldn't tell you. No, I could have. I didn't want to. A man like you?

You wouldn't have spit on me if you'd known. I helped them. Those child rapists. The information I gathered won the case for them. All those children. All those little children. I can't . . ." She stopped talking as if someone were choking her.

He didn't say a word. When she finally raised her head, he knew his eyes were drilling into her. He felt like he could read her thoughts; he was looking for the truth but finding nothing but lies.

"So am I supposed to feel sympathy for you now? You made a mistake. We all make mistakes, but you couldn't tell me? You had to make up a whole phony past because you did one wrong thing? And if you were doing your job, if that's all it was, it wasn't wrong, even if it was immoral. It's the lies: I can't wrap my head around the lies. I don't know who you are, what's true. Are you even an orphan? Is that a lie too?"

"So now, whatever I say, you're going to think I'm a liar. Good for Michael. He's getting his revenge already. I . . . I wasn't an orphan. Not exactly, but I felt like one. I was alone. All the time."

"You weren't an orphan, but you 'felt like' an orphan? Pat, if that's really your name, what the hell does that mean? Who are you?"

"I'll tell you who I am!" she yelled as if he were in another room. "I'm a pedophile by proxy. I'm a hypocritical lowlife who helped to victimize survivors like me. I knew how it felt to be young and to be raped. I knew how it felt to have no one listen to me. I knew what it meant to have your whole life changed because of what your rapists did to you. I was a little overweight as a child, but I was still confident and thought pretty well of myself. But after . . . I knew no one would believe the most popular boy in school would rape the fat girl. And no one did. And it wasn't just him. There were . . . Doesn't matter. My mother didn't protect me. She said I brought it on myself. I was alone. As alone as any real orphan. And hey, it wasn't all bad. In a way, it helped me because I buried myself in my books. I studied and studied and barely slept and took care of myself while my mother was in the streets and gained more weight and had no friends and studied. I took every course I could pack in, so I wouldn't have to think. I aced everything in college, offered a fellowship to Harvard Law." She laughed slightly at the confused look on his face.

"You see, you wouldn't know me anywhere. And you wouldn't love me if I were fat," she spat out bitterly. "Yes, I was there when you were there, the shining star who everybody knew and loved. I was the invisible fat girl making high grades and working to stay under the radar. You think you loved me at first sight? You didn't even notice me at first sight. You never met Patricia-Sue, you never even knew she ever existed."

He backed up and sat on the corner of his desk, still looking at her. "Nathan, go ahead. You can wait outside."

Chen, clearly relieved, stepped briskly to the door.

"Oh, and Nathan," the agent stopped with his hand on the doorknob, "We're going tomorrow. That son of a bitch isn't stopping us."

Chen started to speak, but the President held up a hand, cutting him off. The agent shifted from foot to foot for a moment, nodded helplessly before closing the door softly behind him. Pat walked to the darkened window and stood with her back to him. He couldn't tell if she was seeing anything. She probably wasn't really focused on Dallas at night.

"What happened after the case? How did you end up in Africa?"

"It was horrible. Dark and ugly," she said, her back still to him. "Unarguably the worst days of my life."

She wiped her face with her hand, and he grabbed some tissue from a box on the table and walked to her.

"I had felt like nothing when I was being abused, but after I helped those priests, I felt like less than nothing—a filthy, disgusting piece of garbage. They had a case, they did, and everybody knew it, including those smirking, predator priests." He pressed the tissues into her hand, and she glanced up at him gratefully.

"I admit it; I chose my job and my possible future in the firm over decency and righteous action. And there was still a bit of 'who would believe the fat girl?' operating. I felt like I couldn't do anything. If I had been a stronger person, a better person, I would have said to hell with the consequences and spoken out. But I couldn't and didn't. I decided I would kill her, the low life who didn't act, and create a new woman, a strong, and heroic one who knew how to help people. To stand up for them. So I kept enough of the old to remind me and adopted enough new to start over again. I ended up working in South Africa. It wasn't really work; it was penance that I was happy to do. But I'll never, ever get over the guilt. In ten lifetimes I won't be able to make up for it."

She turned to him, her face a wretched picture of guilty sorrow and said wryly, "Forgive me Father, for I have sinned" before burying her face in her hands and crying like she would never stop. He hesitated only a moment before taking her in his arms.

Chapter 27

FBI Office – Los Angeles

The look on the boss' face when he came out of his office said he was not happy with what he had to say next. "I've heard from the President in Dallas, and they're going ahead with the drive." He held up a hand to quiet the disbelieving comments, "I know, I know," he continued. "They want us there as soon as possible. I'll be taking part of the team. Carter and Jennings, of course, and I'll let you know who else. We'll get into specifics on the plane as we hear from Dallas. Othello, I want you here to keep everybody connected and to process any new leads or research we may get. This is it people—whatever he's going to try, it's going to happen tomorrow."

Harrison couldn't believe what he was about to say, but he had to say it. It had only been an hour or so since the call to the President, but as soon as it was over, he started having doubts. What was Michael's real goal, his actual intent? If he just wanted to kill Pat Mitchell, there were a lot of easier, less protected occasions than the insane circus of the Dallas drive. Something as simple as an accident in the predicted massive traffic jam could screw up his whole plan.

And with Michael, would it be that simple? If they'd figured it out sooner, or if the drive was cancelled, what then? He had been so meticulous with the other reenacted murders, it didn't make sense for him to believe he could somehow get into the book depository or even close to it. He'd be dead or in custody before he could think about it twice. Harrison couldn't help but feel that Michael would have prepared for that possibility. There had to be something else, something more. Something not in Dallas.

Harrison dropped his bomb. "Sir, I . . . I don't think I should go." He saw Jennings' head snap around so fast, he was probably whiplashed.

"You wha' . . . excuse me?" Stanton said.

"I know everything seems to point to it," Harrison said, "But I'm not sure he's there. I'd prefer to stay here and look at some other possibilities."

"Other possibilities? Harrison, you're the one who discovered the target was the First Lady. You and I both think you're right. She's in Dallas. They're going to drive through town in an open vehicle, practically begging for an assassination attempt. How can you have any doubts now?"

"Sir, I can't explain it. Something's not right. This was too easy. Hitchings knows how much security there'll be in Dallas. He knows we're hunting for him. His face is all over the news. The chances of success are almost zero if he's trying to get to the First Lady. He's too smart and too invested to risk failure. And Franks, why would he sell out his best friend, his brother, with such a clear hint? I feel like there's some kind of distraction or sleight-of-hand going on."

"You can't explain, you feel, he's too smart. Harrison," he ran his hand through his hair in exasperation, "maybe it's the near loss of your partner, not to mention Sharon Daniels, but your judgment has been affected. This guy is getting into your head." He turned away from Harrison and spoke brusquely. "Now everyone, I'll see you at LAX shortly, and I expect you to be ready and focused for Dallas." He shot a look at Harrison. "We're going to finish this thing."

As everyone else dispersed, Harrison stood still a moment, awash with indecision. "Harrison?" He could hear the warning in the director's voice, but he didn't know what else to do.

"Boss, I really don't think I should—"

"Stop." Stanton held up a hand. "If you're thinking about refusing a direct order, especially at a time and in a situation like this, don't do it. Now, we're wheels up for Dallas in ninety. Be there or not, but if you're not, you and I are going to have a talk when we get back, and you're not going to like it. Your decision."

He turned abruptly and walked away, and Harrison couldn't help but feel his career was disappearing right along with him.

* * *

Harrison was expecting the shocked look on Othello's face when he walked back in to headquarters over an hour later. He had left to grab a bag on his way to the airport, and then he'd sat in his car for a while. But he knew what he had to do.

"You didn't go," Othello whispered, shocked.

"I know. But I'm right. I'm not sure what's happening, but Hitchings is playing us. He knows exactly what we'll do, and he's making a countermove."

"But why do you believe that?" Othello asked.

Harrison shrugged and said aloud what he'd been thinking. "It's what I would do."

Othello still didn't look convinced.

"I know it sounds as crazy as a ride through Dallas in an open top car with a madman stalking you," Harrison said, "But it's something else. We're looking for something more, something to make him look like he's won after all: the ultimate revenge."

"But what is that?" Othello asked.

"I don't know!" Harrison tried to keep the frustration out of his voice. "We're going to look, and you're going to help me find it, if you're willing. This monster has tried to murder Kate. He's taken Jeanne and . . ." he had to stop.

"And Sharon Daniels," Othello finished for him.

"So are you ready?"

Instead of answering, Othello hung his head and stood there like a preacher's kid who had just stolen from the collection plate. Harrison didn't understand what was going on.

"Othello?" he said impatiently. "I need your help. Are you conflicted because I didn't go to Dallas? You know you aren't going to be blamed. This isn't going to reflect on you or your career in any way. You're just—"

Othello started shaking his head slowly, then he shook it so hard, Harrison expected some of that shock of wild hair to fly off his head.

"What is—" Harrison began.

"It was me," Othello said, looking like he was near tears.

"It? What?"

"The leak. The way MayHem knew things. The person I was supposed to be searching for in her followers. It was me."

Harrison felt like the man had seriously announced he was ready to fly back to his home planet. "What? How do you even know MayHem?"

"She's . . . my girlfriend. Well, she was."

Harrison sat down, completely bewildered. *This kid? No fucking way.*

"Your girlfriend? The one you've been talking about. But . . . but when do you see her? You've been going back and forth to San Francisco?"

"No I . . . well, we . . ." He hung his head, his face a mottled purple, and whispered,

"We never actually met."

"What? Speak up. Did you say you haven't met her?" Othello nodded. "But how?" Othello shrugged, and Harrison pulled a chair in front of him and said gently, "Here, sit down." Othello sat with his forearms on his thighs, nervously picking at his nails.

"Tell me," Harrison said.

Othello drew a breath like he was going to dive into an icy lake and said, "We met online, on her site. We kind of had this connection. She wanted to talk, well, we both did, which led to Skype and FaceTime."

"And what did you talk about?"

"Anything . . . everything."

"The team? The case?"

Othello nodded, eyes closed. "But it wasn't like . . . It's hard to explain. She didn't try to get information or anything, it was, you know, she'd ask how my day went, and I'd ask about hers, and we . . . you know, the way two people talk when they . . . "

"Love each other?" Harrison asked.

"I did," Othello confessed. "Actually, I still do. She said she loved me too. We were going to be together. She was talking about moving here and . . . I'm sorry. I'm so sorry! I don't know how I could have been so stupid!"

"It's okay. Remember, I've met her. In person. Did she ask for team names? Personal info?"

"Of course not! I wouldn't tell anybody stuff like that."

Oh, now he's offended, Harrison thought, grimly amused.

"But I guess whatever I said, she was passing it on to Hitchings," Othello said bitterly.

"Maybe he researched the rest on his own, I don't know."

He stood up resolutely. "I guess this is it. I'm done here."

"What?"

"Well, what I did, the information. He used it to get to Mrs. Daniels. I . . . I helped him to . . . do what he did. It's my fault."

"You can't know that," Harrison said. "Someone like Michael, he probably had information on people here before he ever committed the first murder. He's been planning this for a long time."

"Doesn't matter," Othello said. "I still feel like I helped him. I have to pay for what I did, for being such a stupid jerk."

"I'll tell you how you're going to pay." Harrison stood and gestured to him. "You're going to help me find this guy. He's not in Dallas, I know it. There's something else going on, and we're going to find out what it is. You are going to help me bring him down, and then the account will be paid in full. Let's go."

Chapter 28

FBI Office – Los Angeles

Harrison and Othello had been working steadily for a few hours, painstakingly going back over old territory.

"We have to try and find what his next target will be, which murder he's going to try," Harrison said.

"But, well don't get mad," Othello said, "But why couldn't it be going after Pat Mitchell? I mean, suppose he has an idea to do it some other way, not the historic Kennedy assassination method?"

Harrison shook his head vigorously. "No. No. I kept thinking about that murder shrine he had in the cellar. The one big obvious one that was missing was JFK. No. He wants us out of town, away from what he has in mind. It's not Dallas."

"But suppose it isn't here either? Then you . . ." he stopped himself.

"I know," Harrison replied. "Then I'm screwed. There's no reason why it automatically would be here, but he had that hotel room here, he did two murders here, and he's made it his business to directly taunt our team. What better way to humiliate us than to send us racing south to Dallas and to do a crime right here in our backyard?" He sighed and looked at Othello's worried frown. "But full disclosure—I don't know. He could be across the country. I know we have to keep looking."

Othello nodded. "Well," he said, "you've gone through the court testimony again, we've looked at the priests and the other witnesses, the prosecution and defense. What do you want me to—" He was cut off by a prodigious yawn.

Harrison could see the kid was drooping from exhaustion.

"Next, put all the Psalms that he left behind on the screen for me. I want you to take a break," Harrison said. "No," he stopped Othello's protests. "Grab some coffee and a sandwich or something. Isn't it close to breakfast time? This isn't going to happen right this minute. I'm going to keep going Sherlock Holmes style. We'll keep eliminating possibilities, and what we're left with will be the answer."

"Ok," Othello responded gratefully. "I had a couple of ideas. I might help to locate him, but it'll take a little while. Maybe we'll have something by the time I get back."

Harrison sat and stared at the Psalms for a while, trying to think of some new way of looking at them. He knew, of course, on the surface, each seemed to be connected to the relevant crime scene, like the bridesmaids and king with Sharon's murder. But beyond that? Under it?

Like trying to work a Rubik's Cube, he began twisting and turning ideas in his mind; he could almost hear the cubes clicking. He came up with anagram after anagram, numerical equations using their chapter and verse numbers, even looked at verses backward. He knew the team must be set up and already on it in Dallas. He was about to try yet another idea when his phone rang.

Through his bleary, sleep-deprived eyes, he stared at the display, blinked, and stared again; why would Skip Jennings be calling him? Unless . . .

He clicked on the call then realized it was a video chat request, which he accepted.

"Jennings," he said, trying to sound professional and neutral. The new Skip was just as professional and spoke without a trace of sarcasm.

"Harrison (*Harrison??*), it looks like you may have missed on this one. When we arrived, the local office showed us a list of all the guests; one of them is a woman named Christine Sahay. She checked in a few days ago. We're in her room now. It took no time at all to figure out that that name was just a scrambled version of—"

"Christian Hayes," Harrison said along with him, and felt his stomach turn.

"Yeah, right," Jennings said, clearly impressed. "They're going over surveillance video now to see if they can spot who actually checked in under that name, but it could take a while. Anyhow, well, take a look." He panned his phone slowly around the hotel room. It looked like four obsessively neat maids had just left. And most important, the closet contained men's clothing, slacks, and shirts, and the spaces between each hanger were identical.

"What about the mirror?" Harrison asked.

"Covered," Skip said. "And Harrison, there's this." He turned his camera toward one of the dresser drawers which was open. A bizarre-looking, fuzzy, doll figure was in there. It looked like fistfuls of cut hair and shredded string had been woven and braided into a stick figure—with wild, unkempt hair—that was standing on a hair cloud.

It was a Manson style "blame doll." He knew without looking too closely that some of the color was from baby Malia's pink tee fabric and some was from Jeanne's favorite shirt. He didn't want to think about the hair.

"These were underneath," Skip said. It was Kate's credit card, and beside it was a note, "We're not in Wonderland anymore, Alice." An inside Manson "joke" from Michael.

Othello walked back in, and Harrison beckoned to him and let him look over his shoulder at the screen. Harrison heard a quiet "Uh oh."

"Looks like our boy is here in Dallas," Skip said. He turned the lens toward himself.

"The boss wanted me to show you. We think it's Hitchings. But what do you think? And by the way, the President asked where you were."

Harrison felt time stop for a heartbeat. The President. That doll. *If he had this wrong!* "It looks like it could be his room, and he may have been there. But no," Harrison said. "I don't think he's in Dallas."

Skip paused a moment, "Okay, buddy. Your call. We're going to keep looking. I hope you're right, and he's not really going after the President or the First Lady." *Buddy??* To Harrison's amazement, he sounded like he really meant it.

"Uh . . . yeah. You guys keep working there. We might have a lead here. Either way, the team will find him."

Skip nodded and hung up.

They stared at each other, and he watched the familiar blush happen. He knew Othello was probably thinking he was completely wrong, but instead of saying so, he drew a deep breath and said, "Ok. So what's next?"

"I've been trying to work with the Psalms, to see what other clues they may hold, if any, but no luck yet. Would you . . . ?" He wasn't even sure what he wanted to try next. "I guess, list them in order of how we think the crimes happened."

Othello rearranged them on the screen, and they both looked at them.

Psalm 3:1

I have so many enemies, Lord, so many who turn against me!

Psalm 54:6

I will gladly offer you a sacrifice, O Lord; I will give you thanks because you are good.

Psalm 10:12

O Lord, punish those wicked men! Remember those who are suffering!

Psalm 46:9

He stops wars all over the world; he breaks bows, destroys spears and sets shields on fire.

Psalm 45:14

In her colorful gown she is led to the king, followed by her bridesmaids, and they also are brought to him.

Psalm 69:25

May their camps be left deserted; may no one be left alive in their tents.

Harrison tried to ignore the ache in his back and his stinging eyes.

"Maybe I'm making it too complicated. Is the boss right? Am I giving him too much credit? Could be I'm looking for Rube Goldberg when it's actually Mastermind for Kids."

"Oh, Mastermind, I used to love that game," Othello said enthusiastically. "You're right, sometimes, simpler is better. My favorite kinds of puzzles and brain teasers are always the ones that look much harder than they really are. Then you kind of slap yourself upside the head when you get the answer."

"Simpler," Harrison said, looking back to the screen. "Yeah. Wouldn't that be . . ."

He stood stock still, staring at the board. "No fucking way. Simple as first verse, first word; second verse, second word; third—"

"Oh my God!" Othello said. "It does! It makes a sentence!"

He raced to his computer, highlighted the words in question, and put the resulting sentence on the screen under the Psalms.

"I – will – punish – all – she – deserted."

Harrison frowned. "It's a sentence, but what does it mean? Is 'she' Pat Mitchell? Or 'she' could even be the church. Or maybe it's another clue to lead to yet another mystery."

"Maybe it—" Othello began, when a *ding ding* sounded from his computer. He rushed over, hit his cursor, and brought a map up on his screen. "Did it work?" he asked himself hopefully as he scanned the screen. "It worked! Holy shit, it worked!! Oh, I mean sorry sir. I found something." he said.

"It's ok. What did you find?" Harrison hurried over.

"It's from his phone, at least I think so."

"What? I thought we couldn't track his phone because it was a burner. And wasn't he getting rid of it?"

"We couldn't find out his exact location, but I was able to find the numbers he called. One of them was Franks' of course, you guys had that one. Now Franks only called him on the burner a couple of times, but after Michael ditched that one, a new number appeared on Franks' call list, the only number he called. It had to be Hitchings, right?"

"So I tracked that one: it's still being used. In the San Francisco area and right here in LA yesterday and today. And guess what? There's a number he called twice, and the last one was only a few hours ago. So now I'm . . . Holy shit, look at the zip code! 90024!"

"So he's somewhere right around here? He could be in the building."

Othello was furiously typing. "No, no wait. I'm finding an address for the number he called. Got it! It's not far from here. Look."

He put his cursor on a spot on the map. "Ohmygod, it's on UCLA's campus."

"Seven fifteen Hilgard! Let's see a visual."

The street view on the university campus showed a row of beautiful two-story houses of various muted colors with pristine paint and immaculate decorative hedges and lawns. Each had two or three Greek letters prominently displayed on the front of the house. Seven fifteen was Chi Chi Tau.

"Sorority row," Harrison said as a dread feeling came over him.

"Why would he—" Othello began.

"The verse 'I will destroy all . . .' What if—Nononono!"

"What? What?" Othello asked, panicked.

"Bundy, has to be Ted Bundy." Harrison grabbed his keys and sprinted for the elevator.

"Call the sorority and tell them to get everybody out immediately." He screamed to Othello just as the elevator doors closed.

Chapter 29

Nov. 22nd – Dallas, Texas

Finally, it was happening, he had been planning this day in his mind for years. This was the day that would say to his country and the world: *We're all one again. We actually are the United States. We may disagree on some things, but we are in love with our principles, our ideals, and our place in the world. We're going nowhere from here but to the stars.*

"You're sure about this?" Pat had asked just before their helicopter landed at Love Field. "Absolutely," he said. And he meant it. They needed it: the country needed a bold, mad, purely symbolic moment of positivity that they could hold on to. The hard work wasn't ever going away, but today, for this one day, they were going to pause and breathe and smile and say *we're ok.*

Just like the Kennedys had so many years before, they began to move. He was aware that his heart was racing about ten times as fast as their convoy was traveling. He looked over at Pat, and they each widened their eyes a little and took a deep breath as if they'd rehearsed it. They both laughed, and she took his hand and kissed it. Without looking at him she again said, "I'm sorry. Thank you." He felt her squeeze his hand once then hold it tight. She meant *It's going to be okay.* "Yeah," he whispered to her. "But now it's my turn to make sure you don't feel like I've put you in danger out of anger or childish pique."

"We both know you were going to do this no matter what," she said. "And you have a right to be angry. I should have trusted you with the truth. We may be in danger, but it's okay; I'm with my hero."

They left Love Field and drove the few blocks down Mockingbird Lane. *So far, so good*, he thought and turned and looked back at the motorcade behind him, giving a thumbs up to any of them who could see him.

The Veep was safe at home, of course (he grinned thinking how relieved Gordon looked when he told him about his decision), but Jameson was truly shocked at how many Texas dignitaries were eager to take part. They actually had a few more cars than the original motorcade.

They made a right and began the longer drive down Lemmon Avenue. That's where the crowds started.

"Here we go," Jameson said.

"They do love you," Pat said when one group of excited onlookers broke into spontaneous clapping that turned into a wave of applause as they passed.

"Oh no, they like me, but they love you, Mom."

"Will they love me when they find out who I really am?"

"They know who you really are. They'll forgive you," he said.

As an homage to but not a direct copy of Jackie O's famous pink suit, Pat had decided to wear a rose outfit that somehow made her look even more beautiful to him. He reached over and took her hand. "It's going to be okay. You'll see."

"You good up there, Nathan?" he called teasingly.

"Fine, Sir, thank you. Better later," Chen replied without taking his eyes off the crowd.

They had a lot to talk about, but like his faith in the country, nothing was going to shake his faith in his wife. He understood her even better now, and they were going to be stronger than ever.

As he waved and Pat threw kisses, he read signs and searched the crowd for signs of protest, but he didn't see any. Well, not yet anyway. It was going to be a very good day.

* * *

Almost overnight, it seemed, Make America Greater tee shirts in a variety of colors had appeared, and they were all over today. There were different versions: one group had a graphic of a mountain or pyramid with *M(aturity)* at the bottom left, the *A(gape)* at the top and G(reatness) at the bottom right. His favorite said *M.A.G.nificent*.

Right on Turtle Creek Boulevard, Cedar Springs Road, North Harwood: the few miles zipped by.

They made a right on Main Street, and Jameson knew they were close. A few blocks through shops and cafes and a little college. The JFK Memorial Plaza and right after that, on the corner to their left, was the Old Red Museum building. For one moment, he felt like the beautiful old building with its turrets and many windows was warning him, *Go back. Go back!*

It was time.

They made the right onto Houston Street, and he felt a sudden wave of tension from Nathan and the agent who was driving. It was all there in front of them: the iconic vision had haunted and inspired him for so much of his life. They were at Dealey Plaza, a block from the infamous schoolbook depository turned museum memorial where Lee Harvey Oswald had shot from a sixth-floor window. "There it is," Pat whispered, as if the building could hear her. The big red brick edifice which he had seen so many times looked different today. It didn't feel dangerous or even intimidating. It was, for him, a beacon of hope and a symbol of second chances, of new beginnings. They made the left turn that had preceded the last moments of JFK's life, and Jameson realized Pat's nails were digging into his palm. When they cleared the trees, standing since the time of Kennedy's assassination, there were a few moments of relative quiet because today there was no one on the grassy knoll in front of the depository but police officers and Secret Service. They cruised past the grassy knoll, and he felt the breath of history waft over him. Goose pimples rose on his arms, but it was excitement, not fear, that he was reacting to. It was going to be fine.

"It's okay, honey. We're okay. It's only a ride through a beautiful park."

She nodded, her focus on the simple white colonnade atop the low green hill where Abraham Zapruder had stood when he caught film of Kennedy's assassination.

It all went by in a haze, and almost before he'd realized it, they were past the assassination site: past the book depository and Dealey Plaza and under the railroad overpass. The other side was like bursting out of a wormhole to another world.

People were everywhere, as far as he could see. It appeared to him like one mass of cheering, waving, chanting, sign-carrying humanity.

The crowd roared and waved and applauded hysterically. Pat's death grip on his hand relaxed some.

There were probably many detractors in the crowd, but he didn't see any—not today. He could feel the love and support. They all knew they'd made it out of the dark. They were cheering like he'd won the Super Bowl, the World Series, and about five Olympic gold medals all at once. They understood.

He closed his eyes for a moment. If he'd willed this into reality, maybe he could will some other dreams into being: world peace, 2% unemployment, four more years in office . . . he laughed foolishly, and Pat said, "What?"

"Nothing. Just, this is amazing!" The crowd started a chant, and they joined right in, "M.A.G! You and Me! M. A. G! You and Me!"

Pat, laughing, pointed to her right and said, "Look."

A group of men of various ages and sizes, wearing Pride Flag tees adorned with glitter MAG's and brightly colored wigs, were standing together in a sparkling throng.

The two of them laughed and waved. Jameson knew he shouldn't, but he couldn't help himself: he stood up in the car and began waving with both hands.

When they saw they'd captured the First Couple's attention, the guys jumped up and down, excitedly waving back. A chant started "MAG!! MAG!!" with some countering "Mom! Mom!"

"Jameson! Sit down!" Pat yelled.

"Sir! Sir, you have to sit down!" Chen said sternly.

"Fine," Jameson said like a petulant child. He grinned at his own joke as he took his seat. "You're right. I'm sorry. Not trying to make your job harder, Nathan."

"Thank you, sir," Nathan said.

"As good as you hoped?" Pat asked.

"Better," he responded.

The rainbow crew started what looked like a dance challenge or maybe a choreographed routine and tossed glitter in the air. It came down on their heads like jeweled rain, shimmering in the sunlight. The crowd around them laughed and applauded and of course, began to shoot pictures and video.

Then one of them stopped laughing and stepped forward into the sparkling cloud.

"Uh oh, here comes the Solo," Jameson chuckled.

But he didn't dance.

In one swift move, the man whipped off his wig and threw it into the air, before snatching off his tee shirt. Under it was another tee: black, with huge white letters that said, "I AM MICHAEL HITCHINGS."

As a group, the rest of them did the same and stepped up beside the first man until there was a phalanx of a dozen men standing shoulder to shoulder, right arms pointed directly at their car.

"Oh my God!" he heard Pat say.

"Nathan—" he began, but Chen was already on the walkie, ordering the convoy to speed up.

In one unified movement, the men clasped their hands on their heads like prisoners of war, snapped to an about face, and turned their backs to the street standing shoulder to shoulder. The message revealed straight across all their tees read, "I will visit the iniquity of the fathers upon the children to the third and fourth generation."

"Get us out of here!" Nathan shouted, his gun drawn.

Jameson could see law enforcement had completely surrounded the group and had wrestled them to the ground with no visible signs of resistance.

But just as the driver was about to accelerate, Jameson called out, "No! Wait!!" He didn't know why, and he knew it was crazy, but somehow he felt they were not a threat. "We're not running. Stay the course."

Chen said, "Mr. President! We have to—"

"No!!" Jameson barked. "This is supposed to scare us, to make us think he's controlling things, but he's not. We'll keep going."

"Jameson," Pat yelled, "If all of them are working with him, there could be—"

"No!" was all he said.

The driver looked at Chen who shrugged helplessly and gave new orders. They continued the drive, if at a brisker pace.

Pat dabbed at her eyes, pasted a smile on her face, and began waving once again.

"Damn right," she said. "We'll keep going."

"That's my girl." Jameson kissed her, which brought roars from the crowd.

"I don't understand it. They weren't going to do anything but show that crazy ass message," he mused. "So what's the point? They'll be on the news, of course, but will anyone have a clue what it means?"

She squeezed his hand even harder, cleared her throat, and through her fake smile said, "Yes. Someone will."

"What? Who?"

"Jameson. My love. There's something else I have to tell you."

Chapter 30

Nov. 22nd – Los Angeles, CA

Straight off the elevator, Harrison sprinted to his car and zoomed out of the parking lot and onto Wilshire Boulevard. Like an out-of-control TV detective, he zipped in and out of traffic, ignored stop signs and a changing yellow light, and almost took out a pedestrian as he careened left and zoomed up Gayley, which curved around to the left of UCLA's campus.

The first right was Lindbrook which turned into Hilgard: only a couple of blocks now. His phone rang, and without checking, he hit the button and said, "Othello, news?"

"I couldn't get through to the house, their landline is out. I think LAPD is on the way, but you know they have this protocol about coordinating with campus police first. That may slow things down some. Are you close?"

"Yes, coming up on it now. Keep trying both of them. And no sirens."

Harrison was at the house and out of his car in two minutes. He hit the buzzer on the front door, then impatiently hit it again. "Come on. Come on!" he growled. He was afraid to bang on the door too loudly in case Hitchings was in there, but he didn't know what else to do. He hit the door once, but before he could knock again, it opened, and a twenty-something girl with a long blue and purple braid opened the door and leaned against the jamb. Another girl was right behind her. Both were holding beers.

"Well hello there, tall and serious," purple braid said. "I would have come faster if I'd known—"

"FBI, Miss. Is everything okay in there?"

"What?" she stared at his badge. "Yes. What's going on?"

"Did you say FBI?" the other girl, a smiling Latina with glasses who looked even younger, peered past her. "Welcome to the party FBI. Can I get you a beer?"

He stepped inside and glanced around. It was a large house, rooms with closed doors to the left and right that would be dining and living rooms in someone's home. A staircase, with a landing, was leading to the second floor. He could hear a reporter talking about the Dallas drive coming from a television somewhere.

"Girls, I need you both to focus. Names?"

Olivia was blue braid and the other, Frida. "Okay. Olivia and Frida. There's a potentially dangerous situation going on here. The police are on the way. We need to clear the house now. Where is everybody else?"

"Some upstairs, but mostly right there in the common room," Olivia pointed toward the door on his right.

"Is anyone here who doesn't live here?"

"No. Well we have some guys in there from our brother fraternity, but that's it."

"No one else has been here today? No strangers?"

"No! Well, a plumber, but—"

"We started having problems this morning," Frida said, "and he showed up in a few hours. I don't know who called maintenance."

"What did he look like?"

"Tall, really cute. Kinda like you. He had a limp, though."

"Did you see him leave?"

"No, I . . . I don't know. Maybe somebody else knows."

Harrison threw open the door to the common room and flashed his badge. There were about a dozen students in the room, some watching the Dallas drive or standing and talking.

"FBI. Listen up everybody. Please turn that off." Someone muted the TV, and he saw a guy shrug and grab a couple of beers. "There's a serious and dangerous situation developing here. I can't answer questions now, but I need you to quietly and quickly exit the building. The police are on the way. Olivia do you know how many people are upstairs?"

"Um," she looked around at the group, only some of whom were moving toward the door. "Well, Sophia, she's up there with her boyfriend, and Mrs. Sapp, our house mother, she's here somewhere, and uh—"

"Alison and Juliet," Frida finished off. "Everybody else is out. Do you want me—?"

"Alison? You said Alison?" He grabbed her arm. "What's her full name?"

"What? Ow! Let go of me! What are you—?"

"Palmer," Olivia said. "Her name's Alison Lee Palmer. What difference does it—?"

"Did anyone see the plumber leave?" Harrison demanded. There was head shaking and a chorus of "no's."

A screech from the second floor sent them running into the hall. They looked up to see a wild-eyed girl thundering down the stairs toward them. Harrison's weapon was in his hand immediately. She was shouting incoherently, "Ohmygod she's . . . Mrs.Sapp . . . somebody killed Mrs. Sapp . . . I think she's dead . . . her head is all . . . and a wrench or something . . . all bloody . . . they handcuffed her . . . and Ohmygod the plumber . . . the plumber has her, he has her!" She collapsed and Harrison broke her fall.

"What are you saying? Calm down. What are you saying?" Harrison shook her.

"She's saying the plumber has her, Harrison," a low, male voice called down from upstairs.

"The rest of you, out of here right now!" Harrison barked.

"Come on Juliet, I've got you," Olivia said and threw an arm around the girl, but Juliet sank to her knees, and one of the men scooped her up and carried her, as the remaining students hustled out the front door.

Harrison cautiously crept up a few steps.

"That you, Harrison?" Michael called out. "I know you want to meet Alison, Jr. don't you?"

There was a mirror at the top of the staircase, but Harrison still couldn't see them.

"Why do you keep calling me that?" a female voice demanded. "Let me go!"

"You'd think she knew, wouldn't you, Harrison? Such a little diva princess. With a soft diva princess throat."

"Ow!! Stop it," Alison screamed.

Harrison ran another few steps to the landing, but Michael's "Stop or she dies now!" arrested him in his tracks.

"Michael, don't hurt her," Harrison said, keeping his voice measured and calm. "You know we're here. You want to come out of this alive; I know you do. Let's find a way to make that happen."

A door to the left of the staircase burst open, and a shirtless, sandy haired man, who looked like a linebacker, charged out, followed by a slender girl, who must have been Sophia. She was pulling on a tee shirt over her underwear.

"Let her go!" the athlete yelled toward Michael. "Let her go motherfucker or I'll—"

"No! No, stop! Stay back!" Harrison yelled, but the man charged confidently toward Michael's location. Something flashed toward him, and Harrison heard a sickening "thuk" sound like pounding a meat cleaver into a side of beef.

Sophia screamed, "Hank!" and he stopped, looking incredulously down at the handle protruding from his bleeding abdomen. He took two more steps as he tried to stop the blood flow with one hand while tugging on the knife handle with the other. He gave Harrison a confused look and tried to say something but couldn't. Hank took another step and tumbled sideways down the staircase, landing at Harrison's feet.

He could hear Michael and Alison struggling, and then suddenly there was silence. He jumped over Hank's body, prepared to run the rest of the way, when Sophia yelled, "No, stop, stop, he has a gun!"

She whimpered, looking helplessly from her fallen boyfriend to where Michael was, gathered her courage and said, "Let her go. Please, let her go. Don't hurt her."

"You'd better go while you still can, miss," Michael said to her.

She looked from his direction to Harrison and Hank and finally crept to the top of the stairs and hurried down to her boyfriend. "Tell the cops to wait, don't come in yet," Harrison whispered. She nodded, kissed Hank, and ran down the stairs. Harrison took another step, staying as far to the left of the stairs as he could.

"Michael, is she okay?"

"Why would she not be okay, Harrison? Nothing wrong with a little wrestling and horseplay. Or at least that's what the priests used to say."

"Can I talk to her?"

"Afraid to say her name? Afraid it'll set me off and make me do something ugly?"

"I'm okay!" Alison called out.

"Shut up!" Michael yelled, accompanied by a loud "smack"!

"Ouch, you fucking pig! You have a gun, you don't have to hit me."

Harrison took one more step, and at the far-right edge of the mirror, he could finally see Alison and a man's arm around her neck. Her left hand and hair were covering her face where Michael's hand had probably just made contact, but she didn't seem to be crying. She took several deep breaths and slowly pushed her hair off her face and took her hand down. She raised her head proudly, her jaw set and a look of angry defiance in her eyes.

Even though he suspected, he gasped in shocked surprise. She could have been Pat Mitchell's younger sister. Alison Lee was Patricia-Sue Alison Lee's daughter. And Michael Hitchings had found her.

"Sorry, Michael, you're right. I should use Alison's name. We both should."

He saw her eyes searching for him, but she couldn't move forward with Michael holding her back. He used his badge and wiggled it around enough to catch a little light, and it took only a moment for her to focus on the movement in the mirror. Now she could see him. But could Michael?

"What do you want to do, Michael? It's all up to you. Should we tell her? Is that what you want?"

He motioned to his mouth, hoping she would understand him.

"Tell me what?" she asked, and he nodded and gestured again. *Good. Keep him talking.*

"She doesn't know, but it's on you, Michael. What should we do?"

"Don't act like you're here to help me or like you're on my side," Michael said. "You're the same as the rest of them. You want things from me. You want me to do what you want so you can have what you want. You think you can save her and be the big hero and have a happy life with your lady love just like senior and her knight in tarnished armor."

"Who is senior? Why do you keep calling me junior?" Alison asked.

"I am on your side, Michael. It's all about justice, isn't it? About letting the world know your story? Who can tell it better than you? Shouldn't you live so we'll all know the truth? And wouldn't one small act of mercy show people you're not the monster here? You could let her go."

Alison was looking repeatedly to her right without moving her head. He crept up another step and saw Michael's other hand holding a gun to her right temple.

"Monster? You think I'm the monster?" Michael growled. "Every time she came in the courtroom, she brought them more ammunition. We tried to stop them, to stop it from happening, but we were powerless. Don't you see that a greater power was working for them? I thought I had God, but he was busy. His sorry ass was never there when my ass needed him. They had the Anti-Christ on their side. Don't you see? The first time I read where someone was calling her an angel, I knew it. I recognized her."

"She's a person Michael. A person who's made mistakes, just like the rest of us. She knows it, and she regrets it. Do you want her to speak out about it? I give you my word. You let Alison go and Pat Mitchell will tell your story to the whole world. Little Billy, Frankie, all the others, their truth will be known."

"You're damned right their truth will be known. And she's not just a person. You don't understand who she is; you can't. She has graduated from small evil to great power. She helped to do this one small thing to a few boys, now she's in a position to do great evil to the world. She changed her appearance as Satan does, masquerading as an angel of light."

"And she should pay, Michael. She did it, no one else. You were innocent. All you boys. You shouldn't have to pay for other people's sickness and sins. This girl is innocent too."

"Pat Mitchell? The First Lady?" Alison said. "I don't understand. What does she have to do with me?"

"Same thing she has to do with me: she made us who we are today." He could hear the smirk in Michael's voice. "When she became the power behind the throne, I knew it was a sign. I knew we had to strike back at all of them, every one of them, through her. Now all of you feel the same kind of terror we felt. And rightfully so: you are going to reap the whirlwind."

Alison's eyes darted all over the place like a person having a waking dream, and suddenly they stopped and met his in the mirror searching for his confirmation. He nodded, and he knew that she knew.

"Are you saying . . . are you saying the First Lady is my mother?"

"Isn't it wonderful, Harrison, the brilliance produced by a privileged upbringing?" Michael sneered.

Harrison saw her eyes fill with tears, but she angrily blinked them away. Her chest began heaving and she took a deep breath as if she was working up a banshee scream. *Oh no,* Harrison thought, *She's going to do something.*

But she didn't scream. Instead, through clinched teeth she said, "She is not my mother. My mom's name is Constance Palmer." He saw her jaw working in an odd way like a guy getting ready to spit in the street. *What is she doing?* he wondered. He didn't want her to do anything that would trigger Michael or maybe make him shoot her accidentally.

"Her husband thinks we can get our innocence back," Michael said. "We can somehow go back to the Kennedy Camelot days, and it'll all be okay. But don't they know we children were victims then too? You think America is great, but how can you say that about a country built on rape and destruction and hatred? This country pretends to care about righteousness and justice, but every chance they get, they hand over the power to evil. We kids, we know better."

"Even if it's true, what does that have to do with me?" Alison demanded. "I don't even know her. I don't know you. Michael, if you're going to kill me, at least tell me why? Why are you doing this to me?"

"I will by no means clear the guilty," Michael pronounced, "I will visit the iniquity of the fathers upon the children to the third and fourth generation."

She shot Harrison a look in the mirror, and he knew, whatever it was, it was about to go down.

"You can quote bible gobbledygook all night long, but she is not my mother!! That is a lie!!"

"Stop yelling!" Michael said, "You don't want her to be your mother because mothers like ours abandon us. They throw us in the garbage and never look back. She is your mother alright."

"How could you possibly know that?" Harrison asked.

"A little white heart on her neck," Hitchings mused.

"What?" Harrison and Alison asked as one.

"I noticed it in the court case. She was still a fatty black chick then."

The silence begged him to continue.

"Back when I was in the Reserves . . ." he paused with a faint scoff. "I not only know she's your mother, I know who your biological father is too. There's some genealogy you can be proud of," he leered.

Hurriedly Harrison tried to piece the clues together in the silence of his own urgent thoughts. It didn't take him long to connect the dots.

"Alison, it's true—" Harrison began.

"You're lying! You're lying! I hate both of you!" she screamed hysterically.

"Shut up! Stop it! I said shut up," Michael yelled.

Harrison topped them both yelling, "Alison, be quiet! We're not lying to you! Michael wouldn't lie about that! It's too important! Calm down!"

She began sobbing, "Oh God, it can't be true. Oh, oh no, I think I'm gonna . . . gonna be sick."

"What?" Michael almost sounded panicked. "You'd better not—" She brought her hands up and partly covered her mouth.

"No, I'm . . . I'm not kidding. Oh no! Ooooh. I'm gonna throw up. I real . . . really Bluh – Aaaargh!!" She wretched and spewed the mouthful of spit she had accumulated on Michael's arm. It must have felt like actual vomit because he flinched and moved his left arm, loosening his grip on her throat enough for her to duck her head. She grabbed his right wrist with both hands and forced his arm forward and up as hard as she could.

Bang!! Michael's gun went off, and Alison screamed and fell to the floor, clutching her head.

He brought his arm down aiming at her again, and Harrison dove up the last two steps and fired twice, hitting his chest and arm. Michael dropped to the floor right beside her. Alison groaned, holding her bleeding forehead, and crawled away from him.

Harrison saw Michael's hand inching toward his gun and kicked it away. He knelt down beside him. Michael raised his head groggily, and the two men had eye to eye contact for the first time.

"I could have been you, Harrison," Michael rasped. "You think you're so smart, so special, living your soft, easy life. But I actually am special—beloved by the men who are loved by God." He laughed and coughed up blood, catching some of it with his hand. "So smart," he sneered. "It took you forever to put the pieces together. All these people didn't have to die." With one last burst of strength, he grabbed Harrison's arm and pulled him closer. "You think this is over? It never ends. Judgment day is today."

"What does that mean, Michael?" Harrison said, wresting his arm from the man's bloody grasp.

"Tell them it doesn't come back, Harrison."

Michael turned his head and looked into the mirror. "Oh look," he said and smiled, "it's me."

And he closed his eyes.

Chapter 31

Dallas – Texas

Jameson sipped a little more of his Jack Daniels, leaned back and looked at his wife again. This day had made a roller coaster ride seem like lounging in a heated massage chair. The drive was stupendous. It had surpassed every vision he'd conjured up. Even the Hitchings effect helped rather than hindered. As the word flashed through the crowd, they went crazy about his "bravery" in the face of "danger." He could hardly get through his closing speech at the Dallas-Fort Worth Cemetery because he had to keep stopping for cheers and chants. People appreciated that he wanted to honor the past, the military, and also his own pledge to make this drive end better than the original one. No trip to the hospital this time.

But then, his wife told him . . . what she told him. And before he could recover, they received the call from LA about Hitchings and his attempt on Alison's life.

"You have a daughter," he said for the tenth time. But there was no anger. She had come as a result of the worst night of Pat's life. How could he blame her?

"I know it sounds horrible, but I couldn't keep her," Pat said. "I was allowed to name her, then she was gone – gone from my life forever. In truth, before she was born, every time I looked down at my belly, I was back there, going through it again, fighting them off in my nightmares. I hated them. I hated her. But most of all, I hated me. My mother put it beautifully." Pat slipped into an imitation of her mother's accent, "She said, 'A slut lak yew, bet you're not even sure who's the daddy.' This was true."

She laughed bitterly. "But she wasn't mad that I was pregnant. She didn't care about that. Apparently, I picked the right rapist! 'Ho, if you were gonna open yo' legs to everbody and enybody; at least you found a boy with some money.' I almost wanted to kill her."

"Oh honey, I'm so, so sorry," he said. "I guess you really were kind of an orphan."

"I didn't have to give her up, you know. It was blood money, I knew that. But it gave me a chance in life. It also meant the child would have a chance in life. Even if I did hate her, she was innocent."

"Did you ever consider finding her?"

She shook her head. "Can you imagine? An unpopular, fat teenager like me with a mother like mine trying to take on the establishment? All of them sticking together and claiming I was insane. It would have meant lawyers and the whole town's ridicule and DNA tests. I'm pretty sure Mom wasn't going to foot the bill for those. I wasn't strong enough to even think about doing anything like that alone."

"And yet, despite all that, you gave her your name. Something in you must have wanted her to find you."

"I know. It sounds crazy. But I guess I hoped that somehow I wouldn't always be a loser. Maybe the day would come when I was over it, past it – when I'd risen above. I would be someone she'd be proud to meet." She shook her head and shrugged.

"You're so much stronger than I ever imagined." He pulled her closer beside him. "And you don't have to carry that burden alone anymore."

She rested her head on his shoulder.

"I can't wait to meet our daughter," he whispered.

"Me too. And we also have to meet Agent Carter. If it hadn't been for him . . ."

"I know," Jameson said. "I predict great things for his future—very great things."

He touched her chin gently and turned her face up to his. "Tell me, how do you feel now?"

Pat smiled and said, "Free. I feel free."

There was a soft knock on the door, and a voice said, "Room Service, Mr. President."

"Oh good," Pat said. "I'm starving. I feel like I haven't eaten in two days."

She walked briskly to the door, and something about the lightness of her step made her seem younger than when he met her.

"As soon as we're done, let's make arrangements for us to fly back," she said. "I want to get to Alison as soon as possible. I'll bet Aidan's going to love having a big sis."

She opened the door, and a tall, dignified server, accompanied by Nathan, rolled in a cart with their dinner.

He paused before uncovering the dishes.

"Are you ready to dine now, madam? Mr. President?" he asked in a low, radio announcer sounding voice.

"Yes, but that's okay; you can go. I'm going to serve my husband." She smiled up at Jameson and winked.

The server walked to the door, flanked by Nathan, then stopped and turned back. "Um, Mr. President, if I could just . . .? I was at the drive this morning, and I really need to say something on behalf of a lot of people."

His stern demeanor didn't waiver and Jameson thought, *Uh oh, not a fan.* "Of course. What is it?" Jameson said, hoping he sounded genuine.

"I just . . ." the man said, "You should know that the things you said, the promises you made—they don't all sound believable."

"Oh, well I—" Jameson looked uneasily at Pat, and Nathan took a step closer.

"But I believe it. Every word. I think we've turned a corner. I think we're going to a better place. And you're going to lead us there. I'm proud to have met you, sir."

"Thank you." Jameson grasped his hand and looked at his name tag. "Thank you, Mick. You've made my day."

Mick gave him a solemn nod and quietly exited the room.

"Come on, honey, while it's hot," Pat said and began taking lids off dishes. "This catfish is calling your name."

"And I'm answering," he said. "Nathan, I don't suppose we could talk you into copping a squat and grabbing a munch with us?" He kept his face deadpan straight, as did Nathan, but he saw the twinkle in the agent's eye.

"No sir, thank you Mr. President. No squat copping on duty."

"But seriously," Jameson chuckled, "I want to make sure all you guys get an unforgettably special meal before we go back, so would you let them know they should be prepared to check out the menu downstairs and go wild? Whoever gets stuck with us this evening can have room service."

"Thank you, sir, I'll . . ." he stopped, alert, staring at the door. Jameson heard clearly what he was listening to: loud voices, several male and one female.

Nathan drew his weapon and went closer to the door.

Pat walked up behind him, listened, and started.

Jameson heard a muffled, "Oh my goodness gracious! Oh my goodness gracious!"

"Wait, I know that voice!" Pat rushed to the door and reached for the handle.

"No, Mrs. Mitchell, that's not wise," Nathan said.

"It's okay, I know her," Pat said.

"We can open it, Nathan," Jameson told him.

Nathan pulled the door open a crack and peeked out, but Pat stepped to his left and opened it wider. "Elizabeth," she said, extending both her hands. It was Elizabeth Cash, Pat's transgender supporter from the banquet.

"I'm so sorry! I'm so sooo sorry!" she cried, hardly able to get the words out. "Oh, Miss Pat, I didn't mean! I was only . . . I was on the wrong elevator, I just got on the wrong elevator!"

"It's okay. Come on in," Pat said.

Elizabeth walked slowly into the room, leaning heavily on both her cane and the First Lady.

"Oh my goodness gracious, this is so horrible. Every time I see you, I embarrass myself." She collapsed against the door, closing it with her body, buried her face in her hands, and sobbed.

"Come here, sit down." Pat walked her to a chair and helped her to sit. "It's okay now," she said softly, "You're okay."

"I know it's my fault, making a silly mistake like that, but I don't think those agents had to be so unkind. I had my button on which you gave me and everything. Now that young man," she pointed her wolf's head cane at Nathan, "he seems kinder than those, well, rough fellows outside, but even he is holding a gun on me."

"Agent Chen is very kind," Pat said, throwing a look to Jameson, who signaled Nathan to put his gun away, "but it's their job to be suspicious and careful with everyone."

"Yes," a male voice responded, "maybe you should have been more suspicious and careful."

"What—" was all Pat was able to say before Elizabeth launched from the chair, swiftly grabbed Pat by the throat, lifted her cane, and fired two quiet shots, hitting Nathan in the head and chest. The agent crumpled to the floor, and Jameson tried to run toward Elizabeth, but the next shot hit him in the leg. Elizabeth shoved Pat away and quickly recovered Nathan's gun.

Pat hurried to Jameson, who was on the floor, holding his bleeding leg.

"Not a sound," the male voice said as "she" removed her wig, glasses, and some of the prosthetics on her face.

"Who are you?" Pat asked.

"You don't know me, Mom? After all the meaningful times we spent together in court. Shame on you."

Pat looked confused, and Jameson saw the realization dawn in her eyes.

"Franks. You're George Franks."

"Guilty as charged, Psalm. As are you. Guilty, that is. I bring a message from Michael. He knew he might not see this day for himself. He knew he might not finish his great work, but he sent his disciples to finish it for him. You thought we'd abandoned each other—like you abandoned your daughter—that we took the blood money from those pedophile priests and scurried off into the woodwork. But that money helped us all along the way. Travel, rent, supplies, even costumes." He touched the bodice of his dress. "Too bad Agent Carter isn't here. He'd like this performance much better than the last one I did for him. Now," He raised Nathan's gun and pointed it at Pat, "the reckoning has come, and justice shall be done this day. Your life for all the others."

"George, please," Jameson said, grimacing from the pain, "don't do this. If you spare my wife, I promise to use all my power to help you in whatever way I can."

"There is no promise you can make to stop what must happen today. I must work the works of him that sent me."

"I can't accept that," Jameson said. "There's always a way. Please, George, I'm the President of the United States. I can help you. I can find a way to make your life better. We can come together on this."

"It's too damned late to make my life better. It ended in an orphanage a thousand years ago. It'll never happen. We'll never come together. This kumbaya-love-everybody crap that you keep imagining and talking about, it's never going to happen because people ultimately are hypocrites. They don't care about each other. And she's the proof." He pointed the gun at Pat's heart.

"Mom," he spat out. "Guess you had to kind of grow into the job? Get it right with number two? Fake it till you make another one? Kind of like that first pancake—yeah, make it and throw it away. Kind of like us boys. If you don't even care about your own child, how can you pretend to care about other people? The hypocrisy ends today."

"No, no," Jameson struggled to his feet and stood in front of Pat. "Take me instead. Don't leave our son motherless. You don't want another child to go through what you boys went through."

"Stop Jamie," Pat pleaded, clutching at his arm. "It's okay, my love. This day was always going to come."

"Fine then," Franks said, "Let it be as you have said. Both of you."

He raised the gun and fired, fired again and again. Jameson heard Pat shriek,

"Noooo!!" and felt himself flying through the air and tumbling on his right side. There was a loud commotion, yelling, the door banging open, more shots, and Franks bellowing as bullets struck him again and again. Silence.

Only later did he understand Pat had shoved him out of the way just in time. That she had taken all but the one of Franks' bullets that had entered his arm. That she was gone. He used his good arm to pull himself across the floor toward her, smoothed her hair out of her face, and kissed her. He rested her head on his chest and whispered, "Free. You're free." But there was no freedom for Jameson, only the free-flowing tears of inconsolable pain.

Chapter 32

Five days later – Los Angeles, CA

"I guess he was right: it didn't end like Kennedy," Harrison said. He and Kate were on her sofa watching Pat Mitchell's "Life Celebration," as it was being called. There had been speeches and songs and video and pictures about her life, their life together, her surprise daughter, and here and there, bits about Michael Hitchings and George Franks. There had been nothing else talked about on all media for the last five days.

"Do you think it really did any good? All his faith in us as a country, in people in general?" Kate asked.

"I don't know," he said, "I'd like to think so."

He reached for Kate's hand again and smiled at her. He still couldn't believe how easy it was, how naturally they had come together in the days since Pat Mitchell's death.

He'd walked into her hospital room, and she was looking at the door as if she expected him at that moment. He'd pictured himself stopping at the door, waiting for her to speak first, then walking at a dignified pace to her bedside. But she smiled her crooked, swollen-faced smile and put her hand out. He rushed to take it. He took her in his arms and finally said it over and over, "I love you. I love you. I love you."

"I know, I know," her muffled, raspy voice said. "Stop making me smile, it hurts."

He pulled away from her, concerned. She put her hand on his cheek and laughed, "Ow! Laughing hurts even worse." Then, they both laughed. "Of course you love me. I love you too. Now make it feel all better." And she held her beautiful lips up to his, and finally, finally they kissed.

He'd taken leave for a while, and they had been together every day since.

"Those guys who showed up at the Dallas drive, did any of them get charged with anything?" Kate asked.

"They were checked out and released. They had some damned good lawyers, but they hadn't actually broken any laws. Maybe littering, with those hideous wigs. But even though they were from the orphanage and clearly knew Michael and Franks, there was no evidence that they knew what those two were up to. They were being manipulated, like the poor Marine who delivered the package. We haven't found him so far, by the way. Michael may have done something to him."

"I hope not," she said. "But he didn't think twice about killing the Lyft driver Fred, and he was at the orphanage with him, too."

"I don't know," Harrison said. "Michael seemed to have a method to his madness. Each victim had a purpose, a reason, at least in his mind. I think the marine served his purpose. It wasn't like Michael cared about being identified by that time. He knew we knew."

"And uh," she paused and slid her eyes toward him and back at the TV, "was there any connection with MayHem?"

"Connection? Uh, you mean . . . well we know they knew each other. That is what you meant, right?"

"What else could I mean?" she asked innocently.

He smiled and said, "She's just a lovely lady with a lot of . . . assets. Her many fans appreciate those ass—Ow!" He rubbed his arm where she'd punched him and gave her a surprised and indignant look before breaking into a grin. "You know, for all her creepiness and all that macabre murder fan stuff, she really didn't know him as well as she thought. He'd presented himself to her as a kind of shy, virginal boy man who was completely in awe of her, and she bought it. We wouldn't have found him as soon without her. Of course, she also is kind of awesome." He blocked another punch and kissed her into submission.

The camera switched from archival film of the Mitchell's as a new young couple to the president walking the last few blocks to his wife's burial. Jameson Mitchell was as changed as his friend Malik had been by his loss, but he seemed somehow more presidential: older, more dignified—exuding an air of gravitas instead of good-natured charm. He looked like a president who'd been through a war or his own personal 911.

The shot switched again to an earlier one of the President at the funeral service. "Oh look," Kate said. "They're playing the end of the speech again. Children are going to be learning this one in school."

"Nothing anyone does or says can touch me now," Jameson said. "I am living for my son, my newly found stepdaughter, and for you, my fellow Americans. Nothing else matters. I am determined to be a monument to Pat Mitchell's memory and her beliefs. She made a horrible mistake when she was a young, vulnerable, damaged woman who had never had the chance to heal from the trauma of her childhood. It haunted her to the end, but she spent her life after that mistake trying to make up for it, doing her penance.

Michael Hitchings' full story is out now. We know about the horrors that he experienced. There is no excuse for the things he did, but there is a reason for what he became. Monstrous men with their monstrous acts created an even worse monster. We must, collectively, stop all such monsters from gaining and holding power. We must protect our children, our families, our future. The buck stops at all of us. The responsibility is ours. Please, my friends, my family, my fellow Americans: no more hate, no more judgment. Henceforth and forevermore, let our hearts be fixed on love."

Harrison didn't even realize he was crying until he felt the tear on his cheek. He looked at Kate, and without looking at him, she held out the tissue she had just used for her own tears.

The camera shot switched back to Mitchell walking behind her casket past silent crowds as the reporter repeated details she had already stated a dozen times that day. When she said something about the "supportive and loving citizens, true Americans, standing here in the November cold on behalf of a saddened nation," the camera panned across the crowd standing along the curb.

Kate bolted upright and said, "Oh no! Look! Look at that!"

A man who was at the front holding his coat closed had thrown it open and revealed his tee shirt. It said "I Am Michael Hitchings."

The reporter went crazy, doing a play by play of what the man was doing, the President looking in his direction, the whole funeral procession stopping to stare.

Another man in the crowd said something and pushed the man in the tee shirt who pushed him back. Another man grabbed the tee shirt man from behind and the first man started tearing at the man's shirt while other bystanders encouraged him.

Three police officers and two others Harrison knew must be Secret Service rushed over, and the picture began bouncing as obviously, the camera operator was sprinting right behind them.

The sound improved, so the reporter must have caught up with them. They didn't need her to describe the melee spreading out in the crowd.

Then they heard a familiar voice say, "Stop! Stop it right now!"

The camera swung around to reveal Jameson Mitchell standing there, his arm still in a cast, clearly despondent, yet somehow looking regal and proud. "Leave him alone," he said quietly.

The noise and struggle stopped instantly, and the shocked attackers stepped away from the man whose shirt was now torn. He looked defiantly at the President.

Jameson walked over to him, stood a moment and put both hands on his shoulders. To the man's obvious astonishment, Jameson hugged him and said, "I'm sorry." And he stepped back

The man, along with the rest of the crowd, stood in stunned silence. He bowed his head and slowly closed his coat and buttoned it. "I'm sorry too," he said, so softly that the mike hardly picked him up.

Jameson turned to go but turned back and extended his hand.

"Come with me," they heard the President say. "She'd have liked that."

The man nodded and took his hand. The two of them went back into the street, and the procession continued.

"Did you see?" Kate whispered.

Harrison nodded, putting his arm around her.

"I think we're going to be okay." He kissed her face gently, she lay her head on his chest, and they continued watching together.

www.ingramcontent.com/pod-product-compliance
Lightning Source LLC
LaVergne TN
LVHW051823080426
835512LV00018B/2699